EFFECTIVE ONLINE TEACHING

EFFECTIVE ONLINE TEACHING

FOUNDATIONS AND STRATEGIES FOR STUDENT SUCCESS

Tina Stavredes

JOSSEY-BASS
A Wiley Imprint
www.josseybass.com

Published by Jossey-Bass
A Wiley Imprint
989 Market Street, San Francisco, CA 94103-1741—www.josseybass.com

Readers should be aware that Internet Web sites offered as citations and/or sources for further information may have changed or disappeared between the time this was written and when it is read.

Jossey-Bass books and products are available through most bookstores. To contact Jossey-Bass directly call our Customer Care Department within the U.S. at 800-956-7739, outside the U.S. at 317-572-3986, or fax 317-572-4002.

Jossey-Bass also publishes its books in a variety of electronic formats. Some content that appears in print may not be available in electronic books.

Library of Congress Cataloging-in-Publication Data
Stavredes, Tina.
  Effective online teaching : foundations and strategies for student success / Tina Stavredes.
     p. cm.—(The Jossey-Bass Higher and Adult Education Series)
  Includes bibliographical references and index.
  ISBN 978-0-470-57838-4 (pbk.)
  ISBN 978-1-118-03878-9 (ebk.)
  ISBN 978-1-118-03879-6 (ebk.)
  ISBN 978-1-118-03880-2 (ebk.)
  1. Web-based instruction. 2. Web-based instruction—Social aspects. 3. Distance education—Social aspects.
4. Learning, Psychology of. I. Title.
  LB1044.87.S846 2011
  371.33′44678—dc22

                                                                                        2011011126

Printed in the United States of America
FIRST EDITION

PB Printing   10 9 8 7 6 5 4 3 2 1

The Jossey-Bass Higher and
Adult Education Series

Contents

Exhibits and Figures

This book is dedicated to my husband, Jim Stavredes,
who provides unwavering love, endless encouragement,
and support in everything I do.

Preface

M any colleges and universities are joining the ranks of institutions that offer online learning opportunities. The question that many of these institutions are facing is how to prepare faculty to teach in the online environment and address the motivations, needs, learning styles, and constraints of online learners while achieving the same learning outcomes as traditional, on-ground campuses. A major role for instructors is helping learners overcome constraints and persist in achieving their learning goals.

According to the Sloan Consortium report *Learning on Demand: Online Education in the United States* (Allen & Seaman, 2009):

> Academic leaders at all types of institutions report increased demand for face-to-face and online courses, with those at public institutions seeing the largest impact. In all cases the demand for online offerings are greater than that for the corresponding face-to-face offerings.
>
> - Over one-half (54 percent) of institutions report that the economic downturn has increased demand for existing face-to-face courses.
> - The economic impact has been greatest on demand for online courses, with 66 percent of institutions reporting increased demand for new courses and programs and 73 percent seeing increased demand for existing online courses and programs.

- The economic impact on institutional budgets has been mixed; 50 percent have seen their budgets decrease as a result, but 25 percent have experienced an increase (p. 1).

Because the growth of online education has been rapid, the quality of trained online instructors is inconsistent. Comprehensive training of online instructors is important so instructors understand the variables that have an impact on teaching in the online environment. According to *THE Journal* (2004), "Experts agree that faculty need training to teach online, yet a survey of faculty who teach undergraduate mathematics courses online indicates that most faculty at two-year colleges are still not receiving adequate training. While 89% of the participants in this research received at least some training, about half said that the training they received did not adequately prepare them to teach online. In addition, 60% said that they would have benefited from more training in facilitating online interaction before they began teaching online" (Para. 1).

With the combination of the book *Effective Online Teaching: Foundations and Strategies for Student Success* and training manual, I hope to support the delivery of training to online instructors and staff so they gain an understanding of the needs of the online learner and how these needs affect learners' ability to persist and learn online.

AUDIENCE

The audience for this book is primarily online instructors; however, the concepts and ideas in this book are also applicable to instructors teaching face-to-face or hybrid courses. Many of the principles and techniques presented in the book will also be of interest to professionals involved in the design and delivery of online courses. Individuals involved with faculty development will be able to use this book in combination with the training manual to develop training for instructors and staff.

This book will also be of interest to administrators of distance learning programs to understand important variables that impact online learners as well as effective strategies to support online learners and help them persist in their programs of study. Individuals who manage instructors will gain important insight to support continuous quality improvement of their online instructors.

Finally, this book is applicable to individuals involved in corporate and government training and development. The principles presented in this book will apply to all types of learning and can be used to develop effective online training as well as develop instructors who deliver training online.

This book contributes to the body of knowledge of online teaching by focusing on an understanding of who online learners are, how they learn, and what they have to overcome to achieve their educational goals online. The instructional strategies that I recommend in the book are grounded in theories of learning and cognition and focus on specific strategies to help learners overcome challenges in learning. These challenges can stem from environmental and affective factors, difficulty establishing online presence, and other situations specific to thinking and learning in a computer-mediated learning environment.

ORGANIZATION OF THE BOOK

The book is organized around five parts. Part 1 develops a profile of online learners, including who they are, how they prefer to learn, and why they choose the online environment in which to learn. Chapter 1 describes the diverse characteristics of online learners and includes a discussion of the impact culture can have on learning. Chapter 2 considers how adult learners prefer to learn and looks at social styles and self-directedness of adult learners. Chapter 3 looks at the challenges learners face in achieving their educational goals online. It considers internal factors that affect persistence, including learners' thinking skills and emotional disposition and how they develop presence online. It also looks at external factors, such as the difficulty for an online learner to integrate into the institution because of the computer-mediated environment.

Part 2 presents the foundations of cognition and learning. Teaching is effective when instructional strategies are grounded in an understanding of how learning occurs. Chapter 4 describes three learning theories—behaviorism, cognitivism, and constructivism—and provides an overview of how learning theories have evolved and how they can be used to support instruction. Chapter 5 looks at the foundations of cognition and the mental processes of learning. It discusses how emotions, environmental factors, and cognitive load influence information processes and describes metacognition, which supports the strategies learners use as they think and learn. It also addresses cognitive learning styles, which influence how they learn. Chapter 6 describes motivation theory and looks at how motivation influences learning, including how learners' motivation, locus of control, and self-efficacy play a role in their disposition toward learning. The chapter then talks about the distance learning environment, specifically the transactional distance that the computer-mediated environment imposes and how that affects learners.

Part 3 of the book describes four types of scaffolding strategies that can be used to support learning: procedural, metacognitive, conceptual, and strategic. Chapter 7 discusses procedural scaffolding, which emphasizes how a learner navigates the online environment and uses available resources and tools in the learning environment. Chapter 8 addresses metacognitive scaffolding, which supports the underlying processes associated with the management of thinking and learning. Chapter 9 describes conceptual scaffolding, which supports learners as they reason through complex concepts and problems. Chapter 10 looks at strategic scaffolding strategies, which assist learners just in time, and emphasizes alternative approaches that learners can use to support analysis, planning, strategy, and tactical decisions during learning.

Part 4 considers the development of a community of inquiry in the online class by fostering cognitive, social, and teaching presence that is mediated by appropriate communication tools. Chapter 11 presents ways to develop cognitive presence through using active learning strategies to support critical thinking and knowledge construction. Chapter 12 describes learner-to-learner interaction strategies to help develop social presence and build a community of inquiry. Strategies for developing social presence offer learners an opportunity to engage in critical thinking and knowledge construction through collaborative activity. Chapter 13 describes strategies to develop instructor presence in the course to support learners. Chapter 14 describes communication tools that can be used to establish cognitive, social, and instructor presence.

This book would not be complete if it did not address strategies to help you manage your online course, which are outlined in Part 5, and include strategies to manage your teaching activities, behavior issues you may encounter, and ethical considerations. Chapter 15 offers specific strategies to help streamline your teaching activities. Because behavioral issues may manifest themselves differently in the online learning environment, Chapter 16 describes behavioral problems that arise in the online environment and provides ideas for how to deal with them effectively. Chapter 17 describes ethical issues that you may encounter in teaching online, offers strategies for overcoming plagiarism, and presents important information on copyright.

Throughout the book, you will have examined the profile of the online learning population, the impact that a computer-mediated environment has on thinking and learning, the issue of developing presence online, and the challenges of managing your online course. In the final chapter, Chapter 18, I invite you to revisit your philosophy of teaching and develop a new philosophy of online teaching. This philosophy will provide you with a strong foundation for applying the concepts and ideas from this book as you teach in the online environment and support learners in achieving their educational goals.

ACKNOWLEDGMENTS

I want to thank Tiffany Herder for her amazing insight and expertise in designing online learning environments. Her review helped me expand my ideas and consider additional areas of exploration. Melissa Martyr-Wagner was a warrior in helping me put together the training manual and presentation slides. Her unique perspective in the field of technology helped me stretch my thinking. I also want to thank Mary Breslin, an expert in online faculty training, for the time she took to review the book. Her recommendations were excellent and helped refine my thinking. Finally, I want to thank my family. I could not have completed this book without their patience when I was overwhelmed, their support when I needed help, and their unconditional love.

About the Author

Tina Stavredes has worked for Capella University, an online higher education institution, for over eight years and is part of a leadership team that has continued to strive to build excellence in the delivery of a quality online learning experience for nontraditional adult learners. Currently she is the chair of the psychology program in the School of Undergraduate Studies at Capella University, where she works to manage and train a high-performing team of online faculty. She previously taught in the School of Undergraduate Studies and also served as Capella University's director of curriculum, a role in which she was responsible for creating the Office of Curriculum Development. In addition, she has held the positions of program chair and faculty director in Capella's School of Education. Prior to joining Capella, Stavredes worked as manager of academic technology support for the University of Minnesota's College of Education and Human Development.

Dr. Stavredes has a master's degree in education with a specialization in curriculum and instruction using information systems and technology in teaching and learning. Her PhD is in educational psychology with a specialization in cognition and learning as it relates to computer-based learning. For over 10 years, she has been involved with online education and demonstrated a passion and vision for how to build a quality and sustainable educational experience for online learners. She has an in-depth understanding of online learning communities, as well as communities of practice, from her experience teaching online and understands the pedagogy involved in building learning communities that are relevant and sustainable for the learner. She has also worked specifically with first-year online learners to understand the factors that lead to learner readiness and that affect persistence and retention. In her administrative roles she has developed innovative ways to support quality teaching and help faculty bring their expertise to the online classroom.

EFFECTIVE ONLINE TEACHING

Profile of the Online Learner

Part 1 presents the profile of an online learner and discusses the importance of knowing your online learning audience in order to deliver a quality learning experience that meets the needs of all learners to improve their ability to persist. Chapter 1 examines learner demographics and considers cultural differences that affect online learners. Chapter 2 looks at the general attributes of online learners, including their attributes as adult learners, their self-directedness, and their social learning styles. Chapter 3 considers issues online adult learners face as they engage in online learning and provides an understanding of critical factors that influence their ability to persist in the online environment to achieve their goals. Overall, Part 1 will help you develop an understanding of your learners, what motivates them, and what barriers may prevent them from being successful in an online learning environment. Understanding the characteristics and needs of the online learner may not necessarily guarantee success in an online course, but it may inform your pedagogy to help learners persist.

Characteristics of the Online Learner

From its beginnings, online education has primarily been focused on nontra- ✗ ditional adult learners. However, this is changing, and we are beginning to see traditional learners considering online education. Because of the wide range of characteristics and needs that make up the online learner population, it is critical to understand the diversity of online learners in order to develop unique approaches that support learners and facilitate their ability to persist and learn.

Characteristics of diversity fall into two categories. Primary characteristics are those attributes of a person that do not change over time, such as age, gender, and ethnicity. Secondary characteristics are those that are acquired or change over time and include characteristics such as occupation, income, education, marital status, and parental status, to name a few. Exhibit 1.1 describes the primary and secondary diversity characteristics of online learners.

Noel-Levitz publishes the yearly *National Online Learners Priorities Report,* which includes a comprehensive examination of online learners (Noel-Levitz, 2009). The 2009 study included 68,760 learners from 87 institutions and showed that the online learner population is 68% female and 32% male. The age distribution is 20% 24 years and younger, 32% between the ages of 25 and 34, 26% between 35 and 44, 18% between 45 and 54, and 4% 55 years and over. Ethnicity was not reported in the 2009 report, but the 2005 Noel-Levitz study reported ethnicity of online learners as 74% White, 12% African American, 4%

Exhibit 1.1   Diversity Characteristics of Online Learners.

Primary Diversity Characteristics	Learner
Gender (Noel-Levitz, 2009)	60% Female 40% Male
Age distribution (Noel-Levitz, 2009)	20% under 24 32% — 25–34 26% — 35–44 18% — 45–54 4% — 55 and over
Ethnicity (Noel-Levitz, 2005)	74% White 12% African American 4% Hispanic 3% Asian 7% Other
Secondary Diversity Characteristics	Learner
Enrollment status (Noel-Levitz, 2009)	81% Primarily online 19% Primarily on campus
Work status (Noel-Levitz, 2005)	70% Employed full-time 17% Employed part-time 13% Unemployed
Marital status (Noel-Levitz, 2005)	37% Married with children 18% Married 31% Single 11% Single with children

Hispanic, 3% Asian, and 7% of other races (Noel-Levitz, 2005). The majority of online learners are between the ages of 25 and 44, which is a wide age distribution that has implications for the types of instructional strategies that you use in your online course. Although a large percentage are White, there are a growing number of African-American, Hispanic, and Asian learners, a trend to consider as you determine the appropriate teaching strategies for your online courses.

The 2005 and 2009 reports also describe secondary diversity characteristics of online learners. The 2009 report states that 81% of online learners are primarily online while 19% are primarily on campus. The 2005 report shows 37% of learners married with children, 18% married with no children, 31% single, and 11% single with children. The 2005 report also states that 70% are employed full-time, 17% employed part-time, and 13% not employed. Most of the online learner population are new to online learning, having taken fewer than three classes previously, and take from one to six credits at a time. Most plan to complete their degree online. The top reasons learners choose online learning are convenience, work schedule, flexible pacing, and program requirements (Noel-Levitz, 2009).

The online learner is different from the traditional learner, who is usually under the age of 25, single with no children, and attending school full-time while holding a part-time job. Most online learners have the responsibilities of children and full-time jobs, responsibilities that make it difficult to manage online learning with their already full lives. You will need to set clear expectations for learners along with some degree of flexibility. Being too flexible can result in learners getting behind and trying to catch up toward the end of the course, which can have an impact on persistence and achievement. Not having enough flexibility can cause learners to become anxious and discouraged, which may result in prematurely dropping the course.

CULTURAL DIFFERENCES

As the diversity data show, the online learner population is a heterogeneous group of learners who come to the online learning environment with diverse values, beliefs, and perspectives. Cultural differences can have an impact on how learners engage in the online environment. Culture is the collective mind of a group or category of people that distinguishes it from other people based on a set of values (Hofstede, 2008). Geert Hofstede (Hofstede & Bond, 1984) has researched the effect of culture on psychological functioning, as well as its impact on sociological, political, and economic functioning of social systems. In his studies, he identified four cultural dimensions that influence social systems, including power distance, uncertainty avoidance, individualism versus collectivism, and masculinity-femininity.

Power Distance

Power distance refers to the status position of individuals in society. It also signifies the extent to which less powerful members of a society accept that power is distributed unequally, and individuals of higher power exert influence on individuals or groups of lower power (Hofstede, 2008). Countries such as

China, India, Czechia, Poland, Korea, Japan, Russia, and those in South America have high power distances, whereas countries such as the Netherlands, Sweden, Hungary, and Israel have low power distances.

The effect of power distance on teaching and learning is pronounced. In cultures where there are high power distances, learners tend to be dependent on the instructor to direct the learning experience and initiate all of the communications in the class. Learners treat the instructor with respect because they are considered gurus who transfer personal wisdom to the learners.

Cultures with low power distances are more learner-centered. Instructors and learners treat each other as equals, and learners initiate some of the communications in class. Instructors are viewed as experts who transfer their impersonal truths to learners, that is, they are more of a "guide on the side."

Uncertainty Avoidance

Uncertainty avoidance refers to the degree to which certain cultures are able to tolerate unstructured or ambiguous situations and environments. This relates to how a society deals with conflict and aggression, as well as life and death. Germany, Japan, South American countries, Korea, Russia, Hungary, and Israel have higher uncertainty avoidance, whereas Nordic countries, the Netherlands, China, and India have lower uncertainty avoidance (Hofstede, 2008).

Uncertainty avoidance has an impact on how a learning environment is organized. Learners who come from cultures with high uncertainty avoidance are concerned about knowing the right answers, which they believe the instructor holds. Learners are able to express emotions in class but they feel pressured to conform to other learners.

Cultures with low uncertainty avoidance are tolerant of individual differences; however, there is little tolerance for the expression of emotions in class. Learners enjoy good discussions and it is acceptable for the instructor to not know all of the answers.

Individualism Versus Collectivism

Individualism versus collectivism refers to the position of a culture along a continuum. On one pole is individualism, which refers to a group of people whose concern is looking after themselves and their family. On the other pole is collectivism, which refers to a group of people that look after each other in exchange for loyalty. Individualist societies include Spain, France, the Netherlands, Nordic countries, Poland, Hungary, Italy, German-speaking countries, and the United States. Collectivist societies include Thailand, Korea, Costa Rica, Chile, Russia, Bulgaria, Portugal, China, Japan, Mexico, Venezuela, Greece, and the Arab world (Hofstede, 2008).

Individualist cultures believe the purpose of education is learning how to learn. Learners are encouraged to seek individual goals and are expected to speak up in class when they need or want to. They collaborate with peers who have similar interests. The value of education is to increase one's self-respect and economic worth.

Collectivist societies believe the purpose of education is learning how to do something. Individual goals are not encouraged and learners speak only when the group asks them to. Learners form collaborations based on popularity rather than similar interests. They believe that education will provide them entry into higher status groups.

Masculinity-Femininity

In Hofstede's construct, masculinity-femininity refers to how certain cultures look at differences based on gender differences and value differences. In masculine societies, men are supposed to be assertive, tough, and focused on material success. In feminine cultures, emotional roles of both genders overlap and values focus on caring for others and the quality of life. Countries such as China, Japan, Mexico, Venezuela, Greece, Hungary, Italy, the Arab world, and German-speaking countries are masculine cultures in which men are assertive and the main decision makers. Feminine cultures include Thailand, Korea, Costa Rica, Chile, Russia, Spain, France, the Netherlands, and Nordic countries, where roles overlap between men and women (Hofstede, 2008).

Education in masculine societies is very competitive. It is considered a disaster to fail in school. Instructors are admired for being experts and average learners seek to do their best. Because of the focus on being the best, learners tend to overrate their own performances.

Education in feminine cultures is less competitive. Failing in school is not considered a disaster but merely a minor incident. Instructors are liked for their friendliness, and they focus on praise of weak learners for their efforts. The average learner is the norm, so learners tend to underrate their performance.

IMPACT OF CULTURE IN AN ONLINE LEARNING ENVIRONMENT

Cultural differences can have a large impact on the online learning environment. Exhibit 1.2 summarizes the impact of cultural differences on learning.

Differences in power distance can have an impact on learners' perceived position in the course and may result in some learners not being able to interact as equals with other learners. Bates (2001) describes how culture influences critical thinking skills, debate, and discussion. In an online environment, learners are often encouraged to critically evaluate and debate the content being presented and share their ideas and knowledge in discussion. Cultural differences may affect the degree to which individual learners interact and can interfere with their ability to challenge ideas or express opinions contrary to those of the instructor or other learners in the class (Bates & Poole, 2003). Cultural differences can also affect learners who consider the instructor a higher power. If you participate in discussions and other activities by offering opinions on a topic or issue, a learner who views you as a higher power may find it difficult to offer opinions or ideas that are contrary to your opinions. Instructional activities that are teacher-directed tend to be best for learners from cultures with higher power distance, whereas lower power distance cultures prefer more learner-directed learning strategies.

Learners from cultures with high uncertainty avoidance may not be able to learn in an environment that is open and unstructured and learners work at their own pace and determine the goals they want to pursue in the course. To meet the needs of learners with high uncertainty avoidance, you must provide alternatives to help them achieve the intended goals of an activity.

The element of individualism versus collectivism can affect the goals of learners and their overall motivation to collaborate with other learners. Learners from collectivist cultures may not be able to set goals and may not initiate interactions with other learners. The way you form groups may also be affected by culture. You may consider having learners select their own group to ensure they can successfully participate in teamwork activities with peers.

The issue of masculinity-femininity may have an impact on how learners interact with one another and how they interact with you as the instructor based on gender. For instance, in masculine cultures, men are more dominant and perceived as assertive and competitive, whereas women serve and care for the

Exhibit 1.2   Impact of Cultural Differences on Learning.

Dimensions	Cultural Differences	Associated Countries (Hofstede, 2008)	Teaching and Learning (Hofstede, 2008)
Power distance status—position of person in society	*Large power distance:* Power and wealth unequal with higher power exerting influence over lower power	China India Arab countries	Teacher-centered Dependent learners Teacher initiates communication Teacher respected Teacher is guru who transfers personal wisdom
	Small power distance: Power distributed equally	Netherlands Nordic countries Austria	Learner-centered Learners are equals Teacher is equal Learner-initiated communication Teacher is expert who shares interpretations, experience, and ideas
Uncertainty avoidance—degree to which certain cultures are able to tolerate unstructured or unclear environments	*High uncertainty avoidance:* Cultures where unstructured or unclear environments are not tolerated	Germany Japan Latin countries	Learners need right answers Teacher has right answers Emotions in class can be expressed Pressure among learners to conform
	Low uncertainty avoidance: Cultures where unstructured or unclear environments are tolerated	Nordic countries Netherlands China India	Learners want good discussion Teacher may say "I don't know" Emotions should be controlled Tolerance for differences in class
Individualism vs. collectivism—relationship with others	*Individualism:* Refers to a group of people whose concern is looking after themselves and their families	Spain France Netherlands Nordic countries Poland Hungary Italy Germany United States	Purpose of education is learning how to learn Learners' individual initiatives are encouraged Learners expected to speak up in class when they need or want to Learners associate according to interests
	Collectivism: Refers to a group of people that look after each other in exchange for loyalty	Thailand Korea Costa Rica Russia Bulgaria Portugal China Japan Mexico Venezuela Greece Arab countries	Purpose of education is learning how to do something Learners' individual initiatives discouraged Learners only speak up in class when sanctioned by group Learners associate according to popularity

(continued)

Exhibit 1.2 *(continued)*

Dimensions	Cultural Differences	Associated Countries (Hofstede, 2008)	Teaching and Learning (Hofstede, 2008)
Masculine-feminine — emotional gender roles Masculinity-femininity differences based on gender differences	*Masculine cultures:* Men are assertive and the main decision makers	China Japan Mexico Arab countries Germany	Brilliant teacher admired Best learner is norm Competition in class Praise for good learners Learners overrate own performance Failing in school is a disaster
	Feminine cultures: Overlapping roles where neither men nor women are the most assertive or sole decision makers	Thailand Korea Costa Rica, Chile Russia Spain France Nordic countries	Friendly teachers most liked Average learner is norm Overambition unpopular Praise for weak learner Learners underrate their own performance Failing in school is a minor incident

Source: Hofstede & Bond, 1984.

family. You may find that female learners from masculine cultures are resistant to interacting in the course, so they may benefit from encouragement to interact with their peers. You may also see differences in the competitiveness that is exhibited in male learners from masculine cultures. In feminine cultures, social gender roles overlap, so you will not find so many differences between males and females.

Being aware of cultural differences can help you develop appropriate teaching strategies that consider your diverse learner population. These strategies may include structuring discussions and activities so all learners feel comfortable, and providing specific instructions to help learners understand the expectations of the activities, including the expected level of interaction. Awareness of cultural differences can also help you plan strategies to help individual learners persist. If you find cultural differences in the degree to which learners engage and interact, you may want to consider communicating with them to offer understanding and advice for how to overcome their discomfort.

In this chapter, we looked at the diversity characteristics of the online learner. We noted that the average online learner is female, around 35 years of age, works full-time, and is married with children. The majority are undergraduate learners taking one to six credits online. They are primarily White, but there is a growing population of African-American, Hispanic, and Asian learners. We discussed cultural diversity and how it can influence how learners engage in your online course. As you can see, the online learner may differ from the typical learner in your face-to-face class, which can impact the instructional strategies you develop. Consider the characteristics of the adult learner as you develop unique approaches that support learners and facilitate engagement in your online course.

2

Key Learning Attributes of Adults

Chapter 1 described the characteristics of adult learners in relationship to demographic characteristics and cultural differences. In Chapter 2, we will look at the learning attributes of adult learners. By understanding the characteristics of adult online learners and their learning attributes, you can target your pedagogy to meet the unique needs of adult learners. Such fine-tuning can have an impact on their satisfaction and motivation to persist.

Much of the research on learning does not differentiate adults from children (Merriam, 2001). There was, however, a drive to develop a knowledge base unique to adults, and from this emerged two fields of inquiry to describe how adults learn—andragogy and self-directed learning. Malcolm Knowles (1992), a recognized leader in the field of adult education, coined the term "andragogy." *Andragogy* describes a learner-centered approach to learning in which the adult learner determines the goals for learning and how they will be achieved. Knowles and colleagues (Knowles, Holton, & Swanson, 1998) developed a set of assumptions to describe key attributes of adults, including their need to know, self-concept, experience, readiness to learn, orientation to learning, and motivation to learn.

- *Need to know.* Adults need to know why they should learn something and how it benefits them.

- *Self-concept*. Adult learners may have difficulty with someone telling them what to do and how to think, which may make them resistant to learning in some situations.

- *Experience*. Previous experience is important to adult learners. Adults have a lifetime of experience and want to use and share what they know to enhance their learning.

- *Readiness to learn*. Adults become ready to learn something when they have a need to solve a problem. Older adults may be more ready to learn than younger adults.

- *Orientation to learning*. Learners' orientation to learning can be life-, task-, or problem-centered. They want to see how what they are learning will apply to their life, a task they need to perform, or a problem they need to solve.

- *Motivation to learn*. Although learners may respond to external motivators, internal priorities are more important. Incentives such as increased job satisfaction, self-esteem, and quality of life are important in giving them a reason to learn.

These assumptions should be viewed relative to your learners' individual levels of self-directedness, motivation, and life experience in order to ensure that your instructional approach functions positively in the given learning situation (Merriam, 2001). For learners who have high motivation, an established knowledge base in the subject matter, and life experience to support their knowledge base, many of these assumptions will be useful. For learners new to the subject, with little life experience, or with low motivation, making these assumptions can lead to a poor learning experience and affect their ability to persist. All learners will benefit from contextual descriptions that allow them to understand the need to know the content. They also will respond well to being treated with respect, which can be communicated by the tone of your interactions. As previously mentioned, it can be difficult for an adult to be told what to do or how to think. How you communicate with adult learners can help build a mutual respect, which can have a positive effect on their satisfaction, motivation, and ability to persist and learn.

SELF-DIRECTEDNESS

One of the assumptions of Knowles, Holton, and Swanson (1998) regarding adult learners is that adults are self-directed in their learning. Self-directed learning describes a process in which individuals take the initiative in diagnosing their learning needs, formulating learning goals, identifying human and material resources for learning, choosing and implementing appropriate learning strategies, and evaluating learning outcomes (Grow, 1996). Many online courses are designed based on the assumption that adults are self-directed; however, this is not always the case. David Grow (1996) points out the need to reconsider the assumption that all adult learners are self-directed. He believes that self-directedness is situational; a learner may be self-directed in one situation but may require more direction in another. He makes the assertion that self-direction can be learned and taught, which has implications for the strategies you use to support learners (Grow, 1996).

Grow proposes a four-stage model, the Staged Self-Directed Learning (SSDL) model (Grow, 1996), which suggests how you can support learners in becoming more self-directed in learning. His model takes into consideration a wide range of learner characteristics to help determine the appropriate level of support for learners, as shown in Exhibit 2.1.

Stage 1 represents the dependent learner. This learner generally has little prior knowledge in the subject, is unsure of the focus of his or her learning, and has low self-confidence and motivation. Dependent learners do best when the instructor role is one of an authority figure who will lead them through the activities and instructions and provide them with explicit directions on what to do, how to do it, and when to do it. Dependent learners require more frequent feedback to let them know how they are doing and whether they are meeting your expectations. They may have difficulty sorting through information and making choices. The amount of information presented to a dependent learner may have an impact on their ability to learn, so caution should be taken when determining content and resources. Dependent learners may also find it difficult to make choices on their own. For instance, they may have difficulty choosing a topic of interest, if given an opportunity. Therefore, if you assign an activity in which the learners are to choose a topic of interest to them, be sure to provide dependent learners a list of topics from which to choose.

Exhibit 2.1   Grow's Staged Self-Directed Learning (SSDL) Model.

Stage	Characteristics	Instructor
Stage 1: Dependent learner	• Little prior knowledge in subject • Unsure of the focus of his or her learning • Low self-confidence • Low motivation • Has difficulty organizing information • Has difficulty making decisions	Instructor as authority: • Directs activities • Provides explicit directions • Offers frequent feedback
Stage 2: Interested learner	• Basic understanding of what needs to be done • Not confident • Low motivation	Instructor as motivator: • Provides encouragement • Builds confidence • Gives frequent feedback
Stage 3: Involved learner	• Has skills and knowledge in subject • Has learning goals • Confident • Motivated	Instructor as facilitator: • Facilitates progress through content • Offers appropriate tools, methods, and techniques • Provides choices • Encourages learners to share experiences
Stage 4: Self-directed learner	• Has skills and knowledge in subject • Ability to set learning goals • Confident • Motivated • Good time management skills • Ability to self-evaluate	Instructor as consultant or guide on the side: • Provides self-evaluation strategies • Gives support when needed

Source: Grow, 1996.

In stage 2, learners may have little or no prior knowledge, but they are interested in learning. They have a basic understanding of what they need to do but are not confident that they can achieve the course objectives; therefore, their motivation may be low. They respond to instructors who are motivators. You will need to encourage these learners to build their confidence so that they can accomplish the objectives of the course.

In stage 3, learners have skills in and knowledge of the subject, and they have a sense of where they are going and how the course fits with their goals. They feel confident and motivated that they can get there. These learners respond to an instructor who will help facilitate their progress through unfamiliar content and offer appropriate tools, methods, and techniques to foster success. Learners with knowledge of the subject may prefer having opportunities to customize activities and assignments to their specific needs, so providing several choices of activities to accomplish the objectives can have a positive impact on these learners. In addition, encouraging learners to share their real-world experiences can give them a sense of satisfaction that they are able to share expertise and experience with the rest of the class to enhance discussions.

In the final stage, stage 4, learners are considered self-directed. These learners have skills and knowledge in the subject and can take responsibility for their learning, direction, and productivity. They also have skills in time management, project management, goal setting, and self-evaluation. An instructor is challenged with finding ways to enhance these learners' experience, while at the same time allowing them the freedom to work independently. Providing opportunities for learners to self-evaluate their performance can enhance their critical thinking skills and help them understand the direction they want to go with their learning. It is also important to be available to learners when they have questions or need support.

Grow's Staged Self-Directed Learning is a representative model of the different characteristics of learners that you will find in your online course. It demonstrates the need to adapt your teaching style to match learners' degree of self-directedness in order to provide appropriate support to help them increase self-directedness. This is a critical factor in learners' ability to persist. For this to be successful, you must have an understanding of where your learners are in terms of self-directedness and carefully monitor their progress throughout the course. This will require you to adjust your teaching to meet the needs of learners based on their stage of self-directedness.

SOCIAL STYLES OF ONLINE LEARNERS

Anthony Grasha (1996) defined learning styles as "personal qualities that influence a learner's ability to acquire information, interact with peers and the instructor, and otherwise participate in the learning experience" (p. 41). Grasha's definition is focused on the social styles of learners and the interaction that occurs between peers and with the instructor in a given learning environment, all of which has an impact on learning.

The Grasha-Riechmann Student Learning Style Scales developed by Anthony Grasha and Sheryl Riechmann (Grasha, 1996) describes how learners interact with the instructor, other learners, and the learning environment. Learners' social characteristics have a direct impact on how they will engage in the online environment. The scale spans six categories and looks at preferences

Exhibit 2.2   Grasha-Riechmann Student Learning Style Scales.

Style	Preferences
Independent	• Prefers to work alone • Not interested in discussion and other learner interaction • Not interested in team work
Dependent	• Looks to instructor and learners as guides • Prefers an authority figure to tell them what to do • Prefers highly structured environments
Competitive	• Interested in learning for reward and recognition • Prefers exams to projects
Collaborative	• Learns by sharing and cooperating with instructor and learners • Prefers group work and discussions
Avoidant	• Not excited about attending class or studying • Uninterested • Overwhelmed
Participative	• Interested in class activities and discussion • Works hard • Wants to meet instructor's expectations

Source: Grasha, 1996.

along three dimensions: independent–dependent, competitive–collaborative, and avoidant–participant, as shown in Exhibit 2.2.

Independent learners like to work alone on course activities and are not interested in interaction with learners. Dependent learners look to the instructor and to peers as a source of guidance and prefer an authority figure to tell them what to do. Competitive learners are interested in learning for the sake of performing and are interested in the extrinsic reward of recognition for their academic accomplishments. Collaborative learners learn by sharing and cooperating with the instructor and learners. They prefer small group discussions and group projects. Avoidant learners are not excited about attending class or studying. Generally, these learners appear uninterested or overwhelmed. Participative learners are interested in class activities and discussion and are eager to do as much class work as possible. They typically are interested in meeting all of the expectations that the instructor sets.

You have probably seen all of these preferences in learners. The extent to which they appear in the online environment is different, however. Strategies must be in place to accommodate the different social preferences of learners and provide a variety of activities that offer an opportunity for each learner to feel comfortable. For dependent learners, a highly structured environment that is instructor-directed with little learner choice is preferred. This includes having the content set out in units or modules with specific deliverables and due dates. Independent learners prefer to work independently via projects and individual assignments. They may be resistant to working in teams and may find discussions "busy work." The more you can engage them in activities that allow them to determine appropriate ways to meet the requirements, the greater satisfaction they will have. Competitive learners prefer exams to projects and are interested in grades. Collaborative learners prefer working together in groups and enjoy discussions and other opportunities to interact with others in projects or socially. It is difficult to engage avoidant learners because they tend not to be "present" in an online environment. Posting instructor expectations can help avoidant learners understand what you expect in terms of how often they should be active in the course. Also include the requirements for interactions with peers and specific learning activities. In addition, strict deadlines and consequences for not meeting them will encourage avoidant learners to stay focused. Providing time management strategies will also assist avoidant learners. Participative learners enjoy class discussions and team activities, so the more active the learning environment, the better. You will find that participative learners are the first to post to discussions and serve as guides for dependent learners. They will also be interested in team projects and can serve as leaders.

Although learners may have specific social styles, you are not expected to cater to their social styles. But by providing a variety of opportunities, you can meet their learning preferences and expose learners to new ways of learning and collaborating.

In this chapter, we looked at the learning attributes of adult learners, which set them apart from traditional learners. These attributes include their need to know, self-concept, experience, readiness to learn, orientation to learning, and motivation. Adult learners' level of self-directedness and social style also has an impact on how they engage in the online learning environment. By focusing on learning attributes specific to adults, you can target your teaching to meet the unique needs of adult learners and help improve their satisfaction and motivation to persist.

Challenges That Affect Learners' Persistence

3

We have examined the characteristics of online learners, including who they are and how they learn. Now we look at why learners choose the online learning environment over traditional learning environments and what challenges they face that affect their ability to persist.

The online learning population is a heterogeneous and diverse group from a variety of cultural and educational backgrounds. One of the main reasons they engage in online learning is because of the flexibility it provides to pursue their educational goals along with a number of other roles and responsibilities in their life. Globalization has created an environment in which learners no longer want to be place-bound and prefer flexible, online learning environments that allow them to engage in their educational goals anywhere, anytime (Dabbagh, 2007).

Learners choose online learning because they are able to select a school or program that fits their educational goals rather than having to choose one based on the best options available in their area. Online learners do not have to schedule specific days and times to attend class, so they have the flexibility to engage in learning when it fits their schedule. In addition, they do not have to spend time driving to school, parking their car, and walking to class, so it provides convenience for learners who may not have large blocks of time to learn.

There are challenges online learners have to overcome to be able to persist and successfully achieve their goals, however. Persistence and retention are often used interchangeably, but they are not the same. Retention is the ability of institutions to retain learners from matriculation through graduation. Retention rates measure how many full-time, first-time learners return the second year. Persistence refers to learners' actions as they relate to continuing their education from the first year until completing their degrees. Persistence rates measure how many total learners return from one semester to the next and includes all learners, not just first-year learners. Persistence rates reveal a more complete understanding of how all learners are doing because the comparison is specific to the institution based on the total population of learners. Persistence rates help an institution understand factors that affect learners' ability to persist, and they can be used to provide appropriate support for learners to increase their ability to persist as they progress from one course to the next in their program of study.

Despite the issue with comparing retention data from institution to institution, there is evidence that dropout rates among distance learners are higher than those of traditional, campus-based learners (Allen & Seaman, 2009). Therefore, it is critical to understand the factors that contribute to learners' dropping out and to develop effective strategies in your online course to support learners and help them persist in learning.

PERSISTENCE MODELS

Persistence models can give valuable insight into important variables to consider when developing your teaching strategies to help learners persist. William Spady, Vincent Tinto, and Ernest Pascarella are three prominent researchers who have studied learner persistence and retention. Their models address the traditional student in a land-based institution; however, the models offer an important framework to begin a discussion of the issues that directly affect online learners and provide a historical understanding of how retention and persistence have been studied and applied in practice. Exhibit 3.1 compares these models.

Spady Retention Model

Spady (1970) proposed a sociological model of the dropout process. He proposed five variables—academic potential, normative congruence, grade performance, intellectual development, and friendship support—that contribute directly to social integration. These five variables were then linked indirectly to the dependent

Exhibit 3.1 Comparison of Persistence Models That Address Traditional Students.

Model	Theory Overview	Variables
Spady Retention Model (1970)	A sociological model of the dropout process. Spady proposed five variables that contribute directly to social integration.	1. Academic potential 2. Normative congruence 3. Grade performance 4. Intellectual development 5. Friendship support

Tinto's Student Integration Model (1975)	This model seeks to explain a student's integration process based on academic and social systems of an institution.	1. Preentry attributes
		   Background characteristics
		   Previous educational experiences
		   Individual attributes
		2. Goals, commitment
		   Higher grades
		   Increased intellectual development
		3. Institutional experiences
		   Interaction with peers and faculty

Pascarella's General Model for Assessing Change (1985)	This model assesses student change and considers the direct and indirect effects of an institution's structural characteristics and its environment.	1. Student background, precollege traits 2. Structural, organizational characteristics 3. Institutional environment 4. Interactions with peers, faculty, and administrators

variable, the dropout decision, through two intervening variables—learners' satisfaction with their educational experience and learners' belief that the institution is committed to their academic success. Spady's model looked at the decision to drop out as occurring over time and identified characteristics that influenced student dropouts, including family background, academic potential, ability, and socioeconomic status. He also identified normative congruence, which refers to students' understanding of academic values and expectations in relation to the institution's values and expectations of the academic program. He also included academic variables such as grade performance and intellectual development as important factors in social integration, which increases satisfaction and, in turn, increases institutional commitment to lower dropouts.

Tinto's Integration Model

One of Tinto's Student Integration Models (Tinto, 1975, 1993) has been the most widely discussed model. Tinto explains student dropouts by examining the academic and social systems of an institution. Students' background characteristics, including family background (such as the parents' educational level), previous educational experiences, and individual attributes (such as race, age, gender, and ability), contribute to learners' commitment to educational goals, as well as their commitment to the institution. Tinto (1993) proposes that goal commitment leads to higher grades and intellectual development. These benefits lead to increased academic integration and even greater commitment to goals, which in turn lead to greater institutional commitment to reduce dropout.

Regarding the social system, this model proposes that institutional commitment increases interaction with peers and faculty and results in greater social integration, and fewer dropouts. Tinto attributes goal commitment to institutional commitment in two ways. First, he relates goal commitment to students' characteristics prior to entering the institution and, second, to students' experiences within the institution. A strong student commitment to their goals along with a positive experience at the institution leads to greater academic integration within the institution.

Pascarella's General Model for Assessing Change

Pascarella's (1985) model proposes that students' background and personal traits interact with the institutional mission and goals as evidenced by administrative policies and decisions, size of the institution, admission and academic standards, and other factors that directly influence the college experience. The latter include interactions with peers, faculty, and administrators, as well as cocurricular and extracurricular activities. Educational outcomes such as grades, intellectual and personal development, career goals, and college satisfaction influence institutional integration. His model emphasizes the importance of interaction with faculty and peers to influence educational outcomes.

Commonality of the Three Models

These three models have at least three things in common. First, they describe attrition as occurring over time based on the degree to which learners' background characteristics affect their ability to build a relationship with the institution. This process leads to learners either feeling that the institution is aligned to their goals and needs or not, and affects their decision to stay or drop out. Second, each model is based on the social and academic integration of learners with the institution, which also influences their decision to stay or drop out. Finally, each of the models is complex in order to allow an institution to analyze the specific variables that are relevant to the unique environment of its own institution.

This information can help institutions determine appropriate recruitment strategies, as well as understand specific strategies for academic support and social integration to help reduce attrition. The major issue with these variables is that they focus on traditional learners under the age of 24 who are full-time students living on campus. Regarding persistence of nontraditional students who work full-time, live away from campus, have families, and belong to social groups not associated with their college, however, are the persistence models such as those of Spady (1970), Tinto (1975), and Pascarella (1985) applicable? Other experts have looked at persistence that incorporates their ideas to see how they align with the nontraditional distance education learner.

ADDRESSING PERSISTENCE OF NONTRADITIONAL, DISTANCE EDUCATION LEARNERS

The persistence models of Bean and Metzner (1985) and Rovai (2003) address distance learning students. Bean and Metzner (1985) identified age, especially being over 24, as one of the most common variables in studies of nontraditional student attrition. Students over 24 years old represent a population of adult learners who often have family and work responsibilities that can interfere with successful attainment of educational goals. Other characteristics typically used to characterize nontraditional students are part-time student status and full-time employment. These are congruent to the data we looked at in Chapter 1 regarding the demographics of online learners. The lower persistence of nontraditional students in college has implications for distance education, since students enrolled in programs at a distance are typically viewed as nontraditional. Exhibit 3.2 is a comparison of the two persistence models that address the nontraditional distance learning student.

Bean and Metzner Persistence Model

Bean and Metzner (1985) proposed a model grounded on Tinto's (1975) model and earlier psychological models to explain attrition of nontraditional students. They argue that nontraditional students are not influenced by the social environment of the institution and are mainly concerned with the academic offerings of the institution. Older students have different support structures from younger students. Older students have limited interaction with the college community,

Exhibit 3.2 Comparison of Persistence Models That Address Nontraditional, Distance Learning Students.

Model	Theory Overview	Variables
Bean and Metzner (1985)	Predicts student persistence based on student-institution "fit."	1. Academic variables Study habits Course availability 2. Background and defining variables Educational goals Ethnicity Prior GPA 3. Environmental variables Finances Hours of employment Family responsibilities Outside encouragement 4. Psychological variables such as Stress Self-confidence Motivation
Rovai Composite Persistence Model (Rovai, 2003)	Is based on a synthesis of persistence models relevant to nontraditional students. Better explains persistence and attrition among the largely nontraditional students who enroll in online courses and programs.	Variables Prior to Admission 1. Student characteristics Age, ethnicity, gender Intellectual development Academic performance Academic preparation 2. Student skills Computer literacy Information literacy Time management Reading, writing skills Online communication skills Variables After Admission 1. External factors (Bean & Metzner, 1985) Finances Hours of employment Family responsibilities Outside encouragement Opportunity to transfer Life crises 2. Internal factors Tinto (1975): Academic integration, social integration, goal commitment, institutional commitment, learning community Bean and Metzner (1985): Study habits, advising, absenteeism, course availability, program fit, GPA, utility, stress, satisfaction, commitment Workman and Stenard (1996): Student needs: clarity of programs, self-esteem, identification with school, interpersonal relationships, accessibility to support and services Kerka and Grow (1996, as cited in Rovai 2003): Learning and teaching styles

and their focus for support is from outside the academic environment, that is, from peers, friends, family, employers, and coworkers.

The model of Bean and Metzner (1985) predicts student persistence based on student-to-institution "fit." In their model, factors that affect persistence include

1. Academic variables such as
   - Study habits
   - Course availability

2. Background and defining variables such as
   - Age
   - Educational goals
   - Ethnicity
   - Prior GPA

3. Environmental variables such as
   - Finances
   - Hours of employment
   - Family responsibilities
   - Outside encouragement

4. Psychological variables such as
   - Stress
   - Self-confidence
   - Motivation

An important finding in their research is that environmental variables outside the control of the institution, such as finances, hours of employment, and family responsibilities, may put too much pressure on nontraditional students' time, resources, and sense of well-being and thus may cause the students ultimately to drop out.

Rovai Model of Persistence

Alfred Rovai (2003) synthesized several persistence models relevant to nontraditional learners and developed a composite model that better explains persistence and attrition among the largely nontraditional learners who enroll in online courses and programs. The model differentiates between learner characteristics and skills prior to admission and external and internal factors affecting learners after admission.

Prior to admission, learner characteristics such as age, ethnicity, gender, intellectual development, academic performance, and preparation can affect learner persistence (Bean & Metzner, 1985). Additional skills that distance learners need to acquire to navigate the online environment include computer literacy, information literacy, time management, reading and writing skills, and online communication skills, all of which affect persistence. Learners who lack these skills and do not overcome the deficiency may be in danger of dropping out.

Once learners are admitted to a program of study, there are additional factors, both external and internal to the institution that can affect the ability of a learner to persist. According to Rovai (2003), these external factors include issues with finances, hours of employment, family responsibilities, the presence of outside encouragement, opportunity to transfer, and life crises such as sickness, divorce, and job loss. Internal factors that affect learners after admission include variables researched by Tinto (1975), Bean and Metzner (1985), Workman and Stenard (1996), and Kerka and Grow (1996, as cited in Rovai, 2003). Tinto's (1975) factors of social and academic integration as well as goal commitment, institutional commitment, and the development of a learning community are internal institutional factors that affect persistence. Workman and Stenard (1996) analyzed the needs of distance learners and identified five needs that influence persistence of online learners. These needs include consistency and clarity of online programs, policies, and procedures; learner's sense of self-esteem; ability to identify with the institution and not be regarded as an "outsider"; the need to develop interpersonal relationships with peers, faculty, and staff; and the ability to access academic support and services.

Online learners also expect a pedagogy that matches their learning style, which requires you to consider ways to support adult learners' need for independence and self-direction. Persistence models connect Grow's (1996) model for matching a learner's self-direction ability with teaching style, described in Chapter 2.

If learners experience problems getting answers to their questions and resolving issues, they may perceive an incompatibility between them and the institution.

If learners begin their academic work and find that they are not able to keep up with the workload due to personal issues, they may decide that this is not the right time for them to pursue their education and drop out. In addition, if they begin their coursework and find that they are having difficulties understanding the curricular materials, thinking critically, and writing, or have other deficiencies in academic skills, they may decide to drop out.

Learners enter college with a wide range of academic skills. The challenge is to address the academic needs of learners without labeling them as "remedial," a term that can lower learners' self-confidence and lead to poor performance. In addition, being able to identify issues early in the program of study is critical, as well as having the appropriate support services available to bridge gaps in learners' academic skills.

You must be aware of academically at-risk learners and be able to provide "just in time" resources to meet their needs and help them reach the next level of performance. One consideration for adult learners in distance education programs is that they have limited time available. Learners have to integrate learning into their already busy schedules and adjust to the time commitments needed to complete course activities. In addition, if a learner needs extra help with academic skills, which requires more time, they may become overwhelmed and drop out. The more support you can incorporate into learning activities, the greater opportunity learners will have to gain additional academic skills in a reasonable amount of time.

Upcoming chapters take a closer look at persistence factors described in this chapter that contribute to learners' ability to persist, and discuss specific pedagogical strategies that can be used to help learners overcome barriers to learning and improve their ability to persist in the online learning environment.

Part 1 presented the profile of an online learner. It discussed the importance of knowing your online learning audience in order to deliver a quality learning experience that meets the needs of learners and improves their ability to persist. Chapter 1 examined learner demographics and considered cultural differences that affect the online learner. As the diversity data show, the online learner population is a heterogeneous group of learners who come to the online learning environment with diverse values, beliefs, and perspectives—all of which need to be considered. Chapter 2 examined the learning attributes of online learners, including their attributes as adult learners, their self-directedness, and their social learning styles. By focusing on learning attributes specific to adults, you can target your pedagogy to meet the unique needs of adult learners, which can have an impact on their satisfaction and motivation to persist. Finally, Chapter 3 considered why adult learners choose the online environment and examined issues and challenges that adult learners face as they engage in online learning. It also considered critical variables that influence learners' ability to persist in the online environment to achieve their goals. Understanding the characteristics and needs of online learners may not necessarily guarantee success in an online course, but it may inform your pedagogy as you develop an understanding of your learners and how to support them to overcome challenges and successfully engage in an online learning environment.

Together, these chapters make up the profile of the adult, online learner including who online learners are, how they like to learn, why they choose online learning, and the challenges they face as they engage in online learning. Part 2 looks at cognition and learning to understand how learning occurs, considers factors that affect learning, and discusses instructional strategies that best support learners as they engage in learning.

Foundations of Cognition and Learning

Part 2 presents the foundations of cognition and learning. It is important to have a basic understanding of how learning theories have evolved, as well as a solid understanding of cognition, which is how we think. Both cognition and learning serve as a foundation for our teaching. If instructional strategies are not grounded in an understanding of how learning occurs, they are unproductive and do little to affect learner persistence. Chapter 4 describes the three basic learning theories—behaviorism, cognitivism, and constructivism—and explains how they can be used to support instruction. Chapter 5 examines the foundations of cognition and the mental processes that occur as we think and learn. The chapter describes how emotions, environmental factors, and cognitive load influence information processes and describes strategies we use as we think and learn. It also addresses two cognitive learning styles that influence how we learn. Chapter 6 describes motivation theory and examines its impact on learning. Part 1 laid the foundation of the profile of the online learner. Part 2 provides the foundation of cognition and learning. Together, these two parts present the basis and rationale for the instructional strategies recommended throughout the book.

Learning Theory

4

A basic understanding of learning theory is an important foundation to teaching. Learning is a complex process involving mental processes that are influenced by emotional and environment factors that can support or hinder learning. Learning theories have evolved that take into consideration these complex factors in an effort to explain how learning occurs and prescribe instructional strategies to facilitate learning. If instructional strategies are not grounded in an understanding of how learning occurs, they are unproductive and do little to affect learner persistence. In addition, there is an opportunity to maximize retention and transfer by linking basic research about the process of learning with instructional strategies (Tennyson & Schott, 1997). This approach is important to help learners use the skills and knowledge gained through educational experiences in the real world.

In this chapter, we look at the psychological foundations of learning, including behaviorism, cognitivism, and constructivism, to understand how each of these learning theories contributes to our understanding of learning and the instructional strategies we use in teaching.

BEHAVIORISM

Learning in the 1950s and 1960s was based on behaviorist learning theories. Behaviorism is grounded in the study of observable behavior and does not take into consideration the functions of the mind. When behaviorism was introduced, the mind was considered a black box that could not be accessed. According to behaviorism, knowledge exists outside of a person and is gained through behavior modification. The theory views learning as a change in behavior that can be conditioned using positive and negative reinforcements such as reward and punishment. There are two types of conditioning associated with behaviorism: Ivan Pavlov's classical conditioning and B. F. Skinner's operant conditioning. Pavlov used animals to discover the principles of learning based on natural reflexes that respond to stimuli. Most prominent was Pavlov's work with dogs to teach them to salivate to the sound of a bell. In his experiments, he demonstrated classical conditioning, in which an association is created between two stimuli (Pavlov, 1927). Skinner's operant conditioning experiments conditioned rats and pigeons to press or peck a lever to obtain pellets of food in an apparatus known as a Skinner Box. The experiments were based on the theory that organisms emit responses, which are gradually shaped by consequences. If a response has a reward, it is more likely to occur again and if it does not, it is less likely to occur. Skinner's operant conditioning demonstrated that associations are formed between a behavior and a consequence (Skinner, 1938).

Based on these types of experiments with animals, behaviorists proposed that learning is influenced by associations between behaviors and consequences. Behavior is conditioned by the instructor through rewards or punishment to attain the desired learning outcomes. According to behaviorists, the types of reinforcement are a critical component to learning because individual learners respond to different reinforcement based on their personal motivations. For instance, if the learner is motivated by good grades, a great reinforcement is the use of grades. Poor grades are a negative reinforcement, which provides motivation for the learner to put in more effort in order to receive a better grade.

According to Moore (as cited in Tennyson & Schott, 1997), the goal from the behaviorist perspective was the development of instruction that would enable the majority of students to achieve levels of performance predetermined by behaviorally defined objectives. Learning that involves recalling facts, defining concepts and explanations, or performing procedures are best explained by behaviorist learning strategies, which focus on attainment of specific goals or outcomes. In behaviorist theory, learners are more passive in the learning process. The learners' role is simply to respond to the learning content and demonstrate a level of performance on specific goals and objectives. Pedagogy based on behaviorism focuses on the ability to modify observable behavior to acquire knowledge or skills. The operant model of stimulus-response-reinforcement ensures that prescribed learning outcomes are achieved. In this model, the instructor provides learners with information about the appropriateness of the behavior through frequent feedback. This feedback either reinforces learners' behavior or determines consequences in the form of corrective actions for the learner to achieve the desired performance behavior. This requires continuous monitoring and feedback from the instructor.

According to the behaviorist view of learning, objectives should be developed that focus on the level of learning desired, as well as the type of task. Behaviorists focus on "identifying small, incremental tasks, or sub skills that the learner needed to acquire for successful completion of instruction, designing specific objectives that would lead to the acquisition of those sub skills, and sequencing sub skill acquisition in the order that would most efficiently lead to successful learner outcomes" (Tennyson & Schott, 1997, p. 5).

COGNITIVISM

In the late 1960s and 1970s psychology moved from the study of behavior to the study of the mind, and cognitivism emerged as a new theory of how learning occurs. According to cognitivism, knowledge is still considered to exist outside of the person; however, its focus is on understanding how human memory works to acquire knowledge and promote learning. The theory's foundation is information processes and understanding the memory structures of the mind for knowledge acquisition. In addition, the theory establishes conditions of learning and strategies to incorporate individual differences into the design of instruction, including the use of pretests and more formative assessment strategies. In cognitivism, task analysis shifts from behavioral objectives to performance; the different stages of performance extend from novice to expert (Tennyson & Schott, 1997).

The environment continues to have the greatest impact on learning; however, there is more focus on how learners acquire specific types of strategies for learning, including planning, monitoring, and evaluating, and the influence of prior knowledge, beliefs, attitudes, and values on learning (Tennyson & Schott, 1997). This theory developed a clearer understanding of how information is processed and stored, as well as how prior knowledge is stored in memory structures called schema for retrieval in an appropriate context. According to cognitivism, the transfer of knowledge to new situations is influenced by how information is presented and the relevance of the information. If information is presented poorly or too much irrelevant information is associated with relevant information, the learner may have difficulty sorting and organizing the information. This difficulty, in turn, can have an impact on storage, retrieval, and transfer—functions that are critical to adult learners who have specific professional needs that require them to be able to transfer knowledge to real-world applications in their professional environments.

Learning outcomes that are focused on complex higher levels of learning such as problem solving are best explained by cognitivism because the focus is on breaking down complex problems into component parts and relating the content to be learned with prior knowledge to build higher levels of understanding. Instructional strategies based on cognitive theory consider the organization of content for learning and focus on information processing, including organization, retrieval, and application.

David Ausubel (1960) developed the concept of the advance organizer (information that is presented prior to learning) and researched how use of advance organizers can scaffold the learning of new information. Advance organizers stimulate schema to help learners link prior knowledge with new information. An example of an advance organizer is a summary of the main ideas in a reading passage and explanations of content at a "higher level of abstraction, generality, and inclusiveness than the reading itself" (Ausubel, 1963, p. 81).

Robert Gagne (1985) proposed nine events of learning that correspond with specific cognitive processes. Gagne's nine events are a systematic organizational process for learning and include the following:

- Gaining the learners' attention
- Informing them of the learning objectives
- Stimulating recall of prior learning
- Presenting stimulus in the form of content to be learned
- Providing guidance
- Eliciting performance through instructional activities
- Providing feedback

- Assessing performance

- Enhancing retention and transfer

Gagne proposed that these nine events provide the conditions of learning and define the intellectual skills to be learned, as well as the sequence of instruction. He believed lessons should be organized according to these events so learners could associate new knowledge with existing structures. He also thought the nine events could provide the appropriate level of scaffolding to support learning.

According to cognitivism, learners play a more active role in learning by actively organizing the learning process. The emphasis of cognitivism is on helping learners organize information for successful processing into long-term memory and recall. Cognitive strategies focus on internal learning and thinking processes, including "problem solving, organizing information, reducing anxiety, developing self-monitoring skills, and enhancing positive attitudes" (Tennyson & Schott, 1997, p. 8). The instructor continues to determine learning outcomes and direct the learning with the additional application of specific information-processing strategies to assist the learner in acquiring knowledge. To facilitate learning, cognitivism postulates that the learning environment should be arranged to maximize learners' ability to retrieve prior knowledge relevant to the learning outcomes and organize the content to maximize information processing. Instructors should provide the appropriate context for learners to draw on prior knowledge and fit new information into existing schema. For learners with little prior knowledge, instructors need to provide opportunities to create new schema by relating the new information to something that is familiar to them.

CONSTRUCTIVISM

Constructivism became popular in the 1980s. It describes learning as a process in which learners construct knowledge and meaning by integrating prior knowledge, beliefs, and experiences. According to this theory, knowledge does not exist outside of the person but is constructed based on how a person interacts with the environment and experiences the world (Tennyson & Schott, 1997). Control of the environment is not a focus of the constructivist theory of learning. Instead, it emphasizes the synthesis and integration of knowledge and skills into an individual's experiences. This theory addresses some of the limitations of other learning theories that emphasize components instead of integrated wholes.

There are two types of constructivism: cognitive constructivism and social constructivism. Cognitive constructivism focuses on the individual characteristics or attributes of the learner and their impact on learning. Social constructivism focuses on how meaning and understanding are created through social interaction. Together, they view knowledge acquisition as a means of interpreting incoming information through an individual's unique lens, which includes his or her personality, beliefs, culture, and experiences. Based on interpretations, knowledge has meaning and learners build schema to represent what they know.

Jean Piaget's (1985) theory of cognitive constructivism proposed that knowledge cannot be simply transmitted to a person but must be constructed through experience. Experiences allow individuals to construct mental models or schemas, and knowledge construction is based on a change in schema through assimilation and accommodation. If the incoming information can be associated with existing information, assimilation of the incoming information into the already formed schemas occurs and equilibrium is maintained. If the incoming information conflicts with current thinking, cognitive dissonance occurs; this is an uncomfortable feeling that stems from holding conflicting ideas at the same time. Cognitive dissonance requires a change in existing schemas to accommodate incoming information. In addition, Piaget believed that learning is based on interaction with the environment around us, so real-world practice is important.

Social constructivism emphasizes the social nature of learning. Lev Vygotsky (1978) proposed that learning could not be separated from the social context in which it occurs, nor could accommodation and assimilation occur without the active integration of the learner in a community of practice. He saw learning as a collaborative process, and he developed a theory called the zone of proximal development (ZPD) to explain the collaborative nature of learning (Vygotsky, 1978). This theory distinguishes between two levels of development. One is the level of development that a learner can reach independently. The second is the potential level of development a learner can achieve with the support of an instructor or peers. This theory argues that with help from an instructor or peers, learners can understand concepts and ideas that they cannot understand on their own. It supports an instructional strategy of providing learners just enough scaffolding or support to help them reach the next level of understanding. This scaffolding in turn allows learners to work independently until they no longer can learn without support. Instruction again is supported through the instructor or peers, and the learner continues to reach higher levels of understanding through their guidance.

According to constructivism, memory is continuously under construction as a person interacts with incoming information in unique contexts that require them to draw upon prior knowledge from different sources. Either accommodation or assimilation of new information into existing schemas occurs, which builds deeper levels of understanding and meaning. Transfer involves the use of meaningful contexts that allow the learning to be transferred to a novel situation and applied. Real-world examples, as well as opportunities to solve real-world problems, allow for the greatest opportunity for transfer.

Constructivist theories do not categorize learning into types but hold that all learning is context dependent. One of the problems with constructivist learning theories is the assumption that all learners come to the learning situation with prior knowledge and that the goal of learning is to activate prior knowledge and build additional understanding and meaning. Learners who are new to a field of study may not have prior knowledge, so building instructional strategies that require them to draw on prior knowledge and deal with ill-structured problems can be frustrating and overwhelming. For learners who do not have prior knowledge and experience, there are cognitive strategies such as the use of advance organizers and conceptual scaffolds that can be used to replace the lack of prior knowledge and experience. These strategies are addressed in more detail in Chapter 9.

From the constructivist perspective, learners are not merely passive receivers of knowledge, they are active participants in the learning process and knowledge construction. Instruction should situate the learning in authentic tasks that allow learners to understand why it is important to learn, as well as its relevance to them personally or professionally. Instructors who base their pedagogy on constructivism take on a new role of facilitator rather than lecturer by actively observing and assessing the current state of individual learners and providing learning strategies to help them interpret and understand the content. The facilitator role includes providing relevant context for learners who may not have prior knowledge and experience with the subject to help them organize the content into relevant schemas for acquiring knowledge. The instructor must develop skill in assessing the current state of learners and adapt the learning experience to support their attainment of goals. The instructor must also have an understanding of individual learning styles to provide effective strategies to help learners plan, monitor, and evaluate their thinking during learning.

SUMMARY OF LEARNING THEORIES

As you can see from the presentation of the three learning theories, there has been a progression in our understanding of learning from behaviorism to cognitivism to constructivism. Behaviorism considers the mind as a black box, so its focus is on the study of how learning occurs by observing changes in behavior and prescribed instructional strategies to shape behavior. Cognitivists focus their theories of learning based on the mind and consider the internal workings of memory and information processing to understand how learning occurs. Finally, constructivism considers how learning occurs both internally and externally through a change of structures in memory, as well as the impact of our beliefs, cultures, and environment on how we construct knowledge.

Each of these learning theories provides important knowledge about how we learn, which in turn affects how we teach and the instructional strategies we choose. Now look at the summary of the learning theories in Exhibit 4.1 and consider how you can use strategies from all three learning theories to help build a meaningful learning experience for learners.

Behaviorism, although not always viewed in the best light because it contributes to the ideas of being teacher-centered and passive learning, has contributed knowledge of how to structure content to ensure learning objectives are met and higher levels of thinking are developed. Its contributions include learning taxonomies for cognitive, psychomotor, and affective domains of learning, the most notable being Bloom's taxonomy of educational objectives (Bloom, Englehart, Furst, Hill, & Krathwohl, 1956). This taxonomy classifies the levels of intellectual behavior important in learning as knowledge, comprehension, application, analysis, synthesis, and evaluation. From learning taxonomies came behavioral objectives, which associate specific verbs to each of the six levels to help instructors develop objectives that target the level of learning expected. Objectives helped link instructional goals with assessment. The new Bloom's taxonomy combines aspects of the original taxonomy with a more recent taxonomy that includes the categories of remember, understand, apply, analyze, evaluate, and create (Krathwohl, 2002). Today there is a call for greater accountability from higher education institutions

Exhibit 4.1 Comparison of Learning Theories.

Component	Behaviorism (1950s–1960s)	Cognitivism (1960s–1970s)	Constructivism (1980s)
Study of…	Study of observable behavior	Study of the mind	Study of social construction of knowledge
Knowledge	Outside of the person—gained through behavior modification	Outside of the person—gained through information processing	Knowledge does not exist outside of the person but is constructed based on how a person interacts within the environment and experiences the world
Learning	Change in behavior that can be conditioned using positive and negative reinforcement such as reward and punishment	Change in memory structure through planning, monitoring, and evaluating Acknowledges that beliefs, attitudes, and values influence learning	Learners construct knowledge and meaning by integrating prior knowledge, beliefs, and experiences as they learn
Research	Pavlov's classical conditioning (1927) Skinner's operant conditioning (1938)	Ausubel's advance organizers (1960) Gagne's nine events of instruction (1985)	Piaget's cognitive constructivism (1985) Vygotsky's social constructivism (1978)
Types of learning	Recalling facts Defining concepts, explanations, procedures	Problem solving Breaking down complex problems into components	Emphasis on the whole rather than components
Learner	Passive	Active	Active, Social
Teaching focus	Teacher-centered Ability to modify behavior Use of behavior objectives Outcomes based	Teacher-centered Organizing content Scaffolding learning	Teacher as facilitator Focus on integration of skills and knowledge in real-world practice Scaffolding learning experience Social construction of knowledge
Instructional strategies	Behavioral objectives Bloom's taxonomy (1956) Drill and practice	Advance organizers Nine events of instruction	Active learning strategies Critical thinking strategies Reflection strategies

to demonstrate that learners have achieved the intended outcomes of a program of study, so the contributions of behaviorism continue to play an important role in how we structure learning activities.

We also see the influence of cognitive learning theory in considering how the mind works. The theory has helped us understand the structures of memory and how information processing and storage occur during learning. It influences the way content is developed and delivered to support learning. Textbooks are organized with headings and subheadings that organize material into meaningful parts. Learning materials are structured from simple to complex and sequenced to support the learner in knowledge acquisition.

Finally, constructivism has contributed a more holistic approach to learning that considers the learner as an active participant in the learning process. There has been a move away from read, lecture, and test strategies to learning strategies that engage learners in dialogue. With these strategies, learners can share their knowledge and beliefs and have their knowledge and beliefs challenged by peers. This helps learners understand multiple perspectives and perceive flaws or misconceptions in their thinking, make new connections, and build higher levels of knowledge. There is some controversy about whether learners should be setting their own goals, especially in light of the move to more accountability. There is no debate, however, that individual needs should direct how learners achieve the prescribed learning outcomes. The more relevant learning outcomes are to learners, the greater impact the learning will have on them.

The strategies recommended throughout the book are grounded in learning theory. You will see that understanding all three perspectives can enhance your teaching strategies to help learners persist in learning and achieve the intended outcomes of your course.

5

Understanding Cognition and Learning

In Chapter 4, we looked at the cognitivist theory of learning and defined cognition as the study of the mind and how learning occurs. How we perceive and process information is an important variable to learning, so having a more complete understanding of information processing can help you develop instructional strategies to improve the learning process.

Learners with poor thinking skills have more difficulty in the online learning environment because their ability to process information effectively may be hindered by environmental and emotional factors. This can lead learners to feeling overwhelmed, frustrated, anxious, and a number of other emotions that can diminish motivation and ultimately cause a learner to drop the course. In this chapter, we look at information processing and how learning occurs. We examine metacognitive strategies for learning, including planning, monitoring, and evaluating. Finally, we discuss factors that influence cognition and learning. The goal is to help you understand the connection between cognition and learning so you can develop effective instructional strategies to support learners as they develop thinking skills, persist in their education, and achieve their educational goals.

INFORMATION PROCESSING

How information is processed and stored as memory is critical to learning. If a learner is unable to focus on the right information, it is difficult to hold information in short-term memory long enough for it to move to working memory for processing and storage. In addition, there are emotional factors, including being overwhelmed by the content, feeling anxious, or other emotional responses, that can interrupt information processing and lead to poor storage of new information. Cognition or thinking is fluid and adaptive in order to adjust to any given environmental or emotional condition at any given moment (Tennyson & Schott, 1997).

The information processing system in the brain is made up of four main components, as depicted in Figure 5.1, including sensory memory, which receives incoming information; short-term memory, which holds the information; working memory, which processes the information; and long-term memory, which stores information. This is how we think.

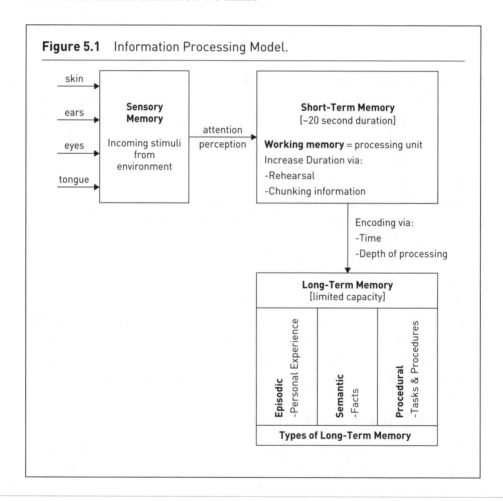

Figure 5.1　Information Processing Model.

Sensory Memory

Information enters the brain through sensory memory receptors located in the eyes, skin, ears, and tongue. Incoming information hitting these receptors decay rapidly and can be easily broken up. In addition, far more information enters the sensory memory receptors than can be attended to, so it is critical for the learner to focus on incoming stimuli from the learning environment in order to progress to the next stage, which is moving the information to short-term memory for processing. Attention and perception are the processes by which the learner determines which information hitting their receptors is important. For learners who are working online, their personal learning environment can have a direct impact on their attention and perception as they learn. If they do not have a private place to study, distractions from their environment that are hitting their sensory memory receptors may impede their ability to attend to important information.

Short-Term Memory

Short-term memory is what we are thinking about at any one moment in time. Short-term memory can last up to 20 seconds unless a rehearsal process is used to maintain the information. For instance, repeating a phone number until you dial it is a form of rehearsal that allows the information to remain in short-term memory past 20 seconds. If a distraction occurs during rehearsal, the information can be lost, so attention is a critical element in retaining information in short-term memory for processing.

Working memory refers to the structures and processes used for temporarily storing and managing information in short-term memory. It includes the processes by which short-term memory is transferred and stored as long-term memory. It requires organizing complex information before encoding it to long-term memory in order to ensure it is retrievable at a later time. It also includes storing new information with existing knowledge to create stronger schemas.

There are limits to the amount of information that can be processed at any one time in short-term memory. Research indicates that the number of units or chunks of information that can be processed is seven, plus or minus two (Miller, 1956). The way information is bundled or chunked can have an impact on retention in short-term memory. A simple example of chunking is in how we organize letters of the alphabet into chunks that form words. For example, if we look at the letters c, a, r, d they represent four pieces of information; however, if you put them together into a word *card,* you now have a single piece of information. If you take that idea further, consider the list below:

Green bean	Apple
Orange	Broccoli
Beef	Chicken
Pork	Pear
Banana	Carrot
Corn	Turkey

Now let's look at the list in chunks:

Vegetables	Fruits	Meats
Corn	Orange	Beef
Broccoli	Banana	Pork
Green bean	Apple	Chicken
Carrot	Pear	Turkey

From this example you can see how chunking the 12 elements into three chunks, each with four elements, allows the items to be classified into groups, which reduces information overload and aids in memory. Organization and presentation of content in your course is critical to learning, so it's important to consider not only the amount of information you present to the learner at one time but also how you organize the information into chunks to enhance memory. Chapter 9 discusses specific cognitive strategies to help organize information to aid learning.

Long-Term Memory

Long-term memory is the repository of all acquired information, known as the knowledge base. It is permanent and the amount of information that can be stored is without limit, although retrieval can be an issue. Information is represented in long-term memory as different domains of knowledge, which consist of a complex network of information organized into meaningful modules called schemata (Tennyson & Schott, 1997).

Types of Long-Term Memory   There are three types of long-term memory—episodic, semantic, and procedural. Episodic and semantic types of memory are associated with declarative knowledge, or what we know about persons, places, or things. Procedural memory is associated with procedural knowledge or the how of knowing. Episodic memory stores personal experiences. These are memories of experiences that you have had and include information regarding who, what, where, when, and why for any given experience. Episodic memory stores the unique experiences that are associated with learning; it requires access to the context, as well as the personal experience, associated with the learning event. Semantic memory stores facts, including concepts, rules, principles, and problem-solving skills, in networks called schemata, as previously mentioned. Procedural memory refers to the ability to perform a task or procedure as a series of steps. Retrieval of information is stepwise, with one step triggering the retrieval of the next, and so forth.

These three systems are not necessarily mutually exclusive; they can interact. In any given learning situation, episodic memory can come into play, especially if a previous learning situation was particularly good or bad. This memory can have an impact on semantic memory. If the previous memories are good, it can strengthen the memory. If the experience was poor, it weakens the memory by creating stress, which interferes with cognitive processing. New information that can be associated with existing schema is easier to retrieve and builds on the current level of understanding. This is the same for procedural memory. As you consider instructional strategies to aid in memory, consider opportunities to situate learning in a context that is relevant and replicates how the learner will experience the information in the real world.

Encoding Information for Storage in Long-Term Memory For information to be stored in long-term memory (LTM), encoding needs to take place. Several factors affect the encoding of information into long-term memory, including the amount of time, depth of processing, organization, and elaboration of information. We have already considered that information can only stay in short-term memory for approximately 20 seconds unless strategies are used to keep it there longer. The more time that the information can remain in short-term memory, the greater chance there is of storing the information in LTM. In addition, depth of processing can lead to better encoding. Depth of processing refers to the way a person thinks about a piece of information (Craik & Tulving, 1975). The more attention the information receives, the greater depth of processing that occurs and therefore the greater chance of storing it in LTM.

Organization of information can be a critical component to storing information in long-term memory. We talked about memory only being able to hold 7 ± 2 units of information at any one time (see discussion of short-term memory, page 45). Organizing information into chunks of related information can increase memory. In addition, reorganizing individual pieces of information into a larger structure or hierarchy can lead to better memory. Finally, elaboration is the depth of processing that results from building connections between pieces of information to develop LTM. The more ways information can be associated with what you already know (or if you have no prior knowledge, the more ways it can be described and explained), the easier it is to properly store the information.

Storage and Retrieval of Information from Long-Term Memory Once information is encoded, it is stored in LTM as a network of information or schemata. If you look at the schema for "cat," for instance, you will find knowledge about physical characteristics of cats, types of cats, scientific information about cats as a species, personal experiences with cats, and so forth. Ausubel (1968) proposed that the most important factor that influences learning is what you already know. As you continue to gain knowledge about cats, your schema for cat continues to evolve, thus resulting in greater knowledge and understanding of cats.

The organization of schemata is also important because greater organization leads to improved learning at a faster rate. In our discussion of constructivism, we discussed Piaget's theory of assimilation and accommodation. As incoming information is related to an existing schema, new information is assimilated into the existing information. If the incoming information does not fit the existing schema, cognitive dissonance occurs, which requires accommodation of new information into the existing framework to build a more organized structure of knowledge. This requires making decisions about the value of the new information in relation to what you already know and may require you to change existing knowledge or organize it in a different way based on the new incoming information.

METACOGNITION

As already discussed, information processing is a complex process. It requires learners to have specific strategies to attend to incoming information, draw on knowledge in long-term memory, and store new information into meaningful schemata that can enhance storage and retrieval. Metacognition is the knowledge of specific strategies we use to think and learn.

Metacognition supports information processing by actively controlling what learners think as they learn. Through the process of self-regulation, learners can use a number of strategies to effectively process information and ensure knowledge acquisition. Strategies include planning, monitoring, and evaluating progress toward a specific learning goal. Because of the self-directed nature of online learning, learners need to have well-developed metacognitive strategies to help them navigate the learning process.

Planning is a critical component of online learning. Many learners begin the learning process without understanding what they need to do and without the skills to critically think through and plan their learning activities. Planning strategies include the following:

- Understanding the expectations of the course in general and activities in individual units of study
- Creating a plan for learning
- Understanding time requirements
- Scheduling time to complete activities
- Drawing on prior knowledge so learners can see what knowledge they already have and where they need to put their efforts to learn new information
- Preparing the environment to make it conducive to learning

Monitoring strategies are critical to ensure that learners are using effective strategies to learn and stay on task. Such strategies include making sure they understand the new information, working toward the intended goals, and meeting the requirements of the learning activity in the allotted time.

Evaluating strategies are those that learners use at the end of an activity to evaluate the effectiveness of the strategies they used during the learning process. This level of reflection can help learners formatively evaluate strategy use and make appropriate changes to improve the quality of the learning process.

Metacognition is situation-specific. Depending upon the type of learning activities, different metacognitive strategies can be deployed. Demonstrating strategies for learning can help learners continue to build their collection of metacognitive strategies to become effective learners. Chapter 8 looks at specific cognitive strategies to help learners plan, monitor, and evaluate progress in the online learning environment.

FACTORS INFLUENCING LEARNING

We examined cognition and learning, which occur through information processing to store information as memories in the brain. We also discussed metacognition, which is our awareness of how we think and learn. Next, we will look at factors that influence learning including emotional and environmental factors, cognitive load, and cognitive learning styles.

Emotional Factors

The emotional response to learning can have a huge impact. Positive emotion can cause more attention to be focused on the learning goal, thus allowing incoming information to be processed in working memory and eventually stored in LTM. Negative emotion can interfere with the learning goal by distracting learners and moving their attention away from learning to managing the emotion that is being felt. Distress interferes with cognition by depleting attention allocation to the learning goal, thereby lowering working memory performance, processing speed, and memory ability. Being able to calm learners' fears and anxiety can help prepare them to engage in the course activities. Reaching out to learners to let them know you are there to help can reduce this anxiety. Also, showing empathy for the difficulty of learning online can encourage learners. Letting them know that you are just a phone call away can help them overcome the emotional response they are experiencing and prepare them for learning. Chapter 7 discusses specific cognitive strategies that can keep learners from becoming overwhelmed.

Environmental Factors

Another factor that can influence information processing is the learning environment. Online learners are not sitting in a classroom, where outside distractions are eliminated. Learners are probably working on their course in an environment in which a number of other things are going on that can potentially distract them. If a learner is not actively attending to the learning task, there is less chance of their moving information from short-term to long-term memory. Although you have little impact on the learner's individual learning environment, be aware that the learning environment can have an impact on learning. If you are working with learners who have difficulty understanding the activities, you may want to discuss where they are doing their coursework. You can recommend that they find a quiet place to learn and that they reduce distractions to help them focus their attention on learning activities. Specific recommendations can include creating a dedicated space for learning, learning at times when family interruptions are at a minimum (for instance, after children have gone to bed), and making sure that there are no additional distractions such as TV. By helping learners understand the effect of their environment on their ability to focus their attention to learn, they can make changes to improve learning.

Cognitive Load

Learners new to an online environment often come to the learning experience with low confidence in their ability to be successful. New learners have to manage the technology, the course environment, the policies and procedures, the vocabulary, and the content. It is normal for learners to have to sift through a lot of incoming information, but when it is a barrier to the goal of learning, it is considered interference. In addition to emotional stress, cognitive load, which is related to the load on working memory during learning, can have an impact on emotion and information processing. If too much new information is presented to learners at one time, an immediate response can be anxiety, which can have an impact on attention and information processing.

According to Sweller and Chandler (1994), there are two sources of cognitive load that have implications for instruction—intrinsic cognitive load and extraneous cognitive load—which are illustrated in Figure 5.2.

Intrinsic cognitive load relates to the complexity of the learning content, as well as the schemata that learners have constructed, and cannot be controlled by design. If the learning content is complex and the learner has little prior knowledge and therefore few or no schemata, then the intrinsic load of the content is high. Extraneous cognitive load is imposed by the design and the organization of the learning materials and has a negative impact on learning; therefore, it should be reduced to maximize learning. If the materials being taught are difficult, then intrinsic cognitive load is high, so the amount of content that is presented and the structure in which it is presented should be simple to reduce extraneous

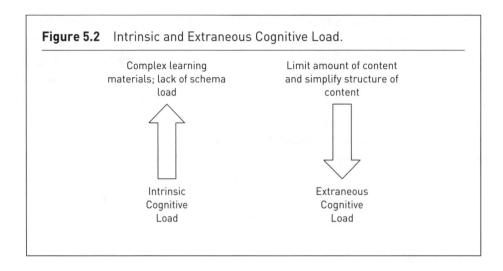

Figure 5.2 Intrinsic and Extraneous Cognitive Load.

Complex learning
materials; lack of schema
load

Limit amount of content
and simplify structure of
content

Intrinsic
Cognitive
Load

Extraneous
Cognitive
Load

cognitive load. Two sources of extraneous cognitive load that cost learners time and effort are split attention and redundancy. Split attention occurs when the learner has to focus on multiple sources of information. Redundancy occurs when learners process duplicate information from different sources. The more you can eliminate redundant materials and arrange information to avoid splitting the learner's attention, the greater the opportunity for learning to occur.

Chang and Ley (2006) describe online learning activities such as navigating the course room, using multiple-linked materials, finding your way back from linked materials to the original place you began, and solving technical issues and connection problems that split learners' attention and increase extraneous cognitive load. Information that is linked from multiple locations within and external to the course can cause extraneous cognitive load for learners. If you choose to link to information, be sure that it opens in a new window and be very specific about what information learners are required to review. For instance, if the information you link to has links to other information, many learners may be confused regarding whether they need to read the information on the main page or whether they need to click on all of the available links and review all information available at the site.

It is also important to consider the amount of information that is presented to the learner at one time if the intrinsic load of the information is high. Try to limit resources to those that are necessary to complete or prepare for upcoming activities. If there are supplemental resources that you feel learners may want to review, specifically label them as supplemental resources. You may also consider putting supplemental resources in a separate location in the course to make sure learners do not become confused with what is required and what is supplemental (Smith, 2008). As you consider how to structure the learning resources, try to locate the resources close to the activities they support. For instance, if you place all of the readings in a single location, the learner will not have an understanding of which readings go with the different activities. Instead, group resources directly with the activities in which they are used. Research demonstrates that extraneous cognitive load in online learning might be reduced by printing online materials, which is a common practice used by learners (Chang & Ley, 2006). Limiting the number of external links to resources and allowing learners the ability to compile and print materials can help reduce cognitive load and organize resources in a way that improves comprehension. Also, consider breaking up information into several chunks of five to seven units, which is the amount of information that can be retained in working memory at one time.

Cognitive Learning Styles

Part 1 describes social learning styles of learners that affect learning in an online learning environment. Cognitive styles also affect learning. *Cognitive style* refers to "an individual's characteristic and consistent approach to organizing and processing information" (Tennant, 1997, p. 80). There are numerous classifications of these styles; however, according to Tennant (1997), two dominant approaches are the Field Dependence/Independence dimension by Witkin (1950) and the Kolb Learning Style Inventory (Kolb, 1976).

Field Dependence/Independence Dimension   Witkin (1950) examined how individual differences and context affect a person's ability to make simple perceptual judgments. Trying to find hidden objects in a puzzle is an example of separating out individual components from a perceptual field. Another example is finding a word embedded in a set of geometric shapes. Witkin found that some individuals' perceptions are influenced by context, whereas context has little or no influence for others (as cited in Tennant, 1997). The common denominator underlying differences in performance of tasks in a perceptual field is the extent to which a person is able to separate a part of the field from the whole field.

Exhibit 5.1 Characteristics of Field Dependent and Field Independent
Learners.

Field Dependent	Field Independent
Perceives globally, perceives field as a whole	Perceives analytically, perceives field as a set of component parts
Cognitive tasks are more difficult	Performs better on cognitive tasks
Has difficulty with ambiguous or unorganized material—needs to have structure imposed	Capable of structuring unorganized or ambiguous material
Needs to have defined goals for learning	Can define own goals for learning
Is externally motivated, needs external reinforcement	Is internally motivated, can provide own reinforcement

Source: Witkin, 1950, as cited in Tennant, 1997.

Field dependent people cannot separate the parts from the whole, whereas field independent people are able to see the individual components of a perceptual field. Exhibit 5.1 lists specific characteristics of field dependent and field independent learners.

Learners who are field independent are perceived as analytical because of their ability to separate the parts from the whole, whereas field dependent learners perceive things more globally. A field independent learner is able to perform better on cognitive tasks and is able to structure unorganized or ambiguous materials, which is more difficult for a field dependent learner. Field independent learners can more easily define their learning goals because they are independent thinkers, whereas field dependent learners tend to go along with the group and need to have their goals defined. In addition, field independent learners are more self-motivated and can provide their own internal reinforcements when needed, whereas field dependent learners need more external reinforcements to keep them motivated. According to Witkin (as cited in Tennant, 1997), a number of studies have shown that cognitive style can be modified (p. 84). Witkin and his colleagues assert that individual differences in field dependence or independence are due to socialization, which suggests that education can modify differences in cognitive style. In other words, just because a learner is field dependent or independent does not mean that you have to teach to his or her style. You can provide learners with a variety of instructional strategies that target a number of different learning styles and encourage learners to use learning strategies outside of their dominant style. We can look to our understanding of the profile of the

Exhibit 5.2 Strategies to Support Field Dependent Learners.

Field Dependent	Instructional Strategies
Perceives globally, perceives field as a whole	Provide opportunities for learners to practice breaking down concepts and ideas into discrete parts
Cognitive tasks are more difficult	Provide metacognitive scaffolds to support learners' thinking
Has difficulty with ambiguous or unorganized material—needs to have structure imposed	Provide graphic organizers, outlines, study guides, etc., to help learners organize difficult or ambiguous information
Needs to have defined goals for learning	Provide learners with goals for learning and structured ways to attain goals using road maps and checklists
Is externally motivated, needs external reinforcement	Use motivational strategies to improve self-efficacy and motivation

online learner, learning theory, information processing, and motivation theory to help learners become more field independent. Exhibit 5.2 describes strategies that can be used to support field dependent learners and help them to become more field independent.

Because field dependent learners perceive a field as a whole and have difficulty separating the parts, provide opportunities for learners to practice breaking down concepts and ideas into discrete parts. Cognitive tasks are more difficult for field dependent learners, so metacognitive scaffolds can support their thinking. They also have difficulty with ambiguous or unorganized materials, so provide them with graphic organizers, outlines, and study guides to help them organize difficult or ambiguous information. Field dependent learners also have difficulty defining goals. Provide learners with goals for learning and structure ways to attain goals using road maps and checklists. They also are extrinsically motivated, so you will need to find ways to help them become more intrinsically motivated, which we will discuss next. Part 3 discusses in detail the cognitive scaffolds to support field dependent learners.

Kolb Learning Style Inventory The Kolb Learning Style Inventory measures cognitive style preferences on two bipolar dimensions: active experimentation versus reflective observation, and concrete versus abstract. The Kolb Learning Style Inventory (LSI; Kolb, 1999) identifies a learner's preference for each of these four learning strategies, and the combination of the scores from the two scales identifies a learner's preferred style as diverger, converger, assimilator,

Exhibit 5.3 Learning Activities Based on Kolb's Learning Preferences.

Style	Preferences	Activities
Accommodators	Prefer concrete experiences Prefer active experimentation Have the ability to carry out plans and get things done	Hands-on or trial-and-error methods Open-ended problems Learner presentations Design projects Subjective exams Simulations
Divergers	Prefer concrete experiences to help them understand ideas and concepts Use experience and knowledge to reflect and see different perspectives Open-minded Have difficulty making decisions May prefer to observe rather than participate	Use of case study videos Peer interaction Motivational stories Group discussion Group projects Subjective tests
Assimilators	Prefer high levels of abstract conceptualization and reflective observation Good at taking in a wide range of information and reducing it to a more logical form Like to plan and define problems Prefer theoretical models and deductive reasoning	Independent projects Lectures Textbook reading Demonstration by instructor Objective exams Concept maps Simulations
Convergers	Prefer high levels of abstract conceptualization Need opportunities for active experimentation Prefer to learn via problem solving, deductive decision making, and direct application of ideas and theories Prefer to solve problems using hypothetical reasoning	Independent projects Problem-solving exercises Simulations Demonstrations

Source: Kolb, 1999.

or accommodator. Exhibit 5.3 shows the preferences of different styles and the activities that fit each learning style.

Learners identified as accommodators or divergers rely heavily on concrete experience. Learners in the accommodator category combine this with a preference for active experimentation and have the ability to carry out plans and get things done. In addition, accommodators like hands-on or trial-and-error methods of learning. Divergers prefer a combination of concrete experience and reflective observation. They are characterized as open-minded and they look at a learning situation from many different perspectives. They often have difficulty making a decision and may prefer to observe rather than participate. Learners falling into the assimilator and converger types share a preference for high levels of abstract conceptualization. Assimilators prefer to combine abstract conceptualization with reflective observation and are good at taking in a wide range of information and reducing it to a more logical form. Assimilators like to plan and define problems; they tend to prefer theoretical models and deductive reasoning, as well as abstract concepts and ideas, over interaction with other people. Convergers combine this preference with a need for active experimentation, and they prefer to learn via problem solving, deductive decision making, and the direct application of ideas and theories.

An understanding of these learning styles can help you develop appropriate teaching strategies in your online course to help learners as they engage in activities. Accommodator strategies focus on experimentation with hands-on or trial-and-error methods such as problem-solving activities. Divergers learn best by being presented with concrete information to help them understand ideas and concepts and then use their experience and knowledge to reflect on and see different perspectives. These styles can be accommodated by using real-world problems. Divergers also prefer instructional methods that include peer interaction because they are interested in the perspectives of other learners. Divergers use these different perspectives to challenge their own thinking and adjust their initial reflection of the experience. Assimilators prefer theoretical models and deductive reasoning. Allowing them to work independently with information can help them to define a problem and develop a plan. Another tool that can be used is concept mapping to allow assimilators to manipulate concepts in visual presentations to show connections or simulations that allow them to build and test models. Finally, convergers prefer working on projects that allow them to plan and organize information and use their hypothetical reasoning skills to solve problems. Simulations are a good tool for testing critical thinking skills to solve problems.

Having an understanding of these preferences will help you evaluate a variety of instructional strategies to engage learners in activities, thereby providing appropriate support and alternative approaches to learners whose preferences are not matched to individual activities. The best approach is to provide the appropriate support as learners engage in activities that do not match their preferences to help them develop new preferences for learning. If there are opportunities to provide a choice of activities for learners to accommodate learning preferences, having an understanding of these preferences can serve as a foundation for developing alternative activities to meet individual learning needs.

In this chapter, we looked at information processing and how learning occurs. The process of moving incoming information into long-term memory is complex, and many variables affect learners' ability to store information in LTM for later recall. We discussed environmental, emotional, and cognitive load variables that affect learning and ways to control these variables to support learning. We also looked at metacognition, that is, knowledge of the specific strategies we use as we think and learn, and described the process of self-regulation to help learners effectively process information to ensure knowledge acquisition. Considering how information is presented can enhance learning and support learners as they navigate the environment and learning materials of a course. Also important is diagnosing learning issues that relate to the learners' environment and emotional state and helping them understand factors that influence learning, as well as strategies to overcome issues that affect learning. Finally, diagnosing learners with poor metacognitive skills and providing them with tools to improve their thinking can enhance learning and help learners persist. Part 3 examines specific cognitive strategies to help learners improve their metacognitive skills.

6

Motivation Theory

Motivation affects the amount of time individuals are willing to devote to learning (Bransford, Brown, & Cocking, 1999). New learners exhibit similar high levels of motivation when they first begin their program of study. I can recollect numerous introductory posts from learners saying how excited they were to be starting their education or returning to school to achieve their educational goals. They talked about their goals of being able to move up in their organization, changing careers, or setting an example for their children and family members. Often they expressed apprehension about not knowing whether they had what it would take to be successful, but ultimately, it did not matter because they were going to do everything they could to make it happen. By the third or fourth week of the course, however, these same learners were saying, "Maybe this isn't for me" or "I can't do this," or some were "missing in action altogether" and some may have even dropped out of the course. I continue to ask myself: What happened? Where did their excitement and motivation go? What about the goals they wanted to achieve?

Some online learners may not have been in school for many years because they were working or raising a family, and may not have had the opportunity to develop the academic skills needed to be successful in the online environment. As already discussed, the first few weeks of the course can be overwhelming because there is so much information to comprehend, along with learners' need to organize the learning activities and arrange for study time in their already full lives. Some learners may not have done well in previous learning experiences. They may have issues with basic academic skills, including reading, writing, and comprehension. These issues can affect their ability to navigate the course environment and to think critically to complete course activities. Other learners may not have realized the amount of time it takes to learn in an online learning environment. They may have decided to begin their educational journey without making any provisions for scheduling "learning time," because after all, they could do it anytime, anywhere. The problem is that "anytime" kept getting pushed back until suddenly there was no time. As issues begin to surface, motivation begins to plummet, confidence drops, and all of a sudden the excitement they expressed in the first week of the course turns to anxiety, apprehension, and general feelings of being overwhelmed, a state of being that can result in learners dropping out.

In this chapter, we take a closer look at motivation theory to help us understand how motivation influences individuals during learning. Effective strategies to motivate learners when they begin to struggle can help learners persist in achieving their educational goals. Motivation drives behaviors, persistence, and goal achievement in learning. Being able to understand factors that influence motivation can help you develop appropriate strategies to keep learners motivated throughout the learning experience to achieve learning outcomes.

Motivation is driven by the need for achievement and avoidance of failure (Snow, 1997). Learners approach the learning environment with a need for achievement, which is driven by numerous factors in their lives. These factors may include advancing in their career or changing careers, as well as the desire to earn a degree. Anxiety stems from fear of failure, which can affect their lives personally and professionally.

INTRINSIC AND EXTRINSIC MOTIVATION

There are two types of motivation—intrinsic motivation and extrinsic motivation. Intrinsic motivation relates to the achievement of personal goals such as building knowledge and skills or for the sheer joy of learning. Even if a reward of a new job or position is involved, when the ultimate goal is learning and there is a strong interest in the content, there are high levels of intrinsic motivation. A need for achievement that is related to external rewards or punishments, however, such as a new job or loss of a job because of lack of skill, is considered extrinsic motivation. Extrinsic motivation is often associated with learner goals that focus on performance as a means to an end rather than on learning for its own sake. When issues arise or the content is difficult, learners who are extrinsically motivated may have a harder time staying focused on their goal and overcoming adversities. This is a common problem and is one of the most difficult to help learners overcome. Learners who do not see the value of learning do everything they can to jump through the hoops, but with little focus on learning. If your online course has a tracking system, you will see learners with extrinsic motivation spending the majority of their time in the discussions going through other learners' posts to try to come up with a response rather than engaging in the content and developing an understanding of information that is presented in the studies. Learners who are extrinsically motivated tend to be performance-oriented whereas learners with intrinsic motivation are learning-oriented, which helps them persist in the face of difficulty (Dweck, 1989, as cited in Bransford, Brown, & Cocking, 1999). In addition, intrinsically motivated learners find relevance that is more personal in learning. As you work with learners who are extrinsically motivated, try to help them focus on the relevance of the content and how gaining skills and knowledge in the content area will change them personally, regardless of the career path they choose.

Developing course objectives that are competency based rather than behavioral can provide relevance to the course activities in the real world, which can help learners develop intrinsic motivation to learn. Behavioral objectives generally focus on acquisition of knowledge and skills but say little about what learners will actually do with the knowledge and skills once they have learned or developed them. Competencies indicate not only what will be learned in terms of knowledge and skills but also how they are applied. Consider how your course objectives are written to determine whether they include components that situate the learning in the real world or on tasks that the learner will need to perform in a real-life setting. If they are written in the form of behavioral objectives, providing an overview of the objectives and relating them specifically to real-world competencies can help learners establish a connection between the course activities and how they can apply them outside of the course.

According to Lenburg (1999), statements of competencies should include the following characteristics:

1. It is worded as a learner-oriented, essential competence (psychomotor, cognitive, and/or affective) to be achieved by the end of the learning period. It is the highest level of competence expected at this level or for this module, unit, or course and subsumes lower level competencies.

2. It is worded in clear, specific, unadorned, and concise language readily understood by the learner and teacher, and is measurable. It is action oriented and begins with the verb that most precisely describes the actual, preferred outcome behavior to be achieved.

3. It is consistent with standards, practice, and real world expectations for performance, i.e., what the practitioner (student) actually needs to be able to do.

4. It contributes to the cluster of abilities needed by the student (graduate) to fulfill the expected overall performance outcomes of the agency or program. (Para 15)

The following is an example Lenburg uses to demonstrate how to convert an objective to a competency:

Objective: Discuss the relationship between individual and family development.

Competencies:

1. Apply (or use) theories about individual and family development as the basis for conducting a family assessment. This is appropriate if the highest level of competence is to apply theories.

2. Conduct a systematic family assessment using theories about family and family development as the basic framework. This is appropriate if the highest level of competence is to conduct something using specific theories as a framework.

You can see that the objective of discussing the relationship between individual and family development was transformed to an application of theories about individual and family development as the basis for conducting a family assessment. This allows learners to demonstrate the competency in the real world by conducting a systematic family assessment by using theories about family and family development as the basic framework.

Stating your course objectives as competencies can motivate learners because they see exactly how they will use the skills and knowledge gained from the course in the real world. Even if you are delivering general education courses that are not specific to a career path, understanding how general competencies can be transferred to real-world applications regardless of learners' career choice can help motivate them to focus on the intrinsic goals of learning.

SELF-EFFICACY AND AN INTERNAL LOCUS OF CONTROL

Instead of looking at the attributes of learners who eventually drop out to determine how to help learners sustain motivation and meet learning goals, discovering the attributes of successful learners can help us understand factors that contribute to motivation and persistence. Attributes that successful learners have include a high level of self-confidence, self-efficacy, and an internal locus of control.

Self-confidence refers to individuals' belief in themselves and their ability to succeed in general (Bandura, 1997). Self-efficacy is a person's belief that he or she can succeed at a specific task or range of tasks in a given domain (Bandura, 1997). Self-efficacy influences the effort that learners put forth, how long they persist at a task when confronted with obstacles, and how they feel about the task. According to Bandura (1986), people tend to avoid engaging in a task in which their efficacy is low and choose to undertake tasks in which their efficacy is high (p. 393). The stronger the perceived self-efficacy, the more vigorous and persistent are their efforts. However, a negative effect of high self-efficacy may result if people do not prepare the way they should because of overconfidence, thus resulting in poor performance. Individuals with low self-efficacy tend to believe that things are tougher than they really are. This belief creates stress and a narrow vision of how best to go about a problem. By contrast, "persons who have a strong sense of efficacy, organize their attention and effort to the demands of the situation and are spurred by obstacles to greater effort" (Bandura, 1986, p. 394).

Locus of control refers to individuals' beliefs about what determines their successes or failures in life. Individuals with an internal locus of control believe that they are in control of outcomes and attribute their successes and failures to their ability to control outcomes through their own actions and efforts. Individuals with an external locus of control attribute their successes or failures to luck, chance, or something in the external environment, such as the power of others or environmental effects, which is outside of their control. An external locus of control can reduce motivation because individuals think that no matter what they do, they will not be able to succeed.

Strong academic self-efficacy coupled with an internal locus of control is a key predictor of success in a distance education setting. Dille and Mezack (1991) studied the profile of learners enrolled in telecourses, focusing on locus of control. They found that locus of control was a significant predictor of success and persistence in distance education courses. Specifically, learners with an internal locus of control were more likely to succeed and persevere to complete the course than learners with an external locus of control.

Self-efficacy can be improved to help learners successfully meet the outcomes of a course. Exhibit 6.1. includes strategies that can increase a learner's self-efficacy during learning.

Build in Success

Success raises efficacy, whereas failure lowers it. At the beginning of the course, structure initial course activities so learners have opportunities to experiences success. This gives them an opportunity to adjust to the course environment and expectations while successfully engaging in course activities. Introductions and discussions that allow learners to consider information that relates to some aspect of their life can allow them to engage in dialogue and get to know their peers and you without feeling overwhelmed. Structure the introductory discussion so that it allows learners to share some personal aspects of themselves with everyone, along with their goals and any concerns they have as they begin the course. This opportunity allows learners to get to know one another and realize that others are feeling some of the same anxieties. They will learn that they are not alone.

Control Content

For learners who are unfamiliar with the content area, the amount of content in a course can be overwhelming and create anxiety. Consider how much information you are presenting to learners, especially at the beginning of the course, and limit the number of supplementary resources. You should also consider the level

Exhibit 6.1 Strategies to Increase Self-Efficacy.

Strategy	Effect	Examples
Build in success	Success raises efficacy, whereas failure lowers efficacy Structure initial course activities so learners have opportunities to experience success	Introduction discussions Discussions that ask learners to draw on their experiences and reflect on what they know
Control content	The amount and structure of information can become overwhelming and create anxiety	Consider the amount of information presented to the learner Consider the degree of challenge Limit supplementary resources Structure information in chunks, so it is easier to process and remember Provide clear directions
Provide verbal persuasion	Verbal persuasion can have a positive influence on self-efficacy by providing learners encouragement that they can succeed and that others feel the same way	Peer encouragement—provide opportunities for learners to communicate with one another informally Instructor encouragement—proactively communicate with learners who appear to be struggling and assure them that through effort, they can succeed
Give continuous feedback	Ongoing feedback can help learners build confidence by communicating specifically what they are doing well, as well as how they can improve performance	Provide feedback in the first few units of the course to help learners gain confidence in their ability Provide actionable feedback to help learners gain needed skills and knowledge to improve performance
Monitor learners with external locus of control	Be aware of statements from learners who attribute failures to a number of things outside their control, a belief that can lead to poor effort	Monitor communications for comments relating failures to external environment Communicate with learners attributing successes to effort, and encourage learners to develop control of their outcomes through their own efforts
Monitor learners with poor performance	Poor performance may be a result of external locus of control and thinking that no matter what they do they won't succeed, so why try	Consider how learner defines effort to ensure effort is spent on effective strategies Work with learner to develop an improvement plan using incremental steps that allow the learner to be successful

of challenge. The content must be at the proper level of difficulty in order to be motivating. Tasks that are too easy become boring, and tasks that are too difficult cause frustration (Bransford, Brown, & Cocking, 1999). In addition, clear instructions can help increase the likelihood of learners succeeding in completing the course activities.

Provide Verbal Persuasion

Verbal persuasion can also have a positive influence on self-efficacy by offering learners encouragement. Providing informal discussion areas where learners can post to other learners gives them an opportunity to describe their anxieties and frustrations. More than likely, other learners are feeling some of the same anxiety, so allowing learners an opportunity to interact with one another and show support and understanding of what their peers are feeling can encourage and motivate them to persist. You, too, should communicate verbally with learners and offer them encouragement. By proactively communicating with learners who appear to be struggling, you can assure them that through effort, they can succeed. It is important to not overexaggerate their abilities but rather emphasize effort over ability, and let them know that you are there to support them. Their persistence and effort will make them successful.

Give Continuous Feedback

Ongoing feedback beginning in the first few weeks of the course can help learners build confidence by communicating specifically what they are doing well and how they can improve their performance. Even if learners' work overall is of poor quality, you can point out that they continue to show improvement and that their tenacity to stay the course in spite of difficulties is admirable. Be sure to relate their success to effort, not ability, so learners believe that by putting forth additional effort, they can successfully achieve the outcomes of the course.

Monitor Learners with External Locus of Control

Monitor communications and be aware of statements from learners who attribute failures to a number of things outside their control. Develop communications that are sympathetic to their circumstances but also offer specific advice that relates to the need for additional effort. Relating performance to effort will help learners understand that the greater the effort they are able to put into their learning, the more positive the impact on their performance. Finally, encourage learners to take control of the outcomes of their learning through their own efforts.

Monitor Learners with Poor Performance

Poor performance may be a result of learners' external locus of control. They may think that no matter what they do, they will not succeed—so why try? It is also important to understand how the learner is defining effort, and make sure that the effort is being spent on effective strategies to navigate the online course content and complete the associated activities. If learners have numerous issues that lead to poor performance, they can become disheartened. Try to develop an improvement plan that allows learners to focus on one issue at a time and improve progressively. Through successive achievements, learners will gain greater self-efficacy and begin to understand that they are in control of their achievements, a realization that can improve motivation and persistence. In addition, offering formative feedback on writing skills can give learners opportunities to improve their writing skills on smaller writing tasks, such as discussions, before they engage in larger writing assignments.

Awareness of learners' self-efficacy can provide you with important information to diagnose issues. This information is critical at the beginning of a course, when learners may be feeling their lowest levels of self-efficacy and highest levels of anxiety. Learners can quickly become discouraged and lose motivation, which may affect the amount of effort they will put forth to successfully complete learning activities. By providing appropriate strategies to help learners improve their ability to persist, you can help increase their confidence, which can increase motivation and effort.

COMMUNICATING ENTHUSIASM FOR THE SUBJECT

You can help motivate learners by how you demonstrate interest in the subject area and show enthusiasm for its relevance to learners. I went into biology as my first career because of an instructor who had so much excitement for the subject that it made me want to go into the field. Showing that enthusiasm for the content is a challenge in the online environment. There are technologies available that can allow you to add audio to a basic PowerPoint presentation. Audio can add life to your presentation and build excitement for the content. Learners can hear intonation as you speak and thus can "catch" your excitement and enthusiasm about a subject or activity.

Presentations can be in the form of an overview of topics and learning activities in which you relate your personal perspective on a topic. Such overviews may help learners understand the importance of the information being presented and motivate them to want to learn more. A presentation can also deliver content in an emotional way that can build excitement and arouse emotion. Consider providing stories or examples of how the knowledge is being used in the real world. This can be done through stories in the news, your own practice in the field, or other examples of how the knowledge is being applied today. Another way to build excitement is to have experts talk about the field of study. YouTube has given rise to numerous video sources that can be used in education to help motivate learners. Any time you can present multiple perspectives via multimedia, you have an opportunity to motivate learners, as well as appeal to different learning styles. There may also be opportunities to have an expert record an audio or video for your course to create excitement about a topic. I taught a course that had a short introduction by the author of the required textbook. I cannot tell you how many times learners mentioned to me how cool that was to hear the author's voice—it brought the book to life!

COMMUNICATION TO MOTIVATE LEARNERS

Understand the motivations of individual learners, and target communications to help them improve or sustain motivation to reach their goals. You need especially to motivate learners when they are unsure of how the activities can help them meet their goals. This requires two-way communication in which you ask probing questions to help determine learners' interests and find ways to adapt the activities to meet their individual needs. Often I find that learners do not know what they are interested in or what their goals are in relationship to their education. One of the ways I communicate with learners who do not have a clear direction is to help them understand that by engaging in the course activities, they can begin to understand their likes and dislikes. I remind them that if they continue through the course and still find little of interest in the content, this is important information that can help them. The course will help them confirm that they are not interested in this area, and they can go on to explore their interests and goals. The key is to keep their experience positive and look at what can be gained from the course rather than focusing on what they are not getting out of the studies. One of the tools I use when I engage in motivating strategies with learners is to keep a spreadsheet of learner-motivation issues, along with the strategies I have used. I go back to my spreadsheets at the end of the course and make notes on whether any of the strategies I used helped the learners, whether they ended up finishing the course, and what grade they received. This allows me to evaluate my strategies for motivating learners and make adjustments when needed or replicate strategies that had a positive outcome. It also can save me time when I am dealing with motivation issues because I can quickly query my spreadsheet when I run into issues and find successful recommendations to use with learners.

THE IMPACT OF ISOLATION ON MOTIVATION

The feeling of isolation in an online course can also have an impact on motivation. Michael Moore (1980) articulated a theory called transactional distance. This theory postulates that distance education is more than simply the geographical separation of the instructor and learners but also includes the impact distance can have on understanding and perceptions, which can affect motivation. Physical separation leads to psychological and communication gaps, which create a space of potential misunderstanding between the instructor and the learner. This is referred to as transactional distance. According to Moore (1991), transactional distance requires specialized organizational and teaching procedures. Teaching variables include dialogue and structure. Dialogue is the interaction between the instructor and learner during instruction. The structure variable includes elements in the design of the course such as content, navigation elements, and multimedia. It also includes communication structures such as e-mail, discussion, instant messaging, and the degree of flexibility that structure incorporates to meet the needs of the learner. High structure along with low instructor–learner dialogue leads to high transactional distance, whereas increased dialogue between the instructor and learner along with a flexible learning environment leads to low transactional distance.

Learners who are new to online learning may feel isolated when they begin their first online course. It is important to manage the feelings of isolation, especially at the beginning of the course, to make sure that transactional distance is minimized. One of the first things you can do is to send everyone a welcome e-mail to acknowledge their presence in the course (Exhibit 6.2).

Take the time to send the e-mail to individual learners and call them by name, so there are no doubts that you are speaking to them individually, rather than sending out a group mail. This also gives learners an opportunity to express any feelings of apprehension they may have and begin a dialogue, which can

Exhibit 6.2   Example Welcome E-mail

Hello Mary,

   Welcome to my class! I realize that you may be feeling a bit apprehensive and not sure of what to expect in this course. Each week I will send out a unit overview that will help orient you to the week's activities. Please be sure to review it each week, so you know what to do. I also will describe any areas where past learners have had problems in order to keep you from having the same problem. Please know that I am here to support you, so please do not hesitate to ask me questions and let me know what I can do to support you. Now relax and enjoy the course☺ Dr. Smith

---

immediately reduce the feeling of isolation. Another recommendation to reduce transactional distance is to check your course mail or e-mail frequently each day to respond to learner communications. If you have an "Ask Your Instructor" thread in the discussion room, monitor the thread several times a day to make sure you answer any learner questions. Providing opportunities for learners to dialogue with one another can also remove feelings of isolation. You may want to include a discussion thread for off-topic discussions to help build a community between learners. Making a requirement to interact with other learners can also create an opportunity for learners to develop relationships in the course. You can also increase socialization by using teams or groups in the course. This structure allows learners to get to know a small number of learners, which is less intimidating than trying to get to know a large group of learners.

   The flexibility of the learning environment can also have an impact on transactional distance, depending on the learning style of individual learners. Some learners may require more structure; others may be more self-directed and prefer independent learning experiences. The critical component of structure is being able to offer a flexible learning environment that meets the needs of all learners. You can build flexibility by allowing learners to choose topics to write on or pick a topic from a recommended list of topics. You may also want to create flexibility by allowing learners to write papers or develop alternative presentations such as slide presentations or other presentation modes using multimedia. You can also create flexibility by giving learners options on participation in discussions. For instance, you may want to consider posting several discussions and giving learners the option to answer the discussion that they are most interested in exploring. Also, consider ways to be flexible with learners when they encounter personal or professional issues outside the course. Remember that most online learners work full time and also have family obligations. Allowing some flexibility can help sustain their motivation and assist them in overcoming obstacles along the way. Overall, the more you can adapt dialogue and structure in the learning experience to meet the needs of the individual learners, the more opportunities you can have to keep them motivated and focused on their overall learning goals.

This chapter discussed motivation theory and the importance of being able to sustain learners' motivation by using strategies to help them develop intrinsic motivation, high self-efficacy, and an internal locus of control. It is also important to consider transactional distance and work to develop a learning environment that has high dialogue between the instructor and learner along with a flexible learning environment to support individual learner needs. These strategies can help maintain learners' motivation to persist in learning, and thus end the course with the same or greater level of excitement about their learning goals as they had when they began.

Part 2 discussed the foundations of cognition and learning, which provided a basic understanding of how learning theories have evolved, developed a foundation of how we think and learn, and provided a basic understanding of factors that impact cognition and learning. The foundations of cognition and learning, along with the profile of the online learning discussed in Part 1, will serve as a foundation for the various instructional strategies recommended in this book. These strategies are grounded in an understanding of how learning occurs in order to support the various styles of learners, which has an impact on their ability to persist.

Cognitive Strategies to Support Learners' Thinking

One of the most important skills an instructor brings to the online learning environment is the ability to help learners build effective learning strategies to improve their thinking. Part 3 examines cognitive scaffolding tools you can use to help learners enhance, augment, and extend their thinking processes, which can result in improving learners' thinking skills as they engage in learning activities (Hannifin, Land, & Oliver, 1999). The online environment provides opportunities to scaffold the learning environment to meet the needs of all learners and provide the appropriate level of support to help learners persist.

Hannifin, Land, and Oliver (1999) describe four types of scaffolding strategies that can be used to support learning: procedural, metacognitive, conceptual, and strategic. Chapter 7 discusses procedural scaffolding that emphasizes how to use available resources and tools in the learning environment. Chapter 8 addresses metacognitive scaffolding that supports the underlying processes associated with the management of thinking and learning. Chapter 9 discusses conceptual scaffolding that supports learners as they reason through complex concepts and problems. Finally, Chapter 10 examines strategic scaffolding that assists learners just in time, and emphasizes alternative approaches that learners can use to support analysis, planning, strategy, and tactical decisions during learning.

Scaffolding tools and resources can be built into the design of the learning environment; however, it is critical to monitor the use of scaffolding by learners and adapt the scaffolds according to the specific needs of the individual. Scaffolding is all about providing the right amount of structured support in the learning environment, keeping in mind that some learners may require little or no support and others may require additional support. If you are designing and developing an online course, the different types of cognitive scaffolds described in upcoming chapters will help you determine appropriate instructional strategies. If you are teaching a course that has already been designed, the cognitive scaffolds can be developed as supplemental resources to support learners as they engage in the course. The scaffolds can also be used as just-in-time resources to help individual learners work through issues to persist in learning.

Procedural Scaffolding

7

Procedural scaffolding guides learners as they learn how to navigate the course environment and engage in learning activities. Learners may have difficulty understanding what to do when they begin an online course. This difficulty is compounded if the online course is not built with a standard design template, because learners must orient themselves to a new navigation structure and location of resources for each new online course. In addition, they have to learn how the content is delivered, how the units of study are structured, what the expectations are for engaging in the course, as well as other features unique to the course. You can eliminate unnecessary frustration and anxiety by scaffolding the learning environment to help learners understand what to do once they begin the course and how to engage with you, the content, and their peers. Procedural scaffolding can help learners persist in learning by orienting them to the course, helping them understand the expectations for engaging in your course, and identifying processes, resources, and tools that will be used throughout the course. There are three types of procedural scaffolds that can help learners persist—orientation, expectation, and resource scaffolds.

ORIENTATION SCAFFOLDS

An orientation scaffold supports learners in understanding the online course environment. It describes the general layout of the course, including the major features of the course environment such as the location of learning

Exhibit 7.1   Course Orientation Template.

Steps of Orientation	Orientation	What to Do
Step 1	Course room tools	Please complete the following activities to ensure you understand what course room tools will be used and where they are located, so you can access them when needed.
Step 1.1	Studies/learning units [location of studies/learning units]	In the [studies/learning units] are all of the materials you will need to complete the course. Each week begin in the [studies/learning unit] and complete all of the activities before participating in discussions or completing assignments.
Step 1.2	Discussion board [location of discussion board]	You are required to use the discussion board throughout the course to engage in discussions with your peers. Please navigate to the discussion forum and post an introduction to me and your classmates in the discussion thread titled [Insert title of discussion thread].
Step 1.3	Assignment box [location of assignment box]	Please navigate to the assignment box and review the assignments for the course and their due dates. Once you have completed your review, make a note of what the first assignment is and when it is due.
Step 1.4	Mail [location of mail]	Please access the course mail tool and read my welcome e-mail. Once you have finished reading my e-mail, send me a reply to let me know that you were able to navigate to the mail area and access my mail to you. Also indicate to me that you know what the first assignment is and when it is due.
Step 1.5	Grade book [location of grade book]	Navigate to the grade book. The grade book is where I will post all of your grades throughout the course.
Step 1.6	Supplementary materials [location of supplementary materials navigation]	Navigate to the supplementary materials area, where you will find additional resources to help you successfully complete the course and/or resources for further reading on any of the topics. Review the following resources: [Insert important resources that learners should review before beginning the course; e.g., research, writing]
Step 1.7	Course roster [location of course roster]	Navigate to the course roster and review some of the information posted by your peers.
Step 2	Syllabus [location of syllabus]	Before you begin the course, please review the course syllabus. Please note: [Include specific features of the syllabus learners should pay close attention to.]
Step 3	Faculty expectations statement [location of statement]	Please review my Faculty Expectation Statement and post an acknowledgment that you have read and understood my expectations for your participation in the course.
Step 4	Due dates document [location of due dates document]	Please access the due dates document and make a copy of it, so you can refer to it throughout the course to ensure you understand when discussions and assignments are due.
Step 5	Insert additional tools and/or resources that are specific to the course you will be teaching	

materials, discussions, assignments, mail, grades, and other major features you may have in your course.

If you are using a course management system such as Blackboard 9.1, there is an orientation feature that allows you to create a custom orientation based on the tools you are using in your online course. This can be an excellent way to orient your learners to your course, so they have a complete understanding of how to navigate your course and where to find the needed materials to complete all of the activities. Some universities also offer an orientation to the online environment, especially if they are using a standard template for the organization of all online courses. If you do not have those two options, then consider creating your own orientation to ensure learners understand the layout of your course and how to successfully navigate the content. Exhibit 7.1 is a template you can use to develop an orientation for your learners specific to the design of your course.

Your orientation should begin by helping learners understand the tools that are used during the course, where they are located, and what learners will find there. You can include activities as learners navigate to each area of the course to ensure they have accessed each of the course tools and understand how to use them (Conrad & Donaldson, 2004). Also include activities that have learners access the course syllabus, faculty expectations statement, due dates document, or other resources and tools that are specific to your course. The key to your orientation is to help learners understand how to access the different features of your course so they can successfully complete activities and engage in interactions. If there is a dedicated place for all resources used in the course, give a description of the location and intended use of the resources. If there are any unique features of the course such as instant chat, they, too, should be described to help learners understand how to access and use them. To help learners visualize the organization of the course you can capture screen shots. The more support you can give learners in navigating the course environment, the less confused and frustrated they will become.

EXPECTATION SCAFFOLDS

An expectation scaffold helps learners navigate the course by addressing expectations they will need to understand before engaging in course activities. Expectations create guidelines for engaging in your course (Boettcher & Conrad, 2010; Palloff & Pratt, 2001). Exhibit 7.2 is a faculty expectation template

Exhibit 7.2 Faculty Expectation Template

Faculty Expectations of [Insert Faculty Name]

Overview
Develop an overview of the course structure including information about:

Describe Teaching Style

- How you will engage in the course

Describe Pace of Course

- Describe how the units fit together [self-paced, weekly units with due dates, etc.]
- Example: The course is a ten-week journey with activities building on one another as you move through the course. Complete the units sequentially (i.e., Unit 1, then 2, etc.). Skipping any unit activity is highly discouraged and, in fact, hinders progress with the course competencies.

Describe the Course Environment

- Location of: learning units, discussions, assignments, etc.

Describe Time to Complete Weekly Activities

- Number of hours learners can expect to engage in the course per unit/per week.
- Encourage learners to allocate enough time to complete all of the requirements.

Syllabus and Learning Units

- Describe where learners can find the syllabus and learning units.
- Encourage learners to review syllabus and learning units prior to beginning the course, so they have a better understanding of how the units of study fit together.
- If you have developed a road map for the course, include information on where that is found and encourage learners to use it to understand the general structure of the course.

Required Course Materials

- Describe required course materials.
- Describe supplemental materials.
- Describe computer hardware and software requirements.

Due Date Document

- You are encouraged to include a due dates document in your course, so describe the document and where it can be found. Encourage learners to save a copy of the due dates document, so they can readily review it each week to determine important activities and due dates.

Instructor Unit Overviews

- If you are providing unit overviews prior to the start of a new unit, include information about the overviews.
- Example: Each week, I will post a unit overview to the first discussion for each unit. It is very important to review these presentations prior to beginning each unit of study because I will go over all of the requirements for each activity and point out areas where I have found learners to have issues or miss important information that can help them as they develop their discussion responses and assignments.

Discussion Protocol

Describe the protocol for discussions:

- Where they are submitted
- Due dates for submitted discussions
- Expectations for number of days of participation in the discussion
- Expectations for when initial post to discussions is due
- Expectations for number of interactions within other learners' posts
- Expectations for when interactions in discussion are due
- Description of discussion grading rubric
    - Expectations for quality of initial response to discussion question
    - Expectations for quality of interactions within other learner's discussion posts
- Expectation for professionalism in the discussion
    - Example: Please keep all responses in the discussion room professional and support all views with published research. Personal attacks are not tolerated and will be reported to the administration. Some questions call for your opinion or your own experience, but please remember not to disclose highly personal information in the course room. This is not a confidential environment, and information posted in this course room is kept and stored for a number of years.
- Guidelines for keeping discussion area warm, friendly, organized, manageable, and professional
    Examples:
    - Give an appropriate subject title for each post. Use concise subject lines to distinguish your main posting from a reply to another learner's post.
    - Include a salutation specifying to whom you are writing.
    - Add your name at the bottom of each post, as you prefer to be addressed in class.
    - Consider that each of your discussion area postings is to be read by everyone. Therefore, the sharing of information becomes exciting and enriching.
    - Your posting compositions need to fully address the instructions and be error free in grammar, spelling, punctuation, and capitalization.
    - Go offline and use Microsoft Word to compose your postings, run the grammar checker, and then check the word count to assure the count is within the guidelines.

(continued)

Exhibit 7.2 *(continued)*

Assignments

- Describe when assignments are due and in what units.
- Describe where assignments are submitted.

Weekly and Unit Due Dates

- Describe due dates for the week or unit.
- Describe what to do if unforeseen circumstances arise.
- Example: Should an unforeseen circumstance arise (e.g., illness, death in the family, emergency at home or work), please contact me immediately and we will work out a plan for catching up. Please note that a late submission may reduce your final grade.

Grading and Instructor Feedback

Grading

- Describe grading criteria, including any general grading rubrics used [i.e., for discussions].
- Describe point/percentage deductions for posting late.
- Describe point/percentage deductions for spelling, grammar, American Psychological Association (APA) or Modern Language Association (MLA) styles, etc. [if applicable].

Instructor Feedback

- Describe how often learners will receive feedback on discussions/assignments.
- Describe where feedback will be given [e.g., course mail, e-mail, assignment box, grade book].

Learner Code of Conduct Policy
Insert Institution's "Code of Conduct Policy."

Academic Honesty Policy
Insert Institution's "Academic Honesty Policy."

Plagiarism
Insert your plagiarism policy for the course.

Example: In this course, plagiarism is not tolerated and if you post a discussion or assignment that is plagiarized, you will earn a 0. The ability to re-do the assignment will be made on a case-by-case basis. If a second occurrence of plagiarism occurs, you will be reported to the university administration for further action.

Questions

- Describe how to ask questions [e.g., Ask Your Instructor discussion thread, course mail, e-mail].

- If applicable, encourage learners to consult a FAQ document prior to asking questions.
- Encourage learners to consult the Ask Your Instructor posts to see whether the question has already been asked and answered.

Preplanned Extended Time Away from Course Room

- Describe requirements for being away from the course room [e.g., inform you in writing no more than 14 days prior to time away].
- Encourage learners to submit work ahead of the time away.

Closing and Signature

---

that can be used to develop a faculty expectation statement for your course. When developing a faculty expectation statement, include information on your personal teaching style. This helps learners understand how you will be engaging in course activities and the types of interactions they can expect from you. Also describe the pace of the course, including whether it is self-paced or if learners are required to accomplish activities by units with specific due dates. If the course is a set pace, include a statement about learners' working ahead and whether they are allowed to post to discussions before they are introduced in the course. One issue I have found with learners is that often they do not have the prerequisite skills and knowledge to work ahead in the course. They end up not doing as well as they could have on assignments because they did not have the opportunity to incorporate my feedback to improve their performance. My recommendation is to let learners work ahead only if they know they will be absent from the course and unable to participate during the scheduled time.

Describe the organization of the course, including where learners should begin, how they move through the content, and where to find information about units, discussions, assignments, mail features, and any other features of your course. Your statement should include the number of hours learners are expected to engage in the course per unit or week. Also describe where your syllabus can be found, and encourage learners to review it prior to beginning the learning unit. If you have developed a road map of the course, include information about where it can be found and how learners can use it.

Describe required course materials and make it clear which materials are supplemental. I recommend that you set specific standards for hardware and software. I have found that many learners begin an online course without a personal computer. Or they may have a computer but do not have Microsoft Office, so they cannot create documents that everyone can open and read.

If you have developed a due dates document for your course, describe the document and where it can be found. If you will be posting unit overviews or summaries each week, include information on when and where they will be posted. Also include a section on discussion protocol, so learners understand the specific expectations for participating in discussions. Many learners will come in and post the discussions and interactions on the last day of the discussion, which does not help to extend the dialogue in a discussion to build knowledge. I recommend that you determine an appropriate number of times per week or per unit learners are required to engage in the discussions, as well as the number of interactions they should have within other learners' posts, and specifically state those expectations. Also consider including a specific day of the week that initial posts to discussions are due. This will also keep learners from posting the last day and allow them to extend the dialogue throughout the week to develop a rich exchange of ideas.

Include information on how discussions are graded and the importance of keeping them professional. Clearly state your policy for making up discussions. I have allowed learners to submit their responses to discussion questions after discussions have ended via course mail; however, I do not allow learners to make up points for interacting within other learners' posts. My personal opinion is that once the unit of study has ended and learners have moved on to the next unit, learner-to-learner interactions have limited value. Also describe assignments, where they are submitted, and the due dates if you have assignments due the same time each week.

Consider including a section on grading and feedback. Describe general information about grading, including any general grading rubrics. Discuss additional point deductions that may not be part of your grading rubrics; for instance, deductions for posting late. I have had learners turn in all of their assignments at the end of the course, so it is critical to make sure that learners understand that your course is not a correspondence course for which everything can be turned in at the end of the course, but requires active engagement throughout the course. Clearly state deductions for each week an assignment is late, so learners understand that turning in all of their assignments at the end of the course may result in a failing grade. If you have expectations for the quality of learners' writing, explain your expectations in detail, including any grade deductions for spelling, grammar, and improper use of American Psychological Association (APA) or Modern Language Association (MLA) formats, if applicable.

Learners must understand the type of feedback they can expect from you. Describe how often learners will receive feedback on discussions and how you will provide it; for example, in course mail, e-mail, private discussions. Also describe where assignment feedback can be found and typically how many days it will take you to return feedback on assignments.

Include your institution's Code of Conduct Policy and Academic Honesty Policy and emphasize their importance. I also recommend that you include a specific statement about plagiarism in your course and the consequences if plagiarism is found.

Describe how learners can find answers to questions; for example, FAQs, reviewing the Ask Your Instructor discussion. Also describe the different ways learners can ask questions; for example, course mail, e-mail, or an Ask Your Instructor discussion. Learners have different expectations for how quickly the instructor will respond to their inquiries, so setting an expectation for response time to questions at the beginning of the course will help alleviate any confusion or misunderstanding. I always try to respond within 24 hours and have thought that it was a reasonable response turnaround; however, in one course I had a learner who complained because his expectations was that he would receive a reply from me within two hours. It made it very clear to me that expectations are different for everyone. The clearer you can be on the maximum amount of time learners will have to wait for a response, the fewer issues will arise from misunderstandings.

Another expectation that you may want to consider in your statement is information about pre-planned extended time away from the course. It is not unusual for me to have several learners take a two-week vacation in the middle of the course or travel for work and have limited Internet connectivity. Stating up front what you expect them to do before they leave on vacation or for business is important.

Establishing a clear set of expectations for learners, as well as what learners can expect from you, can help reduce the number of issues that may arise due to unstated expectations from you as the instructor or from the learner (see

Exhibit 7.2). Also, learners gain an understanding of procedures that can help them successfully engage in the course.

RESOURCE SCAFFOLDS

Resource scaffolds support learners as they engage in course activities. If your course includes specific processes that learners will engage in throughout the course, these should be described in detail early in the course (Boettcher & Conrad, 2010). For instance, you may have learners use a critical thinking process or reflective process as they complete activities throughout your course. A process guide can help learners understand the process and be able to use it systematically during course activities. Creating printable versions of the process guide will make it easily available to learners as they engage in course activities.

Consider the types of supplementary resources and tools you will use to support learners as they engage in course activities. Common support resources include writing and library resources to help learners as they engage in research and writing activities in your course. A plagiarism detection tool can help learners understand the issue of plagiarism and help them properly attribute information to an author. If you are able to embed the tool in your course, it can support learners as they discover how to properly credit their sources.

Consider the location of resources that may be used throughout the course to support learners. If resources are embedded in a specific unit of the course, it will require the learner to remember where the information is and they may grow frustrated trying to locate the information at a later time. Consider having a main resource area where learners can access all resources and tools that are used (Smith, 2008). If you link out to resources on the Web or in a different department or location within your institution, all resources should open in a new window. This allows learners to close the window and return to their original location in the course.

In this chapter, we discussed three types of procedural scaffolds that can help learners persist in learning: orientation, expectation, and resource scaffolds. Procedural scaffolds support and guide learners as they learn how to navigate the course environment and engage in learning activities. By developing a plan for integrating procedural scaffolding in your course, you can eliminate unnecessary learner frustration and anxiety due to not knowing how to begin and where to locate everything they need to engage in the course. You can help learners persist by orienting them to the course environment, helping them understand expectations, and providing them with resources throughout the course.

Metacognitive Scaffolding

Metacognitive scaffolding supports learners in developing thinking skills to manage their learning. Learners who have never been to college, have been away from college for a number of years, or who have never developed strong thinking skills will benefit from scaffolding to build these skills as they engage in learning activities. Learners who do not have well-developed thinking skills struggle more in learning, which makes them extremely vulnerable to dropping out. Metacognitive scaffolding supports planning, monitoring, and evaluating processes to support learners as they engage in learning to ensure they are processing information efficiently and effectively for storage and retrieval. As learners become more aware of their thinking, they can act on this awareness and learn better (Bransford, Brown, & Cocking, 1999).

PLANNING STRATEGIES

Planning strategies help learners establish learning goals, develop a plan to help them achieve the stated course goals and objectives, develop strategies for effective learning, and manage the learning activities in a timely manner. It is important that learners understand the goals and objectives of the course. We have learned that one of the attributes of adult learners is their need to know. If your course is written with behavioral goals and objectives that do not situate the learning in applied knowledge and skills that are needed in the real world, learners may find it difficult to understand the significance of the course for them personally. This may also lead to diminished motivation to accomplish the learning goals.

At the course level, presenting a course overview at the beginning of the course will help learners understand the overall goals of the course and how the learning activities will accomplish the goals. This is also an opportunity for you to discuss the relevance of the course goals and objectives to the knowledge and skills learners will need in the real world. Your overview should include a discussion of the goals of the course, how the activities will help them accomplish the course goals, a description of major activities, and other information that is relevant to helping learners develop a big picture of the course structure.

Another course-level scaffold is a road map that visually illustrates the relationship between the course objectives and the course activities (Exhibit 8.1). This road map can help learners develop a plan for learning. The road map outlines each unit, including objectives, activities, and how they relate to the overall goals of the course, resources needed, estimated time to complete activities and due dates, posting locations for graded activities, and a link to the criteria for grading. This provides learners with a high-level plan for learning throughout the course. The road map also helps learners develop a time management plan to assist them in managing their workload against other responsibilities they have

Exhibit 8.1 Course Road Map.

Road Map of [Insert Name of Course]						
Unit Overview and Objectives	Activity	Rationale	Resources	Estimated Time to Complete	Due Date	Posting Location and Criteria
Unit 1 Overview/ Objectives	Name of Discussion Name of Assignment	Rationale for why these activities are important and how they align with the overall course goals and unit objectives	List of resources needed to complete the activity	Range of time to complete from novice to expert	Date activity is due	Where to post activity and link to assessment criteria
Unit 2 Overview/ Objectives						

outside of the course. It also helps learners review activities in relationship to what they already know about the topic so they can determine where to concentrate their effort.

At the unit level, planning tools can assist learners as they determine a schedule for individual learning activities. At the beginning of a unit of study, an overview can help learners understand the goals of activities and plan their schedule for completing activities. The unit checklist template in Exhibit 8.2 can also support learners as they plan the individual activities within a unit of study. Including time allocations for various activities can help learners plan their schedules to make sure they set aside sufficient time in their weekly schedule to meet the requirements of individual activities.

Exhibit 8.2   Unit Checklist Template

Name of Course _____

  [Unit Number and Name]

  This checklist will help you organize and successfully complete the activities in the unit. If you are having a difficult time determining what needs to be done to complete this unit of study, please go through the list and check the items that you have completed. The checklist is in the order in which each activity should be completed. If you find that you have unchecked items in a section, please be sure to complete them before moving on to the next section. If you find that you are not spending the same amount of time as the estimated times to complete, please consider reallocating time to activities to ensure you are meeting the goals of the activity. In addition, if you find you are going over the estimated time, contact your instructor for guidance on how to complete the course activities within the estimated times. If you have additional questions, please send the checklist to your instructor and include specific questions that you have.

Order of Activities	Activity	Estimated Time to Complete	Status	Questions Regarding Activity
			Mark as complete or incomplete	Note any questions you have regarding the activity to begin a conversation with your instructor.
Step 1	Activity 1— Describe Activity 2— Describe Etc.	Include range from novice to expert	*Learner completes*	*Learner completes*
Step 2, etc.				

Course overviews in the form of presentations, visual course maps, and unit checklists can provide scaffolding for learners to develop strategies for planning and organizing learning activities. These overviews can also be used by you to help determine exactly where learners are struggling so you can establish an appropriate plan for helping learners overcome roadblocks to completing the course activities.

MONITORING STRATEGIES

Metacognitive strategies for monitoring learning include tracking information about how the learner is progressing, whether learners are on the right track and attending to the correct goals, and the potential outcomes of their efforts (Hannafin, Land, & Oliver, 1999). There are several scaffolding strategies that can assist learners in monitoring their progress. Templates, worksheets, and worked examples are effective tools to help learners monitor their understanding. These tools can keep learners focused on the components of a specific task as well as the order in which tasks should be completed. They can also be used as a planning tool to ensure learners complete all of the components of an activity. The checklist discussed in the previous section can aid learners in monitoring progress through the learning activities and determining whether they are on track. If the checklist contains estimated times for completing activities, it can be used to help learners

Exhibit 8.3   Time Log

[Insert Unit Number and Name]

Directions: If you are having issues completing the learning activities each week, use this time log to track your time on task for each activity. If you had issues while completing an activity, note the issue, so that it can be considered by your instructor to help you develop strategies to improve your time on task.

Activity	Estimated Time to Complete	Time to Complete	Issues During Completion of Activity
Activity 1	Include range of time from novice to expert	*Learner completes*	*Learner completes*
Activity 2	etc.		
Activity 3	etc.		
etc.			

monitor time-on-task to determine whether they are spending adequate time in the activities. For learners who are struggling to complete course activities in a timely manner, time logs can be an important tool to help analyze what learners are doing to engage in the activities and how much time they are spending on individual activities (Exhibit 8.3). If they are going over the estimated time, this can be a signal to seek guidance from their instructor to develop more efficient strategies for completing the learning activities.

Scaffolding strategies can also be used to monitor comprehension and understanding. Note-taking scaffolds can help learners organize information as they learn and can be used to monitor their understanding of materials. Microsoft OneNote is an excellent tool for note-taking because it allows learners to type, write, or draw as they take notes. Because it is electronic, they can add, move, or delete pages or sections and reorganize notes. Exhibit 8.4 is a note-taking template that can be used to help learners monitor their comprehension and understanding during learning. As they engage in study activities, they can use the template to record terms and definitions and make notes about information they do not understand. They can also use it to outline information and note important facts in order to monitor their understanding and organize their thinking. Finally, there is a place to record questions they have as they study and can seek out answers to the questions through additional study or by asking you for clarification.

Practice tests via an online quiz feature can help learners monitor their comprehension of major concepts and ideas. It also can be a tool for you to determine areas of confusion and provide additional information to help clarify important concepts and ideas. Many course management platforms have built-in quiz features that allow you to create quiz questions that help learners monitor their understanding of important concepts and ideas.

EVALUATING STRATEGIES

Metacognitive strategies for evaluating learning require evaluation and reflection. This may require revising learning processes, modifying plans based on the end results of the planning and monitoring methods used during an activity, or both. Building in a process for learners to self-evaluate their work against a scoring guide prior to submitting their assignment can help them determine whether they have met the standards of the grading criteria. During their

Exhibit 8.4   Note-Taking Template

Key Terms and Definitions
[List all terms and definitions as you read. If a term is used that you do not understand and it is not defined in the text, include it in the list and look up the definition in the dictionary.]

1.
2.
3.
4.
5. etc.

Outline of Section/Paragraph
[Develop an outline to summarize main concepts and ideas.]

 I. Main heading
   a. Subheading
     i. details
   b. Subheading
     i. details
 II. Main heading, etc.

Facts
[Summarize important facts that you will need to commit to memory.]

Who (important people)
What (important concepts/ideas)
Where (important places)
When (important dates)

Questions
[What information are you unclear about? List specific information that you will need to study in more detail. List questions you have for your instructor.]

1.
2.
3.
4.
5. etc.

Source: Stavredes, 2011.

self-evaluation, learners may find areas where they do not meet the criteria and can make adjustments to their work prior to submitting it. If you have learners turn in their self-evaluations against the scoring guide, you may gain important information to help you target your feedback on their performance. For instance, if a learner turns in a self-evaluation that is rated high on the grading criteria but you consider her performance low or moderate on the scale, this could signal issues related to the learner's overall understanding of the grading criteria or course concepts. In this situation, your feedback may be focused on helping the learner determine what the expectations were for the given criteria to help her see why her work did not meet the given criteria, and provide specific feedback on misconceptions of important concepts and ideas. Another example is a learner who rates himself as moderate or low on an assignment. Generally, such learners will include a comment regarding why they rated themselves poorly. Some comments may relate to difficulty managing time, which signals that you should offer planning strategies to help them manage their time better. Other learners may grade themselves low on the grading criteria because they know they have done poorly on the assignment but they are losing motivation and do not want to put forth additional effort. This may be a signal they are at risk for dropping out. Consider feedback that helps them understand specifically how their work could have met the criteria, along with motivating comments to reengage them and build their confidence so that they can be successful.

Reflective scaffolds allow learners to reflect on their progress after they have completed activities and assignments. An excellent strategy to help learners become reflective is to have them answer a set of questions at the end of an activity that prompt them to reflect on how they planned, organized, and monitored their learning. Based on their reflection, learners can revise their planning and monitoring strategies to improve learning. Chapter 11 describes this strategy in more detail.

Metacognitive scaffolding supports learners as they plan, monitor, and evaluate their performance during learning activities. It also supports learners in developing thinking skills to help them manage their learning, thus leading to greater persistence. Consider ways to support learners' thinking by developing scaffolding to support planning, monitoring, and evaluating processes as they engage in learning to ensure they are processing information efficiently and storing it in memory for later retrieval.

9

Conceptual Scaffolding

Conceptual scaffolding guides learners regarding what to consider during learning. If learners have difficulty understanding course concepts, they can become frustrated and lose motivation. Conceptual scaffolding can support learners as they engage in difficult content by helping them identify key conceptual knowledge and organize it into meaningful structures that support learning (Hannifin, Land, & Oliver, 1999). Strategies include the use of advance organizers, study guides or questions, definitions, graphical organizers, outlines, and hints.

As you review the content of your course, consider ways to introduce major topics and help learners understand how they interrelate. Advance organizers can be used to help learners link prior knowledge with new information to facilitate learning. David Ausubel proposed the use of advance organizers to scaffold the learning of new information (Ausubel, 1960). Advance organizers stimulate creation of schemata to help learners link prior knowledge with new information. An example of an advance organizer is presenting a summary of the main ideas in a reading passage and explaining content at a "higher level of abstraction, generality, and inclusiveness than the reading itself" (Ausubel, 1963, p. 81). It differs from an overview in that it relates content to learners' current cognitive structure, thus enriching existing schemata and enabling learners to link prior knowledge with new concepts. When new information is presented to learners, they use prior knowledge to make sense of new information. Learners who

Exhibit 9.1   Study Guide Excerpt

This study guide is supplemental and can be used to help you understand the organization of the paper and the authors' line of reasoning.

A Defense of Deception on Scientific Grounds
Karen S. Cook; Toshio Yamagishi, *Social Psychology Quarterly*; Sept. 2008; 71, 3; ProQuest Psychology Journals

Page 215

Para 1: In this section the authors define what the use of deception in research includes.

Para 2: In this paragraph the authors argue why banning the use of deception in research will have a negative impact on research into intellectual and scientific issues of importance.

Para 3: Here the authors are discussing the arguments on the opposing side of the issue that deception in research should not be used.

Para 4: In this paragraph the authors are stating their position that deception in research should be used under limited circumstances and that research should not be sanctioned for the use of deception. The authors also state an argument for the use of deception in research, stating, "Important insights into human behavior and decision-making have come from award-winning experiments...."

Para 5: See page 216.

Page 216

Para 5: Here the authors argue why alternative methods to the use of deception are not a valid mode for conducting certain experiments that investigate the elements of choice or behavior.

Para 6: They continue to argue in this paragraph the effects of using other methods as an alternative to deception and how it may influence research findings.

Para 7: The authors present evidence from research studies to support their argument that deception in research should be used in some cases.

Para 8: The authors present evidence from research studies to support their argument that deception in research should be used in some cases.

Page 217, etc.

At End of Guide

Definitions:

Heuristic: A guide for learning, discovery, or investigation.

IRB Board (IRBs): IRBs review research studies to ensure participants of studies are protected by making sure studies are well designed, do not involve undue risk, and include safeguards to protect participants.

Paradigm: The generally accepted perspective of a particular discipline.

Pragmatic: Behavior dictated by practical consequences.

Source: Stavredes, 2011.

---

have little prior knowledge of a subject may comprehend incoming information efficiently because they have not developed schemata or mental structures for the topic. A goal of teaching is to simplify the information or elaborate on the information to help learners activate or build appropriate mental structures to organize and interpret the incoming information and aid recall.

A list of definitions can help learners deal with new terminology and keep them from skipping over information they do not understand. Study questions can help learners focus on important information. They also serve as advance organizers to help scaffold learning and improve cognitive processing by providing appropriate schemata to organize the new incoming information. Study guides can help learners understand major concepts and ideas by providing summaries of reading materials. For example, in an introductory course, you may consider including study guides to journal articles that may be written at a level that is difficult for the learners to understand. A study guide can provide summaries of each paragraph of the article and help point out important ideas and the author's line of reasoning. Exhibit 9.1 shows an excerpt from a study guide that I use to support first-year undergraduate learners.

Visual representations such as diagrams, concept maps, and outlines can help learners organize new information into meaningful schemas and provide a clearer understanding of how concepts are interrelated (Boettcher & Conrad, 2010). As learners engage in the content, visual representations can help learners make sense of the detailed information that is being presented in the readings and allow them to organize incoming information in a structured way for storage and retrieval. Diagrams and concept maps can provide a simple visual at a

Exhibit 9.2   Types of Graphical Organizers.

Type of Information	Graphical Organizer	Examples [Created with Microsoft Word]
Sequential	Cycle	
	Series of Events	
	Flowchart	
Analysis	Spider Map	

Exhibit 9.2 *(continued)*

Comparative	Venn Diagram	
	Comparison Chart	
Conceptual	Concept Map	
	Idea Tree	
Hierarchical	Organization Chart	

high level or can be used as a template to fill in as learners engage in readings. Exhibit 9.2 describes a variety of graphical organizers that can be used to visually organize different types of information. For example, sequential information can be understood via graphical organizers to demonstrate cycles, series of events, and flowcharts. Information that requires analysis can be supported by spider maps. Comparative information can be graphically organized by Venn diagrams and comparison charts. Conceptual information can be organized with concept maps and idea trees, and information that is hierarchical can be organized via organization charts.

If you use Microsoft Office, many of these types of graphical organizer are available in Word and Excel. In addition, there are a number of graphical organizer tools available on the Internet if you do a simple search using the key words "graphical organizer."

Conceptual scaffolding guides learners about what to consider and supports them as they engage in complex concepts and problems. Consider ways to incorporate conceptual scaffolds such as definitions, study guides, outlines, concept maps, and graphical organizers to support learning and help learners persist when they are confronted with difficult concepts. These tools can keep learners from becoming confused and frustrated, and ultimately from losing motivation, which can put them at risk for dropping out.

10

Strategic Scaffolding

Strategic scaffolding emphasizes alternative learning pathways that can be applied to the learning context to meet the diverse needs of learners. Earlier, in Chapter 4, we talked about providing support in the zone of proximal development. We discussed the importance of giving learners just enough support to allow them to reach the next level of understanding. It's important to remember, however, not to provide too much support, such that learners lose motivation to try hard, or too little support, such that learners stop trying because they don't know how to proceed. Strategic scaffolding is a significant tool because it provides just-in-time support to help learners reach higher levels of understanding.

Tailoring instruction to support individual learners requires you to understand individual learning preferences and level of prior knowledge in order to help them meet the intended outcomes of a course activity. For novice learners, cognitive overload may be an issue; strategies to help simplify the content and organize the information into discrete chunks will help learners process the information more effectively. You may also use conceptual scaffolds, such as an advance organizer or alternative presentation modes, to meet learners' learning style.

The use of strategic scaffolds requires you to closely monitor individual learner performance in order to provide support when needed. Alternative explanations can help learners understand course concepts by helping them see different ways of looking at the ideas being presented. Consider ways you can present concepts that target different learning styles. Also consider explanations of the learning materials from your own perspective using relevant real-world examples to help learners grasp difficult ideas.

Probing questions can provide explicit strategic clues for learners who need a place to begin; such questions can also be used in the middle of a problem-solving activity to help learners overcome barriers in order to persist in an activity. As you review discussions, ask probing questions to help learners extend their thinking or move them in the right direction if their posts are not relevant to the discussion questions.

Sometimes learners will need hints to understand the next step in a process or activity, or examples to understand the expectations of an activity to give them a starting point. You may find discussions are not very active early in a unit of study. This may be a clue that learners are waiting for someone to post because they are unsure of how to respond to the discussion question. You can give learners a starting point by providing context for the discussion and possibly hints regarding the types of information that you are expecting them to discuss. Consider structuring projects so there are opportunities to review learners' work, which can be a good time to give them additional hints to help them progress.

Worked examples can also support learners by providing them a way to think through a process to solve a problem. When using examples strategically, you may want to consider allowing learners to progress as far as they can without the examples and then make them available when learners can go no further on their own. It is important that the worked examples are not specific to the activity but allow the learner to generalize from the example to new problems.

Supplementary resources can also help learners strategically to accomplish a learning task by supporting gaps in skills or knowledge. This will require you to diagnose learning difficulties just-in-time and provide specific resources to help the learner overcome the skill or knowledge gap in order to progress in the course activity.

Expert advice can provide support to learners when working with problem-based learning scenarios (Hannifin, Land, & Oliver, 1999). Structuring expert advice around specific questions during a learning activity can help learners think through a problem from multiple perspectives and also demonstrate expert problem-solving skills. The best way to incorporate expert advice is through simulations that present real-world scenarios where learners can engage in

Exhibit 10.1 Cognitive Scaffolding Planning Tool.

Type of Scaffolding	Subtypes	Examples	Use in Course
Procedural—supports learning how to navigate the course environment and engage in learning activities	Orientation	Course orientation at institutional level	
		Course orientation using Blackboard 9.1 tool	
		Develop your own course orientation	
	Expectation	Faculty Expectation Statement	
	Resource	Critical thinking process; reflective process	
		Writing and research resources	
		Plagiarism detection tool	
Metacognitive—supports development of general academic skills to help learners manage their learning	Planning	Course overview	
		Course road map	
		Unit overview	
		Unit checklist	
	Monitoring	Templates, worksheets, worked examples	
		Unit checklist	
		Time logs	
		Note-taking tools	
	Evaluating	Grading rubrics/scoring guides with self-evaluation strategies	
		Self-reflection at end of activity	
Conceptual—supports learners when they encounter new information or information that is difficult to understand		Definitions	
		Study questions	
		Study guides	
		Outline	
		Graphic organizers—diagrams, concept maps, etc.	
Strategic—emphasizes alternative learning pathways that can be applied to the learning context to meet the diverse needs of learners		Alternative explanations	
		Probing questions	
		Hints	
		Worked examples	
		Supplementary resources	
		Expert advice	

content and choose among various experts for advice in solving a problem. The simulation can calibrate the challenge to give the exact amount of support to help learners reach the next level of understanding (Aldrich, 2009). This can also be very motivating for learners. There are many simulations available for purchase. You may also find simulations available through your textbook publisher.

The main goal of strategic scaffolding is to help learners reach a level of understanding that they cannot achieve on their own. Strategic scaffolding requires you to continuously monitor the learning environment, evaluate learners' progress, and diagnose difficulties to provide just-in-time support to help them persist and reach higher levels of understanding. The computer-mediated environment is difficult for monitoring learning because you cannot visually see the learner, so you have to rely on clues from learners to diagnose learning difficulties. Learners who are not engaged in the course may signal learning difficulty, so you will want to proactively reach out to them and ask probing questions about their engagement in learning activities. Discussions can demonstrate learners' difficulty, so closely monitoring discussions can help you diagnose issues and provide strategic support. You also may be able to notice learning issues in informal discussion threads in which learners reach out to other learners for help.

Part 3 looked at cognitive scaffolding strategies and tools to support individual learning efforts as learners engage in an online learning environment. We looked at four types of scaffolding strategies that can be used to support learning: procedural, metacognitive, conceptual, and strategic. Scaffolding tools allow learners to engage in activities for which they may not be prepared on their own. A variety of instructional scaffolding strategies can support learners and have a huge impact on their persistence and achievement. Exhibit 10.1 summarizes the different types of cognitive scaffolds that have been discussed in Part 3; it can be used as a planning tool to ensure that you are considering all four types of scaffolding in supporting learners.

PART 4

Developing Cognitive, Social, and Teaching Presence Online

According to Garrison, Anderson, and Archer (2001), learning occurs within a community of inquiry through the interaction of cognitive, social, and teaching presence. Cognitive presence is the ability of learners to construct knowledge together as they engage in interactions. Social presence contributes to the learning experience because it establishes learners as individuals and helps build interpersonal relationships that can have a positive impact on engagement in learning activities. Teaching presence includes how an instructor facilitates the learning activities to support social and cognitive presence to help learners achieve course outcomes. Cognitive presence, social presence, and instructor presence can be established through a variety of synchronous and asynchronous communication tools.

Chapters 11, 12, 13, and 14 discuss how you can develop a community of inquiry in your online class through the use of cognitive, social, and teaching presence that is mediated by appropriate communication tools. Chapter 11 presents ways to develop cognitive presence through the use of active learning strategies to support critical thinking and knowledge construction. Chapter 12 describes learner-to-learner collaborative strategies to help develop social presence and build a community of inquiry where learners can engage in critical thinking and knowledge construction in collaborative activities. Chapter 13 describes strategies to help you develop presence in the course to support learners. Finally, Chapter 14 describes communication tools that can be used to establish cognitive, social, and instructor presence.

11

Developing Cognitive Presence Through Active Learning Strategies

Cognitive presence is developed when learners share their multiple perspectives to construct knowledge. According to Garrison, Anderson, and Archer (2001), cognitive presence is "the extent to which the participants in any particular configuration of a community of inquiry are able to construct meaning through sustained communication" (p. 5). A community of inquiry occurs when learners work together to construct experience and knowledge by using critical thinking to analyze the subject matter, asking probing questions, and challenging assumptions (Garrison, Anderson, & Archer, 2001). The online experience for learners should be both collaborative and reflective; this is a challenge for online instructors because you must consider ways to develop critical and reflective discourse in a text-based medium.

In this chapter we look at how to develop cognitive presence through critical thinking, reflection, problem-based learning, and debate. Critical thinking skills help learners think through concepts in order to construct knowledge and make decisions. Reflection can help learners actively direct their learning to reach their educational goals. Problem-based learning and debate incorporate active learning and critical thinking as learners engage in a community of inquiry to solve real-world problems or debate real-world issues by using higher-order thinking processes. This can motivate learners by helping them understand the relevance of ideas presented in the course in relationship to the real world. Active learning places the responsibility of learning on the learner. It requires learners to reflect on what they know as they actively engage in reading, writing, and dialogue to make meaning from the content and construct knowledge.

Active learning also has a positive impact on persistence. Chapter 6 discusses motivation theory and the need to move learners from being extrinsically motivated to becoming more intrinsically motivated. This can have a positive impact on persistence because intrinsic motivation leads to more meaningful learning; that is, learning that is not focused solely on performance as a means to an end but rather learning that is transformative in a learner's life both personally and professionally. Active learning strategies are transformative because they focus on meaning-making that is relevant to the learner rather than learning for the sake of meeting course objectives. It is grounded in constructivist learning principles, which consider learning as an active process that engages learners in critical thinking and collaborative learning opportunities to construct knowledge.

CRITICAL THINKING

In today's world, information is changing at a rapid pace. It is not enough to simply transmit knowledge to learners as a primary goal of learning. Because of the dynamic nature of knowledge, learners need to have the skills to work with an active knowledge base and use tools to successfully participate in the ever changing world we live in. Learners acquire knowledge to make sense of the world around them and make decisions about courses of action that need to be taken in their lives. To acquire knowledge, learners need to think critically, which involves "calling into question the assumptions underlying their customary, habitual ways of thinking and acting and then being ready to think and act differently on the basis of this critical questioning" (Brookfield, 1987, p. 1).

Critical thinking skills are a solid foundation for learners to engage in a community of inquiry to construct knowledge by providing them a skill set to help reason through concepts and ideas. According to Stephen Brookfield (1987), there are four components to critical thinking:

1. Identifying and challenging assumptions

2. Challenging the importance of context

3. Being able to imagine and explore alternatives

4. Having reflective skepticism (p. 8)

Critical thinking includes being able to look at multiple perspectives, analyze similarities and differences in other people's thinking, and evaluate the relevance of perspective in the context of the information presented. It helps learners understand people's underlying assumptions and biases, as well as their own, and how these assumptions and biases can influence how they evaluate incoming information.

Critical thinking involves taking in information and reflecting on the information in a critical way to determine its relevance, reliability, and credibility before assimilating or accommodating information into the learner's knowledge base. It requires an active thinking process in which learners ask questions, gather relevant information, and synthesize and analyze information. Throughout this process, learners are also aware of the context in which the information is being presented, to come to logical conclusions from the information (Elder & Paul, 2010). Critical thinking involves the ability to imagine and explore alternatives to the current way of thinking. It requires learners to be able to consider information in the context of their own lives, uncover assumptions that are relevant and irrelevant to their situations, and explore alternative ways to interpret the information and build on the existing base of knowledge.

Another part of critical thinking is reflective skepticism. Reflective skepticism allows learners to become independent thinkers and make their own decisions on the value and worth of information as they experience it. It also allows learners the opportunity to challenge current thinking and make decisions about what to believe or not believe based on their ability to look at the line of reasoning to determine the value of the information.

Pedagogical Approach to Critical Thinking

To allow learners to achieve the type of critical thinking that Stephen Brookfield describes (1987), you will need to create a course environment that encourages learners to examine their critical thinking skills during learning. This can be done by implementing a critical thinking process that learners use to reflect on their understanding as they acquire knowledge through their interactions with information, learners, and you.

One model that I have found to be comprehensive and relevant is the Paul-Elder Model of Critical Thinking (Elder & Paul, 2010). This model presents the concept of critical thinking in everyday language that learners can draw on to improve their thinking in class and in their everyday lives. The model considers the "elements of thought," which include purpose, question, information, inference, assumption, point of view, concepts, and implications. According to Elder and Paul (2010), all reasoning has a purpose and is an attempt to figure something out, answer a question, or solve a problem. Reasoning through a question is based on assumptions that are made from a specific point of view. Information, data, and evidence are used in our reasoning. All reasoning is based on ideas, and inferences are drawn from the information to allow us to come to conclusions, which have implications and consequences.

Elder and Paul (2010) have developed a set of intellectual standards that can be used in combination with the "elements of thought." The standards include clarity, accuracy, precision, relevance, depth, and breadth. . The standards can be used to improve learners' thinking skills and help them as they question ideas to determine whether they should accept them. The standards are a departure from the behaviorist characterization of learners as empty vessels waiting to be filled; rather, independent learners actively use their critical thinking skills to make decisions about the value of information.

Questions based on the standards can be used to aid learners' thinking. They include the following (Elder & Paul, 2010):

Clarity Questions

Could you elaborate further?

Could you illustrate what you mean?

Could you give me an example?

Accuracy Questions

How could we check on that?

How could we find out if that is true?

How could we verify or test that?

Precision Questions

Could you be more specific?

Could you give me more details?

Could you be more exact?

Relevance Questions

How does that relate to the problem?

How does that bear on the question?

How does that help us with the issue?

Depth Questions

What factors make this a difficult problem?

What are some of the complexities of this question?

What are some of the difficulties we need to deal with?

Breadth Questions

Do we need to look at this from another perspective?

Do we need to consider another point of view?

Do we need to look at this in other ways?

Logic Questions

Does all of this make sense together?

Does your first paragraph fit in with your last one?

Does what you say follow from the evidence?

Significance Questions

Is this the most important problem to consider?

Is this the central idea to focus on?

Which of these facts are most important?

Fairness Questions

Do I have any stake in this issue?

Am I sympathetically representing the viewpoint of others?

The Paul-Elder Model of Critical Thinking can be used with learners to help them critically evaluate information during learning and think critically in discussion activities. You can also use the model to probe learners' thinking to move them from surface-level thinking to deep, critical thinking.

Critical Thinking Activities

Critical thinking strategies can be incorporated into learning activities to help learners become aware of the components of thinking and use them during learning. Consider developing activities that require learners to reflect on the components of thinking as they engage in research, discussion, and writing. For research assignments, a research analysis worksheet can help learners analyze the ideas of experts by considering the elements of reasoning as they review research

Exhibit 11.1   Research Analysis Worksheet

Use this worksheet and your understanding of critical thinking and the structure of an argument to analyze the articles on [insert name of topic]. To fill out the worksheet, work your way down through the analysis components and include your responses in the box next to the component and under the column for the article you are reviewing. Once you have completed the analysis, use the worksheet to compare and contrast the opposing positions on the [insert name of topic].

Name:

Analysis Components

[insert name of topic]
[insert APA reference to article]
[insert APA reference to article]

The main purpose of this article is . . . [State as accurately as possible the author's purpose for writing the article. What is the author's position or point of view?]

The main arguments that the author is making are . . . [Determine the main arguments the author makes to support his or her position.]

The evidence or facts the author uses in this article to support his or her arguments are . . . [Identify the facts, data, or resources the author uses to support his or her argument.]

The main conclusion[s] or inference[s] in this article are . . . [Identify the key conclusions the author makes and presents in the article.]

The main assumptions underlying the author's thinking are . . . [Think about what the author is assuming to be true and what might be questioned. To expand on this statement you will need to think about the larger context of the topic.]

If we accept the author's line of reasoning, the implications are . . . [What consequence does the author's argument have on our understanding of current research and/or theory?]

If we reject the author's line of reasoning, the implications are . . . [What consequence does rejecting the author's arguments have on our understanding of current research and theory?]

papers. Exhibit 11.1 is a worksheet that I use to help learners incorporate critical thinking as they research issues.

These questions can help learners examine individual perspectives on issues. If the Exhibit 11.1 worksheet is used to look at a number of authors' ideas on a topic, it can be used to develop an understanding of the diversity of thought on issues. It can also provide learners with a process to analyze, synthesize, and evaluate the information presented to develop their own opinions on a topic of study based on the learners' interpretation of the reasoning of different authors.

Other activities to encourage critical thinking are discussions in which learners interact in a community of inquiry. Discussions allow learners to think critically about the course content and consider their own thoughts and ideas in relation to the opinions of experts and peers. Incorporating critical thinking in discussion activities is discussed in detail in Chapter 12, where we examine learner-to-learner interactions.

Writing assignments can also be structured to ensure that learners are using critical thinking as they construct papers for the course. If you combine the research analysis worksheet with a writing template, you can help learners understand how to write persuasive papers that have sound reasoning. Exhibit 11.2 shows a writing template that learners can use to compose their writing assignments.

REFLECTION

According to Brookfield (1987), reflective learning is an important part of critical thinking. Reflection allows learners to consider where they have been, where they are, and where they want to go. With this knowledge, learners can grow as self-directed, independent learners who are in control of their own learning. Self-reflection allows learners to develop plans for continuous improvement by helping them see both areas of growth and those that need additional attention to improve cognitive development and attain the intended outcomes of the course.

To help learners reflect on previous experiences, begin the course with an activity that allows them to consider the course goals and objectives, determine their current level of achievement in those areas, and identify where they need to focus their attention. One idea is a discussion that relates the course goals and objectives to real-world practice and allows learners to reflect on specific

Exhibit 11.2   Writing Template

Introduction
Share something of interest to capture the reader's attention and introduce the issue. The introduction should include a statement of purpose for writing the paper and identify the problem or issue in question. It should also describe your position or point of view on the issue (thesis) and introduce the reader to the arguments you will make to support your position.

Section Heading for Argument 1 [level one heading is bold and centered]
Each section in the body of the paper will present an argument to support your position. Begin each section by stating an argument and construct an analysis of the argument to support your position. Next provide several pieces of evidence such as data, experience, examples, or illustrations to support your argument. The analysis should be based on your interpretation of the evidence rather than simply the presentation of the evidence and can include comparisons or contrasts to build your position. It should also include a discussion of the assumptions that are being made to support your argument, and include an analysis of counterarguments presented in the research with specific rebuttals to the counterarguments to build credibility for your opinions. If you use quotations, be sure to follow the quotation with an analysis of it and the specific point it makes for your position. Finally, summarize your argument and how you have reasoned through your argument, and lead the reader into the next section of the paper, which is your second argument.

Section Heading for Argument 2 [see directions above]
Section Heading for Argument 3 [see directions above]
Summary and Conclusion
Begin by restating your position and restate the most important points or arguments that you have presented to support your position. You should also discuss your conclusions and the implications if someone fails to take this line of reasoning seriously or the consequences that could follow for ignoring your reasoning.

---

objectives they need to focus on to achieve their personal goals for the future while also engaging in the course activities.

Throughout the course, there should be additional opportunities for learners to reflect on how they are doing. This can be accomplished through reflective exercises at the end of major activities and assignments that allow learners to reflect on the intended outcomes of the activities, understand the process they used to accomplish the activities, and realize where they had the most growth. The exercises should also be forward looking to identify where learners need to focus more effort and attention. By having learners reflect throughout the course, they have a better opportunity to achieve the intended outcomes.

A reflective activity at the end of the course about the course goals and objectives can help learners see how well they met each objective and their overall growth as they engaged in course activities. It can also allow learners to determine areas they need to continue to focus attention on, which can help them make decisions on future courses and identify academic skills they need to strengthen to achieve specific course objectives.

Consider the following types of reflective questions to ask learners:

At the Beginning of the Course

1. Why did I take this course?
2. What do I hope to gain from taking this course?
3. How will this course help me in the real world?
4. On a scale of 1–10, what is my current knowledge and skills in relationship to each of the objectives of the course?
5. What objectives will I need to focus more attention and effort on?
6. What are my academic strengths?
7. What are my academic weaknesses?
8. What type of support will I need from the instructor to help gain additional academic skills?

As Learners Complete Major Activities and Assignments in the Course

1. What did I learn from this activity?
2. What confuses me?
3. Where do I need to spend more time on concepts?
4. What knowledge and skills did I use to complete the activities?
5. What knowledge and skills do I need to work on?
6. What strategy did I use to make sure that I understood the requirements of the activity?

7. What strategy did I use to break down the components associated with the activity?

8. What strategy did I use to ensure I remained on task?

9. What strategy did I use to ensure I was learning?

10. What strategy did I use when I was not sure about what to do or when I needed clarification or elaboration to understand something?

11. What was the most enjoyable part of the activity?

12. What was the least enjoyable part of the activity?

13. How could the activity be improved?

At the End of the Course

1. Consider your rating of the course objectives as the beginning of the course and rate your level of knowledge and skills for each objective at the end of the course.

2. What objectives were you most successful at achieving?

3. What objectives do you need to continue to develop?

4. What strategy did you use throughout the course to ensure you understood the course content and associated activities?

5. What strategy did you use to ensure you met the criteria of the assignments?

6. What academic skills did you use to successfully complete the course?

7. What academic skills do you need to work on to improve your learning?

8. What did you enjoy the most about this course?

9. What did you enjoy the least about this course?

10. How could this course be improved?

These questions can help learners become more self-directed and set personal goals for learning. Consider setting up individual private journals in the discussion room for learners to post their reflections. This can allow them to easily refer to goals they have set throughout the course and continue to reflect on activities to see growth and areas that need improvement. These questions can also help you by providing an opportunity to reflect on specific activities to determine whether there was commonality in the types of successes and failures that occurred. This knowledge can be used to improve the quality of the course content, activities, and support structures for learners.

PROBLEM-BASED LEARNING

In teaching we often break down problems and issues into parts in order to help learners understand what is happening; however, the parts do not always reveal the complexity of the individual pieces and how they interact as a whole to produce a specific result. Problem-based learning can help learners understand the complexity of problems and develop learners' cognitive processes. In addition, often learners are not motivated to learn because they do not see the relevance of the activities to the real world. The use of problem-based learning can provide a real-world understanding of an issue by demonstrating the dynamic relationship among variables. Learners can understand how the interaction among individual variables results in specific situations and behaviors. If developed well, problem-based learning can entice learners to actively seek knowledge to solve a problem, that is, they take control of their learning.

Problem-based learning is grounded in constructivist learning theory as described in Chapter 4. According to Savery and Duffy (1995), the instructional principles for problem-based learning are derived from constructivism. Principles include the need to

- Anchor all learning activities to a larger task or problem
- Support the learner in developing ownership for the overall problem or task
- Design it as an authentic task that reflects the complexity of the environment in the real world
- Give learners ownership of the process used to develop the solution; support and challenge the learner's thinking
- Encourage testing ideas against alternative views and contexts
- Provide opportunity for reflection on the content and the process (p. 3)

Barrows and Kelson (1993) describe core characteristics of problem-based learning, which include the need for learning to be student-centered and occur in small groups under the guidance of a tutor who acts as a facilitator or guide. In addition, problem-based learning activities should occur in the context of an authentic problem to achieve the required knowledge and problem-solving skills.

Problem-based learning provides learners with concrete representations of relevant concepts and ideas situated in real-life experience outside of the classroom. It allows them to critically analyze information and come to conclusions. It also encourages dialogue in a community of inquiry among learners to promote alternative ideas and solutions. This requires learners to use critical thinking and active learning to evaluate the information presented. Problem-based learning focuses learning around a real-world problem, question, issue, case, or project. It requires learners to actively use knowledge in the content domain in tasks that require them to solve, resolve, and interpret as they engage in learning activities.

Pedagogical Approach to Problem-Based Learning

According to Barrows and Kelson (1993), there are six objectives that learners should be able to achieve in a problem-based learning activity:

1. Develop a systematic approach to solving real-life problems, using higher order thinking skills (problem-solving, critical thinking, decision-making).

2. Acquire an extensive, integrated knowledge base that can be recalled and flexibly applied to other situations.

3. Develop effective self-directed learning skills, identifying what they need to learn, locating and using appropriate resources, applying the information back to the problem, and reflecting on, evaluating, and adjusting their approach for greater efficiency and effectiveness.

4. Develop the attitudes and skills necessary for effective team work with others working on a task or problem.

5. Acquire the life-long habit of approaching a problem with initiative and diligence and a drive to acquire the knowledge and skills needed for an effective resolution.

6. Develop habits of self-reflection and self-evaluation that allow for honest appraisal of strengths and weaknesses and the setting of realistic goals (p. 2).

For learners to be motivated to engage in problem-based learning activities, the problem should be interesting and relevant and not constrained by being too structured with specific solutions. Consider problems or issues that are ill-structured with the potential of multiple solutions. In addition, problems or issues should reflect real-world practice; they should be based on problems that practitioners face in their field or issues that are of concern in our real lives. The University of Delaware has a Problem-Based Learning Clearinghouse at https://primus.nss.udel.edu/Pbl/ that has a collection of problem-based scenarios and articles to help instructors use problem-based learning. All of the problems have been peer reviewed by experts in the field of problem-based learning. Each problem scenario includes instructor notes and materials to help instructors use it in a course. The Clearinghouse is free; however, you have to sign up to access the database, and it takes approximately a week for your request to be approved.

Setting Up a Problem-Based Activity

Problem-based learning is knowledge based; it requires learners to apply knowledge and skills as they research and develop solutions to a problem (Barrows & Kelson, 1993). It is also process oriented with learners having to plan, organize research, analyze, and solve as they complete a problem-based learning activity.

At the beginning of the activity, you will need to frame the issue or problem and make sure that learners understand its relevance. Learners can then internalize the problem and be motivated to solve it in order to gain knowledge and skills they can use in the real world. You should also describe the learning problem in detail and make sure that learners understand the parameters of the problem, as well as the learning goals. Details should include the purpose, setting, characters, storylines, and resources to describe the problem-based learning context (Exhibit 11.3):

The Problem-Based Learning Process Once learners have an understanding of the parameters of the project, they will need to begin processing the information about the problem. Learning activities should include

- Identifying or defining the problem
- Analyzing underlying factors
- Considering solutions, alternative courses of action, or both
- Making decisions about courses of action and recommendations to solve the problem

Exhibit 11.3   Setting Problem-Based Learning Context

Purpose

Describe the main goal of the activity and the specific goals and outcomes that will be achieved. This will help motivate learners. Make sure that outcomes relate to real-world practice, so learners see the connection between the activity and how they will be able to apply it in real-world applications.

Setting

Describe the specific setting in which the problem takes place and include all relevant information, so learners can imagine themselves in the specific situation being described. The setting should include the place, whether it is a business, organization, institution, or other location. It should also include the product or service that the organization provides, as well as any background information about the setting, including information such as mission, goals, values, and beliefs.

Characters

Describe each character in the setting and specific traits of the individuals that are relevant to being able to address the issue or solve the problem. The description should include the role the individual characters and any relevant information about the characters, including expertise, issues they have encountered, positions on the issue being addressed, and any additional information about the characters that is important to understand in order to solve the problem.

Storyline

The storyline should describe what takes place from beginning to end of the problem scenario. It should include, at a minimum, the

- Time
- Sequence of events
- Actions of each of the characters
- Results of the actions

Resources

Include any resources to help learners as they try to solve the problem. This can include correspondence, reports, memos, and relevant research, as well as other documentation or interactions that learners can consult during the activity to acquire additional information that may be relevant to the problem. Learners should determine the relevance of the information as part of their analysis.

Exhibit 11.4   Problem Analysis Worksheet

Use this worksheet to break the problem into parts by considering the factors associated or contributing to the problem. For each factor, determine what you currently know about it, any assumptions you have made, evidence you have to support what you know, and information that you will need to gather to determine how the factor contributes to the problem and solution to the problem. Also consider the best place to find the information you will need to investigate each factor.

Problem Statement	Factor	Factor	Factor	Factor, etc.
What do we know about this factor?				
What assumptions have we made?				
What evidence do we have to support what we know [research data, experience, etc.]?				
What information do we need to find to fill the gaps in knowledge and/or evidence?				
What potential resources can we use to investigate this factor?				

To identify or define the problem, learners will need to break down the information they have into factors associated or contributing to the problem, thus framing the problem and leading to a solution. For each factor, learners will need a process for organizing information to investigate it. Exhibit 11.4 is an example of a worksheet that can provide learners a process for organizing information needed to solve the problem.

Learners will need to develop a plan for finding relevant resources to fill any gaps in knowledge in order to understand the issue or problem. Through the Internet, information is available at learners' fingertips. Since anyone can post information online, it is important to include a process for helping learners evaluate resources they find on the Internet. Consider credibility and reliability criteria as part of the process for evaluating resources (Exhibit 11.5).

During the analysis phase, learners will need to organize the information they find relating to the factors associated with the problem. They should look at multiple perspectives to understand the extent to which each factor affects the problem. During the analysis phase, the goal is to find the real cause of the problem by analyzing the underlying issues and causes and considering alternative courses of action. Consider ways to help learners organize information for analysis.

Exhibit 11.5   Credibility and Reliability Criteria for Evaluating Resources

Author: What is the credential of the author? What is the author's area of expertise? Does the author appear to have a bias [e.g., is he or she representing a company that is selling a product or idea]?

Currency: Many resources are put on the Internet; however, rarely are they removed, so it is important to discover when the information was created and consider how relevant it is today. When was this resource created? Has it gone through multiple versions?

Peer Review: Has the content undergone a peer review process?

Accuracy and Verifiability: Does the author use citations and a reference list to support the information presented?

Relevancy: Is this source relevant to the problem at hand?

Exhibit 11.6   Research Analysis Worksheet

Once you have completed researching each of the factors related to the problem, use this worksheet to organize your research and analyze the information related to each factor. Consider what you know as facts, perspectives of stakeholders, and evidence that you have to support what you know.

Factor	Facts	Perspectives	Evidence	Assumptions

Exhibit 11.6 is a worksheet that can be used to analyze factors related to a problem including facts, perspectives, supporting evidence, and assumptions that support the information.

In addition, the use of graphical organizers can help learners visually depict a problem and analyze its underlying causes. As discussed in Chapter 9, there are a number of graphical organizers that can be used to organize information, such as cycles, flowcharts, fish bone and spider maps, Venn diagrams, comparison charts, concept maps, and organization charts.

The final phase is the solution phase, where learners will analyze potential solutions or courses of action to the problem and pick the best one based on their

Exhibit 11.7 Solution Analysis Worksheet

Use the following worksheet to think through potential solutions, courses of action, or both, to the problem. List all solutions and consider the pros and cons to implementing each of the solutions or courses of action. You may want to consider including a rating of the solution or course of action from 1–5 [1 = least likely solution; 5 = most likely solution] as a way of determining which solution is the best.

Solutions or Courses of Action	Pros to Solutions or Courses of Action	Cons to Solutions or Courses of Action	Solution Rating 1 = least likely; 5 = most likely

research and analysis. Consider the worksheet in Exhibit 11.7 to help learners look at potential solutions and courses of action.

Also consider debriefing strategies to reflect on the success of the problem-based learning activity. Reflection is described in more detail later in the chapter.

Collaborative Strategies   The goal of collaboration in problem-based learning is to develop a community of inquiry where learners use critical thinking to engage in discourse to build knowledge and understanding of the problem. Discussion threads can be used with learners to dialogue about the problem and interact with other learners to describe their perspectives on the problem, issues, causes, solutions, courses of action, and recommendations. Having them see multiple perspectives of other learners in the course, and how they have interpreted the information presented, can help them think deeper and challenge their own conclusions. In addition, participants can learn to communicate their ideas persuasively by telling a compelling story using information and reasoning.

Another collaborative tool for problem-based learning is a wiki, which can be used to help groups plan and organize activities, explore a problem through research activities, integrate learners' knowledge and understanding of the problem, and come to a solution through discourse. In a wiki you can link pages together to organize information and activities, which can be a challenge in a discussion thread. All members of a group can edit documents, so it is an excellent tool for collaborating and sharing files because there is no need to pass documents back and forth and control the versions of a document. In addition, it has communication capabilities to allow a group to share ideas and manage tasks.

Instructor Role in Probem-Based Learning The role of the instructor in problem-based learning is to facilitate the activity and help learners understand the goals and tasks, process information effectively, assess learners formatively to ensure they are meeting goals, and provide additional support to help learners achieve the intended outcomes of the activity. This requires you to continually monitor learners individually and in groups and provide just-in-time support to motivate, explain, clarify, and redirect.

At the beginning of the problem-based learning activity, it is important to dialogue with learners and go over any questions about the activity, including the problem, the process, resources, tools, and other questions that learners may have. This can be accomplished with communication tools to hold a live meeting or via a discussion thread where learners can post specific questions after reviewing the requirements of the project. Throughout the project, as learners engage in activities, you can support learners by providing hints or cases to help learners who may not have experience to draw on understand specific aspects of the problem. You can interact with learners within discussions to provide examples from the field or hints for how to proceed. Hints or cases can also be developed in advance of the activity and be a part of the resources available to learners as they plan, research, analyze, and solve the problem. The key is to allow learners to work independently and be there to support them if they run into roadblocks.

You can also support learners by helping them use critical thinking skills as they engage in the learning activity. This can include prompts to help them incorporate the Paul-Elder "elements of thought" (Elder & Paul, 2010) as they generate ideas, draw inferences, summarize results, and draw on implications. Also, consider prompts to help learners focus their attention on important aspects of the problem and direct them to relevant resources, when needed.

A critical component of instructor interaction should be in the form of feedback throughout the activity to help individual learners or groups understand the effectiveness of their planning, organizing, researching, and analyzing processes and provide recommendations for improvement to help them reach the goals of the learning activity. If there are flaws in how learners are representing the problem, they may end up solving the wrong problem, so it is important to challenge the learners to adequately explain the reasoning behind their decision making.

Problem-based learning is an active learning strategy that develops cognitive presence by incorporating critical thinking as learners engage in a community of inquiry to solve real-world issues and problems. It allows learners to understand how the concepts they are learning in the course are relevant to real-world practice; this can increase motivation because learners see the value of learning and the application of the knowledge and skills.

DEBATE

Debate is an active learning strategy that allows learners an opportunity to discuss issues with divergent points of view. Debate allows for an in-depth analysis of an issue from opposing sides using reasoned arguments based on sound evidence. In a debate, learners take one side of an issue and use critical thinking to effectively communicate their position on an issue. Learners formally engage in a debate with peers and try to persuade them that their position is valid and deserves consideration. The goal is to develop critical thinking and communication skills to effectively persuade the opinions of others.

Debates can be structured as an individual activity or a team activity. Individual debate activities require learners to do their research independently and participate as an individual in the debate discussion. Team debates help learners build collaborative skills as they work together to organize, research, and plan the debate. Whether an individual or group activity, debate can help learners develop critical thinking skills as they engage in opposing positions of an issue to help them determine their own stand.

Organizing the Debate

Learners should be introduced to the issue that will be debated by providing them with a general description of the issue and the different views that exist on the issue. Once learners have a general understanding of the issue and the different perspectives on the issue, learners should choose one of the opposing positions on an issue. If the debate activity is a team activity, then learners will need to be divided into teams based on their chosen perspective on the issue.

The next step is to have learners explore the issue from their chosen perspective or position by conducting research. You may want to provide a list of resources that can be used to research the issue. This is especially helpful for dependent learners, so they can focus more of their time and attention on analyzing the research and coming to a more in-depth understanding of the issue and the different lines of reasoning there are for their position. If one of the goals of the course is to make sure that learners can use the library and develop effective research strategies, then consider having them find several resources on their own. This allows learners to learn how to access the library, use appropriate databases, and develop appropriate search strategies to find relevant resources on an issue.

Pre-Debate Activities

For team debates, the first activity should be the assignment of roles for each individual. For each activity, roles will need to be assigned to accomplish the associated tasks. I recommend that you also include lead roles for each activity. The lead role is the person who is accountable for organizing the specific activity and making sure that all team members working on the activity are accountable and understand the tasks, deliverables, and timeline. If the debate is an individual activity, this step in the pre-debate activities will not be needed.

Research is the next pre-debate activity and it requires the individual or team to analyze relevant resources that support their position on the issue. Research should also consider the opposing positions in order to develop strong counterarguments to their positions. Once the research is completed, if the debate is a team project, the team will need to share the information they have found on their position. Next is the development of the position statement, arguments with evidence to support position, counterarguments for the opposing position, and refutations to what the opposing team may say against the position. Consider using a Debate Preparation Worksheet (Exhibit 11.8) to help learners organize information to prepare for the debate. If learners are working in a team, they can use the worksheet to collaborate and prepare for the debate. If the debate is an individual activity, each learner will complete the worksheet to prepare for the debate.

The Debate

During the debate, the individual or team will post a position statement for the team. If the debate is a team project, the team will need to determine who will post

Exhibit 11.8   Debate Preparation Worksheet

Use this worksheet to synthesize what you have learned from your research to prepare for the debate.

1. Position Statement
Construct a personal position statement that reflects your perspective on [fill in topic].

Components of Position Statement:
Include in your Position Statement the following:
* Description of issue:
* Description of perspective:
* Brief summary of arguments that you will present to support your position:

2. Summary of Supporting Arguments and Evidence to Support Your Position
Supporting Argument 1:
* Evidence, experience, example, illustration 1:
* Evidence, experience, example, illustration 2:
* Evidence, experience, example, illustration 3:

Supporting Argument 2:
* Evidence, experience, example, illustration 1:
* Evidence, experience, example, illustration 2:
* Evidence, experience, example, illustration 3:

Supporting Argument 3:
* Evidence, experience, example, illustration 1:
* Evidence, experience, example, illustration 2:
* Evidence, experience, example, illustration 3:

   Add additional supporting arguments as needed.

3. Rebuttal Strategies
What our opponents might say against you: Things you could say back:

(continued)

Exhibit 11.8 *(continued)*

4. Counter-Arguments

| What other learners might say for their position: | Things I could say to challenge them during the discussion: |

5. Summary Statement

Construct a preliminary draft of your summary statement. You will not be able to complete your statement until you have participated in the debate and analyzed the outcomes of the debate; however, you can begin to construct your statement based on what you will present during the debate.

Components of Summary Statement:

Include the following in your summary statement:

- Statement of issue
- Statement of perspective
- Summary of supporting arguments
- Summary of opposing arguments
- Statement of why your position is the most valid and reasonable

---

the team position statement. All team members can post counterarguments to opposing teams' positions and arguments, as well as rebuttals to opposing teams' counterarguments to their team's position and arguments. The final post will be a summary statement that will need to be assigned to one of the team members. Regarding the debate discussion, I recommend that you require specific standards for posting the different parts of the debate, including how to title the subject line and what to include in the message box (Exhibits 11.9–11.11). This will help keep the discussion thread from becoming disorganized, so it is easy to follow the logic of the debate structure and flow.

Instructor Role in Debates

I recommend that you play the role of moderator of the debate. In the online environment, this includes making sure that the threaded discussions remain organized based on the standards you have set up for the debate activity. If

Exhibit 11.9   Discussion Posting Standards

Position Statement: Position statements should include a discussion of the issue, a detailed description of the perspective, and individual arguments that you have developed to support your position. An example of a standard for posting a position statement is as follows:

Subject: Position Statement — Name or Team Name
Message:

- Describe issue.
- Describe perspective.

Include each argument with evidence to support it.

Exhibit 11.10   Counterargument Posting Standard

Counterargument: Each counterargument should include at least one piece of evidence to support it. The standard for posting a counterargument is as follows:

Subject: Counterargument — Your Name
Message:

- Details of counterargument.
- Evidence to support counterargument.

learners do not uphold the standards of how to post in the debate discussion, you should ask them to edit their posts to meet the standards set forth. Another role of the moderator is to ensure that the debate is respectful and learners attack the issue rather than other learners. This requires you to continuously monitor the debate to ensure that standards of posting and discussing the issue are met. If the debate is an individual activity, make sure that all learners have peers engaging in their position statements, arguments, and counterarguments. You can encourage learners to post to other learners to make sure everyone has an opportunity to interact. In addition, if the debate fizzles out, you can provide prompts or probes to re-ignite the debate.

Exhibit 11.11   Summary Statement Posting Standard

Summary Statement: A summary statement should be posted at the end of the debate. Consider setting up a separate discussion for the summary statements and assign a different due date, since it will require the team to come together to form a summary statement. If it is an individual assignment, the individual will post a summary of the debate without engaging in a discussion with other learners about the outcome.

   Subject: Summary Statement—Individual or Team Name
   Message:

- Statement of issue
- Statement of perspective
- Summary of supporting arguments
- Summary of opposing arguments
- Statement of why your position or your team's position is the most valid and reasonable

---

In this chapter we discussed the importance of creating an environment for the online learner to encourage cognitive presence through the use of active learning strategies that engage learners as a community of inquiry to create knowledge and understanding. Active learning places the responsibility of learning and acquiring knowledge on the learner; it can be transformative because it focuses on meaning-making that is relevant to the learner rather than learning for the sake of meeting course objectives. We discussed the need for learners to have critical thinking skills to work with an active knowledge base and described specific strategies to help learners build critical thinking skills. We discussed the importance of reflection to help learners actively direct their learning to reach their educational goals. We described problem-based learning and debate strategies that integrate active learning and critical thinking as learners engage in a community of inquiry to think about real-world problems and issues. This integration can motivate learners because it helps them understand the relevance of the concepts presented in the course to the real world. Incorporating these instructional strategies can support learners as they engage in the online learning environment, improve persistence by allowing learners to control their own learning, and improve motivation by using authentic tasks that are applicable in the real world.

12

Establishing Social Presence Through Learner-to-Learner Collaborative Strategies

Social presence establishes learners as individuals and, through the process of relationship building, allows learners to engage in a community of inquiry. The more learners are able to establish themselves with other learners, the more trust they will build. Trust helps learners feel comfortable with sharing their thoughts and ideas without the fear of being wrong or being criticized. As the level of interaction increases, a greater sense of community can occur, where learners can share their divergent thoughts and perspectives to construct knowledge and understanding.

In today's workforce, employees need to have the skills to work together as a team to be innovative and solve problems. Collaborative learning strategies build higher-order thinking, critical thinking, and problem-solving skills by allowing learners to share multiple perspectives and challenge one another's thinking (Garrison, Anderson, & Archer, 2001). In addition, collaboration enhances learning outcomes and diminishes the potential for learner isolation, which can be a problem in an online learning environment (Palloff & Pratt, 2005). Collaboration also supports the creation of a learning community that can extend and deepen learners' experience by allowing them to share new ideas with a supportive group and receive critical and constructive feedback (Palloff & Pratt, 2007).

Collaboration offers learners an opportunity to build interpersonal relationships with peers. Workman and Stenard (1996) analyzed the needs of distance learners and identified the need to develop interpersonal relationships with peers as a significant influence on persistence of online learners. Tinto (1975) describes social and academic integration, as well as the development of a learning community, as internal institutional factors that affect persistence. How you develop learner-to-learner collaborative learning activities will have an impact on learner satisfaction and persistence. Therefore, it is important to understand factors that influence successful collaborations between learners and structure your collaborative activities to maximize the potential for building a community of inquiry.

In the online environment, it is more difficult to create a sense of presence. Kehrwald (2008) defines social presence as "an individual's ability to demonstrate his/her state of being in a virtual environment and so signal his/her availability for interpersonal transactions"(p. 94). Without the awareness of other learners' presence, it is nearly impossible to develop relationships with peers. Some learners may want it that way; however, knowledge construction does not occur in isolation, so you will need to develop strategies to encourage learners to be present in the course. The key is to create opportunities for interactions between learners that are stimulating, allow learners to express themselves, and have significance in the learners' life (Lehman & Conceição, 2010).

As discussed in Chapter 1, many learners bring a wealth of knowledge to the learning environment. Creating an atmosphere that allows learners to share their knowledge and experience can enhance learning and lead to the collaborative creation of new knowledge. Some learners may have little or no experience; collaborative strategies can allow them to learn from more experienced learners and understand how the knowledge and skills acquired through learning activities apply to real-world environments. In this chapter we look at several strategies that promote collaborative learning, including discussion, team or group projects, and peer reviews.

DISCUSSION

Discussion is an integral part of the online learning environment. According to Brookfield and Preskill (2005), "discussions are ideal for exploring complex ideas and entertaining multiple perspectives" (p. 236). It is through collaboration between learners that higher-order thinking skills can be developed, including critical thinking, creative thinking, and problem solving. Multiple perspectives that present new or different interpretations and explanations of a topic of study can help develop learners' conceptions and inform them of their misconceptions during learning.

I have often said that I did not know how much I really knew about a topic until I started writing or talking about it. Through written and verbal communication, we are able to express what we know. Sometimes we may find that we are at a loss for words right in the middle of what we are saying or writing, because we do not have the extent of knowledge that we thought we had on the subject. This experience allows us to evaluate our learning and determine where gaps exist. We can then develop strategies to gain additional knowledge to fill the gaps. Through discourse, learners can discover viewpoints different from their own; through this discovery learners may learn to question their own conceptions and resolve conflicts between opposing ideas.

The structure of discussion is critical in building strong collaborative skills and developing higher-order thinking skills. A well-structured discussion question should allow learners to use their knowledge and comprehension of a subject at the levels of application, analysis, synthesis, and evaluation. In addition, discussions should be interesting and relevant to elicit broad participation. Without a diversity of thought, learners are unable to practice expressing their ideas persuasively, and the discussion group lacks the diverse viewpoints it needs to make multiple connections effectively (Brookfield & Preskill, 2005).

Types of Discussion Questions

When deciding on the type of discussion to use in your online course, try to stay away from questions with a single or few answers and no room for interpretation. Such questions leave learners frustrated if they enter the discussion late and find that all of the potential responses have already been posted and there is little to add to the discussions without repeating someone else's ideas. In addition, such questions defeat the purpose of using discussion as a collaborative activity for knowledge building. Instead, consider questions that have a number of different ways they can be answered or questions that are open-ended and have no "correct" answer. The best type of question should pose a question or issue of interest in the form of a problem statement. The discussion question format should require learners to understand multiple perspectives on the question or issue, and the learners' response should require them to take a position and discuss the implications of their line of reasoning. Questions should allow learners to integrate their knowledge and comprehension of concepts and apply, analyze, synthesize, and evaluate them in real-world scenarios. Application questions allow the learner to apply course knowledge to solve real-world problems. Analysis questions allow learners to discover relationships between concepts and ideas and compare similarities and differences of ideas. Analysis questions also allow learners to break down information to discover causes, assumptions, motives, and make inferences. Analysis questions can also probe issues or problems and ask learners to discover the root cause. Synthesis discussions allow learners to incorporate information in new ways to plan, design, or solve problems in the real world. Finally, evaluative questions allow learners to judge, critique, or defend their interpretation of concepts.

Consider Exhibit 12.1 to develop discussion questions at all levels of thinking.

How Learners Interact in Discussions

Once you have developed your discussion questions, you will have to consider how you will structure the discussion to encourage engagement. Brookfield and Preskill (2005) describe the need for learners to take a critical stance in discussion to demonstrate they are committed to questioning and exploring ideas and beliefs. This requires learners to enter discussions with an open mind and be willing to adjust their views in light of persuasive arguments that are supported with evidence (p. 7). As previously noted, a discussion question should allow learners to contribute their own thoughts, experiences, and ideas, as well as use "evidence" from experts to support their own ideas to build greater credibility. The structure of discussions should discourage learners from "talking off the top of their heads" without incorporating course concepts and ideas. Yet discussions should also make it difficult for learners to simply state course concepts and ideas without including their own interpretations.

Exhibit 12.1 Stems for Discussion Questions.

Level of Knowledge	Discussion Question Stems
Application questions	Plan, design, solve, utilize, implement, apply
Analysis questions	Compare, contrast, differentiate, outline, distinguish, discover, classify
Synthesis questions	Dispute, justify, support, verify, integrate
Evaluative Questions	Solve, predict, improve, judge

Strategies for Building Critical Thinking in Discussions

Learners should express opinions in discussion by taking a position, building arguments, using evidence or experience to support their arguments, and presenting a case for why their line of reasoning should be followed. This is the foundation for building critical thinking, which can lead to higher-order thinking skills of analysis, synthesis, and evaluation. One of the ways I have structured discussion interactions to ensure they support the development of critical thinking skills is to encourage learners to use the "elements of thought" from the Paul-Elder Model of Critical Thinking (Elder & Paul, 2010), discussed in Chapter 11, as they respond to discussion questions and interact with other learners. Exhibit 12.2 describes the different elements of thought, along with questions to consider to ensure that learners examine a problem or issue from multiple perspectives and think critically to develop an opinion (Elder & Paul, 2010).

Learner-to-Learner Interactions in Discussions

A critical component of discussion is the interaction among learners. As previously discussed, learners need to be able to express their thoughts and ideas and be able to support them or be willing to change them if other compelling evidence is presented to make learners think or feel differently. However, there needs to be a discipline to discussions to ensure that the outcome of the discussion results in learners' changing their thinking or adding to their knowledge. Without a disciplined discussion, interactions among learners can be shallow and include statements such as "good job," "I like that idea," and "interesting comment," which do not add to the collaborative creation of knowledge.

To begin with, to develop an engaging discussion environment you will need to consider ways to make learners feel comfortable in sharing their thoughts and ideas. Brookfield and Preskill (2005) describe a set of dispositions that learners should consider to be more collaborative and respectful participants in discussions. These dispositions include hospitality, participation, mindfulness, humility, mutuality, deliberation, appreciation, hope, and autonomy (p. 8). *Hospitality* makes learners feel welcome to participate and safe to express their ideas and opinions. *Participation* encourages contributions from all learners to add depth and subtlety to the discussion. *Mindfulness* encourages learners to spend time to understand the opinions of other learners and be respectful of their diversity of thought. *Humility* allows learners to admit the limitations

Exhibit 12.2   Paul-Elder Model of Critical Thinking.

Thought Element	What to Consider
Point of view	How am I looking at this situation? Is there another way to look at it that I should consider?
	What exactly am I focused on? In addition, how am I seeing it?
	Is my view the only reasonable view? What does my point of view ignore?
	Have you ever considered the way _____ (Japanese, Muslims, South Americans, etc.) view this?
	Which of these possible viewpoints makes the most sense given the situation?
	Am I having difficulty looking at this situation from a viewpoint with which I disagree?
	What is the point of view of the author of this story/article?
	Do I study viewpoints that challenge my personal beliefs?
Purpose	Take time to state your purpose clearly.
	Distinguish your purpose from related purposes.
	Check periodically to be sure you are still on target.
	Choose significant and realistic purposes.
	What is your purpose?
	What is the scope of your purpose—what is and is not included?
	Is your purpose significant and realistic?
	Throughout the reading/discussion, are you still on target with your purpose?
Question	What is the question I am trying to answer?
	What important questions are embedded in the issue?
	Is there a better way to put the question?
	Is this question clear? Is it complex?
	I am not sure exactly what question you are asking. Could you explain it?
	The question in my mind is this: How do you see the question?
	What kind of question is this? Historical? Scientific? Ethical? Political? Economic? etc.
	What would we have to do to settle this question?
Information	What information do I need to answer this question?
	What data are relevant to this problem?
	Do I need to gather more information?
	Is this information relevant to my purpose or goal?
	On what information are you basing that comment?
	What experience convinced you of this? Could your experience be distorted?
	How do we know this information (data, testimony) is accurate?
	Have we left out any important information that we need to consider?
Interpretation and inferences	What conclusions am I coming to?
	Is my inference logical?
	Are there other conclusions I should consider?
	Does this interpretation make sense?
	Does our solution necessarily follow from our data?
	How did you reach that conclusion?
	What are you basing your reasoning on?
	Is there an alternative plausible conclusion?
	Given all the facts, what is the best possible conclusion?
	How shall we interpret these data?

Exhibit 12.2 *(continued)*

Thought Element	What to Consider
Concepts	What idea am I using in my thinking? Is this idea causing problems for me or for others?
	I think this is a good theory, but could you explain it more fully?
	What is the main hypothesis you are using in your reasoning?
	Are you using this term in keeping with established usage?
	What main distinctions should we draw in reasoning through this problem?
	What idea is this author using in his or her thinking? Is there a problem with it?
Assumptions	What am I assuming or taking for granted?
	Am I assuming something I should not?
	What assumption is leading me to this conclusion?
	What is . . . (this policy, strategy, explanation) assuming?
	What exactly do sociologists (historians, mathematicians, etc.) take for granted?
	What is being presupposed in this theory?
	What are some important assumptions I make about my roommate, my friends, my parents, my instructors, my country?
Implications	If I decide to do "X", what things might happen?
	If I decide not to do "X", what things might happen?
	What are you implying when you say that?
	What is likely to happen if we do this versus that?
	Are you implying that . . . ?
	How significant are the implications of this decision?
	What, if anything, is implied by the fact that a much higher percentage of poor people are in jail than wealthy people?

Source: Elder & Paul, 2010.

of their knowledge and opinions. *Mutuality* encourages learners to be concerned not only about their own learning but the learning of their peers. *Deliberation* encourages learners to offer arguments and counterarguments supported by evidence, data, and logic in a thoughtful discussion of an issue. It includes the understanding that their views may be changed as a result of the arguments presented by peers. Learners express their *appreciation* to peers for their thoughtful comments and insights. *Hope* encourages learners to stay the course regardless of the time, effort, and roadblocks they may encounter knowing that the results will be a transforming learning experience. *Autonomy* allows learners to stay committed to their opinions and beliefs and argue assertively for them. Posting these dispositions at the beginning of a course can set the stage for mindful discussions and encourage respectful dialogue (Brookfield & Preskill, 2005).

In addition, as you monitor discussions, consider to what extent these dispositions are being achieved, and remind learners of these dispositions throughout

Exhibit 12.3 Dispositions of Discussion.

Consider the following dispositions as you engage in thoughtful dialogue with your peers and build a community of inquiry in the course.

Hospitality	Make other learners feel welcome to participate and safe to express their ideas and opinions.
Participation	Engage in the discussions to add depth and subtlety to the discussion.
Mindfulness	Take time to understand the opinions of your peers and be respectful of their diversity of thought.
Humility	It's OK to admit the limitations of your knowledge and opinions.
Mutuality	Be concerned about your own learning but also the learning of your peers.
Deliberation	Offer arguments and counterarguments supported by evidence, data, and logic as you engage in a thoughtful discussion of an issue.
	It's OK to change your views as a result of the arguments presented by peers.
Appreciation	Don't be afraid to express your appreciation to peers for their thoughtful comments and insights.
Hope	Stay the course regardless of the time, effort, and roadblocks you may encounter, knowing that the results will be a transforming learning experience.
Autonomy	Don't be afraid to stay committed to your opinions and beliefs and argue assertively for them.

Source: Brookfield & Preskill, 2005.

the course to ensure learners are collaborative and respectful in discussions. These dispositions can also discourage flaming in discussions, discussed in more detail in Part 5 of the book. Exhibit 12.3 describes discussion dispositions that can be posted in your discussion to encourage thoughtful dialogue among learners as they develop a community of inquiry.

Discussions should also be disciplined in order to ensure learners use critical thinking as they engage in discussions. Brookfield and Preskill (2005) describe the idea of creating disciplined discussions: "discussion is disciplined when participants stay focused on the topic, offer evidence to support their point of view (or explain the basis for that view), recall and summarize some of the multiple viewpoints that have been shared, attempt to identify connections between contributions already made, and show how the discussion has changed their thinking or added to their knowledge" (p. 238).

To help bring focus to participants' contributions, Brookfield and Preskill (2005) recommend using a strategy called circular response. Circular response is a discussion strategy that has learners begin their discussion response by commenting on the previous posts to the discussion question and use the observations of other learners as a springboard for their own comments on the topic

(Brookfield & Preskill, 2005). This type of discussion strategy encourages learners to integrate the multiple perspectives of learners in the discussion and provides learners an opportunity to demonstrate their critical thinking skills.

Learners can also use the Paul-Elder intellectual standards that were described in Chapter 11 to engage with other learners (Elder & Paul, 2010). Exhibit 12.4 describes the different ways learners can incorporate critical thinking as they engage in discussions with their peers. Encourage learners to incorporate as many of the standards as they can when reflecting on the contributions of other learners in relation to their own ideas.

Exhibit 12.4   How to Incorporate Critical Thinking in Your Discussion Interactions.

Intellectual Standards	Questions to consider
Clarity: understandable, the meaning can be grasped	Could you elaborate further? Could you give me an example? Could you illustrate what you mean?
Accuracy: free from errors or distortions, true	How could we check on that? How could we find out if that is true? How could we verify or test that?
Precision: exact to the necessary level of detail	Could you be more specific? Could you give me more details? Could you be more exact?
Relevance: relating to the matter at hand	How does that relate to the problem? How does that bear on the question? How does that help us with the issue?
Depth: containing complexities and multiple interrelationships	What factors make this a difficult problem? What are some of the complexities of this question? What are some of the difficulties we need to deal with?
Breadth: encompassing multiple viewpoints	Do we need to look at this from another perspective? Do we need to consider another point of view? Do we need to look at this in other ways?
Logic: the parts make sense together, no contradictions	Does all this make sense together? Does your first paragraph fit with your last? Does what you say follow from the evidence?
Significance: focusing on the important, not trivial	Is this the most important problem to consider? Is this the central idea to focus on? Which of these facts are most important?
Fairness: justifiable, not self-serving or one-sided	Do I have any vested interest in this issue? Am I sympathetically representing the viewpoints of others?

Source: Elder & Paul, 2010.

Grading Discussions

According to Brookfield and Preskill (2005), "the establishment of unequivocal criteria for participation is of the utmost importance" (p. 40). If you believe discussion is critical to learning, emphasize this in the grading structure for your course. This will motivate learners to participate more fully in discussions. In

Exhibit 12.5   Critical Thinking Grading Rubric for Discussions.

Criteria	Nonperformance	Basic	Proficient	Distinguished
Applies relevant concepts, theories, or materials to argue or support a point of view and posts initial response to discussion by midweek to extend the dialogue. (30%)	Does not include a point of view or point of view is not developed. (0–15%)	Does not use relevant course concepts, theories, or materials to argue or support a point of view. (16–21%)	Applies some relevant course concepts, theories, or materials to argue or support a point of view. Posts initial response to discussion by midweek to extend the dialogue. (22–26%)	Applies and analyzes most concepts, theories, or materials to argue or support a point of view. Posts initial response to discussion by midweek to extend the dialogue. (27–30%)
Applies relevant information [facts, data, evidence, or real-world examples] to support point of view with implications and/or consequences of reasoning. Relevant information is cited and referenced to APA format. (30%)	Does not apply relevant information [facts, data, evidence, or real-world examples] to support point of view. (0–15%)	Applies information [facts, data, evidence, or real-world examples] to support point of view, but lacks relevance and does not address implications of reasoning. (16–21%)	Applies relevant information [facts, data, evidence, or real-world examples] to support point of view. Relevant information is cited and referenced. Does not address implications or consequences of reasoning. (22–26%)	Applies relevant information [facts, data, evidence, or real-world examples] to support point of view. Includes a discussion of implications and/or consequences of reasoning. Relevant information is cited and referenced to APA format. (27–30%)
Collaborates with fellow learners, relating the discussion to relevant concepts over at least two days to extend the dialogue. (30%)	Does not collaborate with fellow learners or collaboration is not relevant to discussion (i.e. good job posts). (0–15%)	Collaborates with at least one fellow learner, relating discussion to the relevant course concepts. (16–21%)	Collaborates with at least two fellow learners, relating the discussion to relevant course concepts but does not participate in the discussion over at least two days to extend the dialogue. (22–26%)	Collaborates with at least two fellow learners, relating the discussion to relevant course concepts over at least two days to extend the dialogue. (27–30%)
Applies proper spelling, grammar usage, and mechanics. (10%)	Has six or more spelling, grammar usage, mechanics errors in discussion post. (0–5%)	Has four to five spelling, grammar usage, mechanics errors in discussion post. (6–7%)	Has two to three spelling, grammar usage, mechanics errors in discussion post. (8%)	Has zero to one spelling, grammar usage, mechanics errors in the discussion post. (9–10%)

addition, establishing a clearly defined grading rubric can help learners understand the exact expectations that you have for their participation in discussions. If the purpose of discussion is to build critical thinking, consider using a grading rubric that allows learners to receive feedback on the extent to which they incorporated critical thinking in their interactions in the discussion. Exhibit 12.5 offers criteria that can be used to assess the critical thinking of learners and give them important information to continue to improve their critical thinking skills throughout the course. The rubric takes into consideration collaboration with other learners. It is critical that you set the expectation of what it means to collaborate with other learners in order to keep learners from posting shallow comments just to receive credit for learner collaboration. In addition, you will notice that the rubric includes points for spelling and grammar. I have seen a lot of poor spelling and grammar in discussion posts, which can cast a shadow on what the learner is trying to say and often leads to fewer interactions with other learners who draw conclusions about the learner based on his or her writing skills. In order to help learners build credibility, it is critical to set high standards for writing and help learners with poor writing skills improve the quality of their writing in order to be able to communicate their thoughts and ideas effectively.

TEAM OR GROUP PROJECTS

I am sure that many of you have heard from learners that they do not like team projects, but if set up correctly, team projects allow learners to experience real-world applications of knowledge in a dynamic environment. In addition, with more and more organizations becoming dispersed, there is a need for learners to have the skills to effectively work with others at a distance. Providing learners an opportunity to work together on projects allows them to have more interactions and build stronger relationships with other learners in the course. Team projects also give learners an opportunity to learn how to work effectively on collaborative projects and to develop skills for working on virtual teams. Team projects provide learners with a framework for learning from one another and sharing their experience. In teams, learners challenge one another's thoughts and opinions to develop new knowledge. It also offers additional opportunities to get together with peers and develop interpersonal relationships.

There are critical elements that need to be in place for a virtual team project to be successful. Consider the following:

- *Clearly defined roles.* Each member of the team must have a clearly defined role, so there is no misunderstanding about who does what. In addition, learners should not be penalized for the accomplishments or lack of accomplishments of other team members. Roles that have individual deliverables allow the learner to work outside of the team, thus providing a degree of independence.
- *Clearly defined tasks and time lines.* There should be a clear time line that indicates each of the team tasks and deliverables, who is responsible for each deliverable, and when each deliverable is due. Rubrics should be provided to define the criteria for each individual deliverable to make sure all team members are aware of the criteria on which their work will be graded.
- *Team guidelines.* It is important to have clear guidelines for team activities. All teams need to understand the assignment and have a clear understanding of the purpose of the team project. Decisions will need to be made, and each team needs to know which decisions can be made by an individual and which decisions should be made as a team. There should also be specific statements of expectation about meetings and other communication requirements during the project. Be specific about how many meetings or communications are required per week, as well as expectations for learners if they are unable to make meetings or collaborate during the project. In addition, there should be specific guidelines for what to do if a member of the team does not participate or does not turn in his or her deliverables during the project. One of the ways I have advised teams when they had a team member who didn't participate and turn in deliverables is to have them state that the part of the project that was assigned to the nonparticipating learner has been outsourced and will not be addressed in the project document. This takes the burden off the team to do extra work and helps reduce anxiety and frustration among team members. If outsourcing is not a solution based on the project, then additional information will need to be provided to the team so they are prepared for these kinds of issues.
- *Flexibility.* Many learners choose to take courses online because their schedule does not allow them the flexibility to be in class at a specific day and time. When setting up teams, have alternative ideas for how the team can work

together asynchronously and include a process that allows those members who are unable to meet synchronously to have input and review what takes place in any synchronous team meetings. In addition, have some flexibility for how the team will work together. Consider providing them with a number of collaborative tools to choose from based on the different skill levels teams may have. Chapter 14 discusses a number of collaborative tools that can be used to support groups or teams. Be sure to be flexible when the team presents ideas for different ways of accomplishing the team project. Allowing teams opportunities to customize the experience can build more autonomy.

Instructor Role in Group Projects

Play a role in team projects to ensure learners stay on task and work through any conflicts that may occur within the team. Act as a facilitator and be involved along the way to set the stage, create the environment, and model, guide, and evaluate the process (Palloff & Pratt, 2005).

- *Setting the stage.* You should begin by setting the stage for the team project and communicate a clear understanding of the expected learning outcomes of the team activity. You should also ensure that the critical elements discussed in the previous section are communicated to learners, including the process that will be used, the rules and guidelines for the project, and specific instructions for completing the project.
- *Creating the environment.* There are many tools that teams can use to construct an environment for the project. Be specific about where and how teams should collaborate. This should include a description of the tools available, including team discussion threads or other collaborative technologies, both synchronous and asynchronous, to help learners meet together as a team and share resources and documents.
- *Modeling the process.* Throughout the project, the interactions you have with teams should model the process. In other words, your interactions should model the interactions you hope learners will have with their teams, respect the teams' ideas, and negotiate change as needed.
- *Guiding the process.* It is critical that you monitor all team discussions and answer questions on an ongoing basis. You may want to include a discussion

question thread for each team, so learners can post questions that you can readily see and answer in a timely manner. I also recommend that you ask teams to post any transcripts or notes of team meetings that occur outside of the course, so you can understand the extent to which teams are working collaboratively together.

• *Evaluating the process.* One of the issues that learners have with teams is their grade being impacted by other learners' performance; therefore, the total grade should not be based solely on a final team product. Learners should be able to earn a top grade for their contributions even if all of the members of the team are not fully engaged. Consider grading individual deliverables by team members rather than the project as a whole, so individual learners who have done their part will not be negatively affected by issues that may occur within the team. When grading the team, consider criteria that relate to what makes a good team member, including

> *Team environment.* Contributes to building a constructive team environment by participating in the team activities on a regular basis and contributing to team meetings.
>
> *Integrity.* Builds trust with team members by acting ethically and putting the team above his or her own individual contributions.
>
> *Accountability.* Follows through on agreed-upon tasks and responsibilities as required by the project.

By focusing on criteria that relate to being a good team member, learners can be satisfied that those learners who choose not to participate fully will not be able to earn the same grade as those who do, which can lead to greater satisfaction with team activities. Consider having team members complete their own self-reflections of the grading criteria. You also may want to have team members reflect on a weekly basis the degree to which they are meeting the criteria of building a constructive team environment, building trust with team members, and following through on agreed-upon tasks and responsibilities in order to help them make changes along the way to ensure their contributions support the team.

Conflict Management

Issues and conflicts can quickly destroy team cohesion and result in a poor learning experience. Having clear guidelines for managing conflict is critical to the success of a team project. Conflicts generally occur for a number of reasons. Palloff and Pratt (2005) describe challenges that face teams, such as inactive learners, cultural differences, decision-making issues, communication issues, technical difficulties, aggressive team members, and passive team members.

As described in Chapter 1, cultural differences can have a huge impact on learners' level of engagement in the online environment in relation to power distance, uncertainty avoidance, individualism-collectivism, and masculinity-femininity. Power distance examines the status position of people in society, where individuals of higher power exert influence on individuals or groups of lower power. It is important to monitor team interactions to ensure all team members are treated equally. Uncertainty avoidance relates to the degree to which certain cultures are able to tolerate unstructured or unclear environments. Many team activities are based on ill-defined problems, which can be problematic for learners who come from cultures with high uncertainty avoidance. The more structure you can provide by using templates, checklists, and worksheets, the easier it will be for learners with high uncertainty avoidance to actively participate in team projects. Individualism-collectivism refers to how learners collaborate. Some learners may want to form teams based on popularity while others prefer to form teams based on similar interests. Providing opportunities for learners to choose teams may provide more satisfaction. Masculinity-femininity refers to the ability of certain cultures to look at differences based on gender differences. This may cause male learners from masculine cultures to feel they have power over female team members or the opposite may occur when female learners from masculine cultures may feel they cannot participate as an equal with the male members of the team. These four dimensions can have an impact on how the learner interacts in a team environment, so setting expectations regarding how learners collaborate as a team can help resolve some of the issues that relate to cultural differences. This is also an area that you should be aware of and monitor team interactions to ensure that cultural differences are not having an impact on individual learners.

Consider developing specific processes for teams to use when confronting conflict or issues (Exhibits 12.6 and 12.7). If the team has a project manager, the project manager should be in charge of handling team conflicts. If the project manager is unable to resolve the conflict, you will have to step in and work through the issue to come up with a resolution.

Exhibit 12.6   Conflict Resolution Process Guide

1. What is the issue or conflict? Allow each member of the team involved in the conflict to describe what he or she feels the issue is from his or her own perspective. Review "Team Guidelines" to determine if it is addressed in the guidelines. If not, go on to step 2.
2. What are the potential solutions? Again, have each team member involved in the conflict describe his or her ideas for solving the problem.
3. From all potential solutions, ask each member to describe those solutions that he or she are not willing to consider and those that he or she will consider.
4. From the list of solutions that all members will consider, have team members collaborate to come up with a solution that will satisfy all parties.
5. If time is an issue, agree upon a specific time line for resolving the issue with the chosen solution.
6. The project manager should develop a written summary of the issue from all perspectives, along with the final resolution and time line for implementing the resolution, and send it to all team members to ensure that the issue and solution have been properly represented.

Notes:

1. You may have to put a time limit on the discussion in each step in order to reach a resolution in a timely manner.
2. If this process does not resolve the conflict, the next step is to bring it to the instructor for further review and resolution.

PEER REVIEWS

Peer reviews are an excellent learning strategy that involves collaborating with learners and sharing their individual expertise and perspective in the review of other learners' projects or papers. Not only does the feedback help the learner whose paper is being reviewed, but it also allows the reviewer to reflect on his or her own work from a different perspective.

Many learners complain about the reviews they receive from peers because they do not receive concrete feedback to help improve the quality of their work. For the peer review to be successful, there should be a prescribed process for the review, including specific questions that each reviewer needs to answer as he or she reviews the work of other learners. Consider a peer review criteria for this

Exhibit 12.7   Process for Resolving Issues with Inactive Team Members

1. Reach out to the inactive team member via available communication channels (team discussion thread, course mail, e-mail, telephone).
2. Discuss expectations with team member regarding participation. Be very specific regarding participation [i.e., you are required to check into the team workspace (daily, every other day, etc.), you are required to attend all meetings, etc.], referring the inactive learner to the "Team Guidelines."
3. Listen to the inactive learner's explanation of the reason he or she has not been active. If it involves a conflict with team members or with the project, use the Conflict Resolution Process to resolve the issue.
4. Ask the learner what the team can do to support him or her to improve participation in the team project.
5. Recommend ways to help the learner participate more fully, including providing additional support to help understand the requirements of the project, reassigning roles and responsibilities that he or she can accomplish, and so forth.
6. Reiterate the expectation for participation and explain, in detail, a time line for the inactive learner to catch up on any missing deliverables.
7. The project manager should develop a written summary of the issue from all perspectives, along with the final resolution and time line for implementing the resolution, and send it to all team members to ensure the issue and solution have been properly represented.

Notes:

1. You may have to put a time limit on the discussion in each step in order to reach a resolution in a timely manner.
2. If this process does not result in engaging the inactive learner, the next step is to bring the issue to the instructor for further review and resolution.

---

process. The criteria should be based on the grading criteria of the assignment, as well as basic structure and format for the type of assignment. For instance, if the assignment is a research paper that needs to be formatted according to APA, then as part of the peer review, there should be review criteria for formatting standards for the paper (i.e., double-spaced, heading styles, length of paper, in-text citation formats, reference formats, etc.). In addition, there should be criteria for the structure of a research paper, including the required sections of the paper and

Exhibit 12.8   Peer Review Questions

Formatting Standards

1. Is there a cover page that includes name of paper, name of student, name of course, name of instructor?
2. Is the paper 3–5 pages in length?
3. Is the paper double-spaced?
4. Are there an introduction, at least three titled sections in the body of the paper, and a conclusion?
5. Are there citations in the body of the paper to give credit to the ideas of others?
6. Is there a reference list on a separate page at the end of the paper?
7. Are all citations included in the reference list?
8. Are all references cited in the body of the paper?

Content Standards

1. Introduction:
   a. Does the introduction gain the reader's attention?
   b. Does it introduce the topic?
   c. Does it provide a narrow and specific thesis statement that introduces what the learner will explore and defend?
2. Background:
   a. Does the paper provide sufficient information to understand the context of the issue or problem being addressed?
3. Analysis of main ideas:
   a. Does the paper establish several main points or arguments to support the thesis statement?
   b. Is there evidence to support the arguments?
   c. Is there an analysis of the evidence, including pros and cons, comparisons, or contrasts?
4. Conclusion:
   a. Does the conclusion summarize the main points of the paper?
   b. Does it draw logical conclusions from the arguments put forth in the paper?
   c. Does it look at future direction or next steps?

how each section should be developed to support the thesis, including main arguments and evidence to support the arguments. Consider the peer review questions in Exhibit 12.8 as you determine a process for peer reviews.

Consider having learners self-select whose paper they review. You can do this by posting a discussion thread where learners can post their drafts and other learners can respond to the learners' request for a review, stating they will review their paper and when they can expect their feedback. When grading peer reviews, base the quality of the peer review on the extent to which the reviewer has addressed the criteria of the peer review questions.

Instructor Role in Peer Reviews

You will also want to consider the role you play in peer reviews. Having the peer review remain between learners can build more autonomy and self-directedness. If learners self-select whose paper they review, you will want to monitor the discussion to make sure that all learners have reviewers, so everyone gets feedback on their work. Also monitor the discussions to ensure that all reviews are returned to learners in a timely manner and, if needed, reach out to learners and encourage them to post feedback in a timely manner.

Collaborative learning strategies provide opportunities for learners to develop social presence and build higher-order critical thinking and problem-solving skills by allowing learners to share multiple perspectives and challenge one another's thinking. In this chapter we looked at several strategies to promote social presence, including discussion, team or group projects, and peer reviews. As you consider the approaches you will use in your online course to engage learners in collaborative activities, consider a variety of strategies that will allow learners to share their knowledge and perspective. Collaborative activities also allow learners to see the diversity of thought based on the interactions they have with learners as a community of inquiry, which can help them reflect on their own opinions and ideas and consider alternative ways of looking at an issue that may influence and expand their own thinking. Social presence can help learners feel socially and academically integrated into the environment and help learners develop interpersonal relationships, which are key factors that help learners persist.

13

Establishing Instructor Presence Through Instructor-to-Learner Interaction Strategies

Instructor presence is critical in establishing a community of inquiry. The different ways you interact with learners can have a great impact on developing social presence, which affects cognitive presence. Your presence can encourage interaction and help develop thinking skills. The different opportunities you create for interaction can have a large impact on establishing a community of inquiry.

Instructor-to-learner interaction is a critical component of learner satisfaction and the lack of it can have a negative impact on learner persistence. As discussed in Chapter 3, one important factor that contributes to persistence is the learner's ability to develop a relationship with the faculty to feel connected. In Chapter 6 we discussed Moore's (1991) theory of transaction distance and how increased dialogue between the instructor and learner leads to low transactional distance, which diminishes learners' feelings of isolation. Other factors that contribute to low persistence include poor academic skills, density of concepts being taught, and the pace and manageability of the course that can potentially lead to learners withdrawing (Rovai, 2003). The bottom line of all this is that you must continuously monitor and engage with learners to help them persist. The quantity, timeliness, and quality of your interactions with learners are critical to helping them persist in the course and achieve the course outcomes.

This chapter introduces specific interaction strategies that you can use to develop a relationship with learners to encourage participation, knowledge construction, and critical thinking. It offers strategies to monitor learner progress and provide just-in-time interactions to help learners engage in the course and overcome roadblocks. Finally, it looks at interaction strategies to assess performance and discusses interactions to help learners become more self-directed. All of these strategies can result in increased dialogue between you and the learners in your course, thus diminishing learners' feelings of isolation and helping them persist.

INSTRUCTOR AS A FACILITATOR

Instructor interaction in an online learning environment is very different from the traditional learning environment. Traditionally, the major interaction that an instructor has with learners is through the transmission of content via lecture. In an online learning environment, the delivery of course content is not the instructor's primary activity, so you will need to be able to transition from being the "sage on the stage" to the "guide on the side." As a guide you will support learners as they construct knowledge by engaging in facilitative and knowledge-sharing strategies to help learners develop critical thinking skills and construct knowledge. Interaction should be continuous, with the goal of being able to engage learners, give encouragement, help them develop critical thinking skills, and provide specific feedback to help them improve their performance.

According to the Merriam-Webster Online, a facilitator is someone "who helps to bring about an outcome (as learning, productivity, or communication) by providing indirect or unobtrusive assistance, guidance, or supervision." As a facilitator, you will encourage participation and work with learners to help them utilize the content to acquire the stated outcomes of the course. This includes helping them develop critical thinking skills and empowering learners to be self-directed and in control of their learning. As a facilitator, you will encourage collaboration and discussion to support learners in knowledge construction and help learners build relationships by creating a supportive environment that produces ongoing mutual respect and trust. Finally, you will monitor course activities and help learners complete the activities in a timely and efficient manner. This includes assessing their progress, evaluating their performance, and celebrating their successes.

INTERACTIONS TO ENCOURAGE PARTICIPATION

Learners who are new to online learning may feel isolated when they begin their first online course. It is important to manage the feelings of isolation, especially at the beginning of the course, to make sure that transactional distance is minimized (Moore, 1991).

At the beginning of the course, communications should be welcoming and personable. Try to focus your interactions with learners on developing rapport and encouraging learners to participate. Offering learners an opportunity to introduce themselves will help give them visibility, so they do not feel like they are an outsider and can begin to develop relationships with you and other learners. You can encourage introductions by posting your own personal introduction, which will help learners establish a relationship with you. Giving information about yourself on both a professional and personal level can help learners identify with you as an expert and as an individual and discover more about your expertise, as well as things you have in common. Along with an introduction to all learners, individual communications early in the course can demonstrate your acknowledgment of them as individuals. A built-in course mail feature or e-mail can be used to contact learners individually, welcome them to the course, and encourage them to interact with you. It is important to take the time to send these types of messages individually, using the learner's name in the salutation. This helps establish a personal relationship with learners, and communicates your interest in their participation and your acknowledgment of them individually. It also opens up the communication to allow learners to express any feelings of apprehension and ask questions they may have. Communication should be supportive and ensuring to help learners feel comfortable in the learning environment.

INTERACTIONS TO ENCOURAGE KNOWLEDGE CONSTRUCTION AND CRITICAL THINKING

One of the most important interactions you will have with learners is to encourage knowledge construction and critical thinking. Anderson, Rourke, Garrison, and Archer's (2001) model for assessing teaching presence in an online course describes the importance of facilitating discussion to maintain the interest, motivation, and engagement of students in active learning. The ability to encourage knowledge construction and critical thinking requires a blending of facilitation skills and direct instruction to provide leadership and share knowledge of the subject matter with learners (Anderson, Rourke, Garrison, & Archer, 2001).

When considering how to interact with learners to encourage knowledge construction and help build critical thinking skills, you will need to make a decision on the types of strategies you will use to engage learners in discussions. Chapter 1 discussed how different cultures view people of power (Bates, 2001), such as an instructor, so it is important to be aware that sharing too much of your own opinion and perspective early in the discussion may influence learners' own thinking on the topic. It may also keep some learners from posting their ideas that might be contrary to what you have presented in the discussions. Consider allowing the discussion to initially flow between learners and use techniques to keep the discussion going and help learners develop their critical thinking skills.

One of the best-known methods of interacting with learners is the Socratic method, which is based on the thoughts of the philosopher Socrates. It is grounded in the idea that in order to be a critical thinker, you need to question ideas to determine whether to believe them (Elder & Paul, 2010). The best types of discussion questions are those that do not have a single answer. Using the Socratic method can help extend learners' thinking to help them reach higher levels of understanding about topics. Instructor interactions should be a blend of facilitation and knowledge sharing, which can include the use of prompts, elaboration, clarification, weaving, perspectives, inferences or assumptions, implications, and summaries to encourage discussion, build knowledge, and develop critical thinking.

Prompts

Often learners are hesitant to be the first to respond to a discussion question or may be unsure exactly what the instructor is expecting in a response. If you find that learners have not posted to a discussion after one or two days, post a prompt to the discussion to help encourage discussion. If you think learners are unsure of what the question is asking, a prompt can include specific directions about how to go about answering the question. You can also give an example of a proper response to the discussion to help learners see a concrete way to answer the question. Also consider providing a more concrete or real-world example to help learners understand the question more clearly.

Elaboration

Asking learners to elaborate on their thoughts and ideas can help them achieve the goals of the discussion and build a better understanding of what they need to include in their response to the discussion question. A request for elaboration also encourages learners to think deeper about the issue and extend their critical thinking skills. Asking learners to expand on their ideas can help them build a better understanding of their own thinking on the issue or topics. Be very specific about what you would like the learner to elaborate on by asking questions to help elicit the type of response you are looking for.

Clarification

If the response from the learners or their line of reasoning is difficult to follow, ask them for clarification to help flesh out their ideas more clearly. Strategies can include asking them to state the response in a different way, extend the response for a more complete thought, or provide illustrations and examples to help clarify their thinking. For learners who are posting off topic, asking how what they have said relates or connects to the topic or issue can move them back on topic.

Weaving

Weaving can point out important contributions from a number of learners and provide a foundation for deeper understanding by showing connections between multiple perspectives on an issue and pointing out areas of agreement and disagreement to stimulate further discussions. If you find learners are getting off topic or the discussion is disorganized, weaving can be used to get the discussion back on topic and organized. You can summarize points on topic as well as those that are off-topic and help learners reorganize the discussions to focus on the discussion question. Consider ways to incorporate your own knowledge in real-world examples. Weaving is also a way for you to demonstrate your presence in discussions if you do not participate in discussions one-on-one with learners. By coming into the discussion a couple of times and weaving the different perspectives on an issue, you can show that you are actively reviewing the discussion. You also gain the opportunity to provide real-world examples or your own personal experiences to add additional perspective.

Perspectives

Taking perspectives can help learners extend their thinking. Often learners will discuss an issue only from their viewpoint and ignore evidence that does not support their view. One strategy you can use is to interact in the discussion, take an alternative perspective on the issue, and ask questions that allow learners to consider multiple perspectives. As an alternative to taking another perspective, ask them to consider whether there is another way of looking at the issue they have not thought of. This allows them to discover multiple perspectives on the issue on their own, thereby expanding their understanding of the issue from all sides.

Inferences and Assumptions

Asking learners about the inferences and assumptions they are making can help them understand statements that may be dependent on other things being true or valued based on certain beliefs. By challenging the inferences and assumptions learners make to build their arguments, they can build stronger arguments based on verifiable evidence. In addition, if discussions analyze issues from the perspective of experts in the field, helping learners determine the inferences and assumptions made by the experts can extend their thinking to come to more reasoned conclusions.

Implications

Asking learners to consider the implications of their line of reasoning helps them see the impact of their reasoning. As you ask learners to consider the implications of their line of reasoning or the line of reasoning of an expert, ask them to extend this not just to the immediate implications but to also consider the secondary and tertiary implications for the present and in the future on persons, places, or things.

Summaries

At the end of a discussion, you may want to provide a summary of the discussion to help learners understand important ideas about the issue and point out any reasoning that may have been inaccurate. This is also a great time to interject your own personal opinions on the topic and provide additional examples of the issue and its impact from your personal experience.

Exhibit 13.1 lists the types of interactions we have discussed and offers examples of how they can be used.

Exhibit 13.1 Instructor Interactions to Encourage Knowledge Construction and Critical Thinking.

Instructor Interaction	Examples
Prompts	I have been monitoring the discussion and have not seen any posts, so I wanted to give you a little more information to get you started. Consider the following elements as you compose your discussion response this week [list elements]. For example....
	Consider the following scenario [to put the discussion in a context]....
	Let me give you a more concrete example....
	From my experience, an example to help you understand the concept is....
Elaboration	You have a great start on the discussion this week. Can you elaborate on your thoughts and ideas and consider the following in your response [list areas where learner has not responded fully to the discussion question]?
Clarification	I appreciate your comments about....
	Can you clarify your response, so we can clearly understand your thoughts and ideas?
	Can you provide an illustration or example?
	Can you state this in a different way?
	I appreciate your comment; however, I am unclear how this relates to the discussion question. Can you provide more information to help us see the connection to the topic we are discussing this week?
Weaving	I really appreciate the multiple perspectives on the issue we are discussing this week. John, Sue, and Nancy believe.... While Paul, Jerry, and Carrie believe....
	How do you reconcile the different views?
	Is there compelling evidence to support one view over the other?
	Are there other ways of viewing this issue that have not been considered?
	For example, in my experience....
	One aspect of the readings that has not been discussed is.... What impact does this have?
	Off-topic weaving:
	I really appreciate the points that have been on the issue including.... It appears that some of the points do not relate specifically to this topic such as..., so please be sure that you consider...as you discuss the topic to ensure that all of your comments help us develop a deeper understanding of the topic or issue.
Perspectives	Consider the following alternative scenario.... How would this influence your view of the issue?
	According to...there is another side to this issue. They cite...as evidence for their perspective. How does this information fit with your perspective on the issue?
	Is there another way of looking at this perspective from a different lens? What if you were faced with....? What would you do if...occurred? How would you feel if...?
	From my experience, I have found....
Inferences and assumptions	Can you discuss the specific inferences and assumptions you are making from this perspective?
	For this to be true, then...would also have to be true. Have you considered this?
	For this to be true, then you must believe that....
	What evidence do you have to support the inferences and assumptions you are making?
	What inferences and assumptions does the author make to lead to his conclusions?

(continued)

Exhibit 13.1 *(continued)*

Instructor Interaction	Examples
Implications	Can you discuss the implications of your line of reasoning on this issue?
	If this is true, how will this influence the present conditions? What will that mean for the future?
	If this is true, what actions must be taken today? In the future?
	What groups will this line of reasoning affect?
Summaries	I have really appreciated the depth of thinking that has taken place during this discussion. It appears that many of you believe . . . , while others feel that. . . .
	The examples that you have used to support your opinions have been excellent, and as a group you have followed the author's line of reasoning and uncovered many of his [her] inferences and assumptions.
	You have done a great job of demonstrating your understanding of the implications of the different lines of reasoning from the multiple perspectives of the authors in the readings.
	Some of the gaps that still exist are. . . .
	There was some confusion about. . . .
	Some of the interpretations did not support. . . .
	From my experience, I believe. . . .
	I have used. . . .
	From my experience, an example of this is. . . .

Instructor interactions to encourage knowledge construction require the use of a variety of types of interactions, including prompts, elaboration, clarification, weaving, perspectives, inferences and assumptions, implications, and summaries to encourage discussion, build knowledge, and develop critical thinking. As you engage in discussions, consider these types of interactions in relationship to the discussion topics and plan appropriate interaction strategies to help learners extend their thinking and expand their understanding of the concepts and ideas being discussed.

INTERACTIONS TO MONITOR PROGRESS

It is important to interact in a timely manner with learners who are behind or not making progress toward the course goals in order to help them understand issues and provide opportunities for them to improve performance. This requires you to monitor all course activity and keep an accounting of individual learner progress and performance. If the course is set up with few graded activities, weeks can go by before a graded activity reveals a learner issue. Consider monitoring learner activities on a weekly basis to determine the extent to which individual learners are progressing through the activities. If you find that some learners are struggling or behind, just-in-time communications can help them overcome learning issues.

Some learners may exhibit writing difficulties that are first discovered as they engage in discussions. If you monitor discussions for writing issues, you can bring the specific writing issue to the learners' attention and provide them with guidance to help improve their writing skills. Be as specific as possible about what the writing issues are and how to correct them. At the beginning of the course, you may want to spend a little extra time to copy and paste discussion posts with writing errors to the learners' course mail or e-mail to demonstrate the specific errors and how to correct them. Also recommend to the learner specific resources that you have found or developed or writing support resources developed by your institution to help them improve their writing skills. By pointing out errors early in the course, you can help learners understand the expectations for writing and allow them to improve their skills before they have to write major papers. Try to sandwich the writing issues between positive comments about what they are doing well to keep them motivated and build their confidence.

Interact on a regular basis with learners who are inactive in the course or having academic issues. In the text-based world of the online learning environment, we sometimes forget that there are other ways to interact with learners. A phone call from you can often be very motivating to the learner, so consider setting up one-on-one meetings over the phone to discuss progress and troubleshoot issues. Because of the importance of documenting communications, follow up all phone calls with written correspondence that details the issue(s) discussed, explanations by learner and faculty, and a specific plan and time line to overcome the issue(s). Ask learners to respond to the correspondence, indicating they agree with your recollection of the phone conversation and the actions they need to take.

INTERACTIONS TO COMMUNICATE FEEDBACK ON PERFORMANCE

Throughout the years of teaching online, I have found that learners want frequent feedback on their performance. They are especially interested in knowing how they are doing on the discussions and assignments and where they need to invest additional time and effort to do better. It is critical to be able to provide formative feedback that specifically discusses how learners can improve their performance and learn better. In the beginning of a course, when learners may not be sure of the expectations of course activities, interact with learners on a weekly basis to discuss their performance. The feedback that is communicated, however, can be a key motivator or it can discourage learners and lead them to drop out of the course. As already mentioned, try to sandwich recommendations for improvement in between positive comments, so learners do not feel that everything they are doing is wrong. For instance, on the one hand, if learners are interacting in a timely manner and posting not only their discussions and assignments but also making an effort to interact with other learners, you can lead with positive comments about this and then follow up with ways to improve the quality of their responses. On the other hand, if learners are responding well to the discussions but are not timely with their posts or not interacting with other learners, lead with the quality of their responses and follow up with recommendations for posting in a more timely manner and interacting with other learners to build a community of inquiry. As discussed in Chapter 6, to build learners' confidence, be sure to stress effort over ability because that is something within their control. Be very specific about how they can improve. End the feedback by telling learners that you are confident that with additional effort, they can continue to improve their performance and successfully complete the activities.

Other considerations for assessing learners' performance include being prompt about grading assignments. Learners are always anxious to know how they did, so the quicker you can grade and send feedback to learners on their assignments, the higher satisfaction they will have. Be clear and concise about the feedback you give to learners so they can act on the feedback to improve their performance. If your course platform has a grade book feature, post grades in the grade book so learners can look at their progress over time. Remember that posting the grade does not mean that you do not need to post individual feedback, because the grade does not communicate the breakdown of the grade on specific grading criteria. If you use rubrics and checklists, provide feedback based on the criteria in the rubrics and checklists. Again, it is not enough to demonstrate the level of achievement. You also need to give learners clear, concise, and specific feedback to help them improve their performance on the criteria.

INTERACTIONS TO ENCOURAGE SELF-DIRECTEDNESS

You should also encourage learners to be self-directed and in control of their learning. Chapter 2 discussed Grow's (1996) concept of self-directedness and looked at a model to help learners move from being dependent learners to becoming independent and in control of the outcomes of their learning experience. As you engage in interactions to encourage self-directedness, consider specific communication strategies based on the learners' current stage of self-directedness (Exhibit 13.2).

Stage 1 is the dependent learner who is characterized by the need for the instructor to lead him or her through all of the learning activities. Dependent learners require more frequent feedback to let them know how they are doing and whether they are meeting the instructor's expectations. Feedback should include prompts to help dependent learners become more independent. I recommend that

Exhibit 13.2 Communications to Encourage Self-Directedness.

	Understand the different stages of self-direction (Grow, 1996) that learners are in and use appropriate strategies to encourage them to be more self-directed.
Stage 1: Dependent learner	Learners require more frequent feedback to let them know how they are doing and if they are meeting the instructor's expectations.
	Feedback should include prompts to help dependent learners become more independent.
	Include process for overcoming roadblocks as they engage in the learning activities, including road maps, checklists, due date document, outlines, rubrics, and any other resources available to support a dependent learner.
Stage 2: Lack confidence and motivation	Be encouraging and acknowledge that the learners' willingness and enthusiasm for learning will help them be successful.
	Help learners build their confidence so that they can accomplish the objectives of the course.
	Help learners expand on explanations and encourage learners to review their work prior to submitting it for grading.
	Encourage learners to ask questions early on instead of struggling with activities and assignments; this can help alleviate frustration and stress from not being sure of the requirements of the activities.
Stage 3: Confident and motivated	Help learners expand their thinking by having them explore higher levels of thinking on the subject.
	Help learners apply their understanding in novel ways.
Stage 4: Self-directed	Provide specific feedback on learners' assignments that points out excellence and why it is excellent.
	Help learners self-evaluate their performance to enhance critical thinking skills and determine any gaps in learning. From the self-evaluation, they can develop a plan to fill any gaps to continue to build their knowledge and skills.

with your feedback you help them develop a process for overcoming roadblocks as they engage in the learning activities. This can include using the resources you have developed in the course to scaffold the learning activities such as road maps, checklists, due date documents, outlines, rubrics, and any other resources available to support dependent learners.

In stage 2, learners have a basic understanding of what they need to do but are not confident they can achieve the course objectives; therefore, their motivation may be low. Communications from you should be encouraging and acknowledge that the learners' willingness and enthusiasm for learning will help them be successful. Help learners build confidence that they can accomplish the objectives of the course. Ask learners to expand on their explanations in assignments and review their work prior to submitting it for grading. Encourage learners to ask questions early on instead of struggling with activities and assignments; this can help alleviate frustration and stress from not being sure of the requirements of the activities.

Stage 3 learners have skills and knowledge in the subject and have a sense of where they are going and how the course fits with their goals. They feel confident and motivated that they can get there. Help learners expand their thinking by having them explore higher levels of thinking on the subject. You can also encourage them to apply their understanding in novel ways to develop their critical thinking skills further.

In the final stage, stage 4, learners are self-directed. They have skills and knowledge in the subject and can take responsibility for their learning, directing course activities, and being productive. They also have skills in time management, project management, goal setting, and self-evaluation. Your challenge is finding ways to enhance learners' experience, while allowing them the freedom to work independently. The key teaching strategy for these learners is providing specific feedback on their assignments that points out excellence, and why it is excellent, and provides additional information to help them expand their thinking and understanding. Providing strategies for learners to self-evaluate their performance can enhance their critical thinking skills, help them find gaps in skills and knowledge, and develop a plan to fill the gaps.

There are general strategies that you can use in your communications with all learners to encourage self-directedness and independence. If you have grading criteria posted for all of the assignments, encourage learners to do their own self-evaluation of the criteria before they submit their assignments to make sure they have met all of the criteria. Consider giving weekly feedback for the first few weeks on the learner's participation in discussion. After a few weeks, move away from individual feedback to posting grades for discussions in the grade book and asking learners to reflect on their performance based on the feedback received from you to date, as well as the criteria of the discussion grading rubrics to analyze their posted grades. Encourage learners to ask you questions if, after reviewing their performance, they do not understand the grade they received to ensure they understand how to improve their performance. Let learners know at the beginning of the course the strategy you will use for giving feedback. Also discuss self-directedness and the importance of learners' being self-reflective and the driver of their own learning. In regard to assignments, give specific feedback to help learners understand to what extent they are demonstrating the objectives of the course and ways to improve performance so they can meet the goals of the course.

COMMUNICATION CHECKLIST

Exhibit 13.3 is a planning checklist that can be used to ensure that your interactions with learners encourage participation, knowledge construction, and critical thinking; monitor progress and communicate feedback on performance; and, finally, encourage learner self-directedness.

In this chapter, we discussed specific interaction strategies that you can use to encourage participation, knowledge construction, and critical thinking. We also described strategies to monitor learner progress and provide just-in-time interactions to help learners engage in the course and overcome roadblocks. Finally, we looked at strategies to assess performance and discussed interactions to help learners become more self-directed. The quantity, timeliness, and quality of your interactions with learners are critical to helping them persist in the course and achieve the course outcomes. Interactions should be continuous, with the goals of being able to engage learners, provide them encouragement, help them develop thinking skills, and give specific feedback to help them improve their performance toward the course goals.

Exhibit 13.3 Communication Checklist.

Purpose of Interactions	Types of Strategies
Encourage participation	Introduction discussions, including personal introduction of yourself
	Individual course mails or e-mails to welcome learners and acknowledge them individually
Encourage knowledge construction and critical thinking	Use the following types of interactions in discussions to monitor level of participation, knowledge construction, and critical thinking:
	Post prompts to stimulate discussion
	Ask for elaboration
	Ask for clarification
	Weave discussion threads
	Take alternative perspectives or ask learners to take alternative perspectives
	Ask learners to consider inferences and assumptions of line of reasoning
	Ask learners to consider implications of line of reasoning
	Post summaries of discussions and include personal opinions and other real-world examples, if applicable
Monitor progress	Actively monitor individual learner activity to determine progress and performance
	Intervene in a timely manner to encourage participation
	Use proactive communication strategies to communicate with learners at risk
	Consider a phone call to help alleviate issues and motivate learners to reengage. Follow up with written communication to ensure your phone call is documented and learner agrees to what was discussed
Communicate feedback on performance	In first few weeks of course, send out actionable feedback on discussion participation
	Include feedback on writing to encourage learners to develop their writing skills
	Always communicate timely and actionable feedback on all assignments submitted by learners
	Use scoring guides [rubrics, checklists] to communicate criteria for grades
	Encourage learners to do their own self-evaluation of the criteria before they submit their assignments
	Post grades in a grade book if available
Encourage self-directedness	Understand the different stages of self-direction that learners are in and use appropriate strategies to encourage them to be more self-directed
	Stage 1:
	Learners require more frequent feedback to let them know how they are doing and whether they are meeting the instructor's expectations
	Feedback should include prompts to help dependent learners become more independent
	Include process for overcoming roadblocks as they engage in the learning activities, including road maps, checklists, due date documents, outlines, rubrics, and any other resources available to support a dependent learner.
	Stage 2:
	Communications from instructors should be encouraging and acknowledge that learners' willingness and enthusiasm for learning will help them be successful
	Use communications that will help learners build their confidence so they can accomplish the objectives of the course
	Communications should expand on explanations and encourage learners to review their work prior to submitting it for grading

Exhibit 13.3 *(continued)*

Purpose of Interactions	Types of Strategies
	Communications should encourage learners to ask questions early on instead of struggling with activities and assignments; this can help alleviate frustration and stress from not being sure of the requirements of the activities
	Stage 3:
	Communications should focus on:
	Expanding their thinking by having them explore higher levels of thinking on the subject
	Apply their understanding in novel ways to further develop their critical thinking skills
	Stage 4:
	Provide specific feedback on assignments that point out excellence and why it is excellent and provide additional information to help learners expand their thinking and understanding
	Provide strategies for learners to self-evaluate their performance to enhance critical thinking skills and find gaps in skills and knowledge

14

Communication Tools to Support Cognitive, Social, and Teaching Presence

Cognitive presence, social presence, and instructor presence can be established through a variety of synchronous and asynchronous communication tools. Choosing the appropriate tools can have a large impact on presence and lead to more opportunities for learning. The "extent to which cognitive presence is created and sustained in a community of inquiry is partly dependent upon how communication is restricted or encouraged by the medium" (Garrison, Anderson, & Archer, 2001, p. 93). Research indicates that asynchronous communications encourage more in-depth thinking whereas synchronous communications may facilitate increased interaction in which learners share ideas and explore alternative ways of knowing.

In the online environment, where there is no face-to-face, it takes a greater effort to develop presence with peers and the instructor. Many learners have never experienced the online environment and there is a void when they first come into an online course room environment because there is no physical presence. This can lead to feelings of isolation and can have a negative impact on motivation and persistence (Moore, 1991). Providing learners with opportunities to interact makes them feel a part of a class instead of alone in a virtual sea of learning materials. Not only does interaction diminish the feelings of isolation but it is also, from a social constructivist perspective, critical to learning because it provides an opportunity to negotiate meaning and construct knowledge.

Chapter 6 described the theory of transactional distance (Moore, 1991), which postulates that distance education is more than simply the geographical separation of the instructor and learners but also includes distance in regard to understanding and perception. This can have an impact on motivation and subsequently persistence. The physical separation can lead to communication gaps, which create a space of potential misunderstanding between the instructor and the learner, which is referred to as transactional distance. According to Moore (1991), to minimize transactional distance, instructors must be able to increase dialogue via various communication tools.

In this chapter we explore the types of communication tools available to increase presence, build community, and support knowledge construction. As you consider the types of communication strategies, consider how you will build community and promote learning. Also determine the tools you will use to meet the needs of all learners. The more deliberate you can be about planning interactions and using the appropriate communication tools for the interactions, the more you can enhance the opportunities to build a learning community that will assist learners in staying motivated and persisting and ultimately achieving the learning outcomes of the course.

DEVELOPING PRESENCE

Throughout Part Three, we have explored how to develop a community of inquiry through cognitive presence, social presence, and teaching presence (Garrison, Anderson, & Archer, 2001). Cognitive presence is the ability of learners to construct knowledge together as they engage in interactions. Social presence establishes learners as individuals and helps build interpersonal relationships that can have a positive impact on engagement in learning activities. Teaching presence includes how you facilitate the learning activities to support social and cognitive presence to support learners in achieving the course outcomes.

Ijsselsteijn, de Ridder, Freeman, and Avons (2000) describe four modes of presence—realism, immersion, involvement, and suspension of disbelief—that can make the boundaries between the real and virtual environment transparent (p. 18). Realism is a mode of presence that allows the learner to engage in experiences that reflect the real world. It provides learners an opportunity to engage in learning by using their senses of vision, hearing, and touch. Immersion creates a sense of presence through the illusion of reality in a virtual environment. Learners are able to navigate an environment, interact with peers, and learn through the simulation of a real-world environment. Involvement allows learners to interact with peers via asynchronous and synchronous technologies that create a greater sense of presence in the online environment. Finally, suspension of disbelief allows learners to create their own reality in their mind even though they are aware that in reality it is not true. This can allow learners the opportunity to engage in experiences that, even though the characters are not real, offer rich engagement and learning. Regardless of the technology used, "the important aspect of the experience for the learners is to provide a sense of 'being there,' a feeling that they are present in the total learning experience" (Lehman & Conceição, 2010, p. 20).

SYNCHRONOUS AND ASYNCHRONOUS COMMUNICATION

Before we consider specific communication tools for developing a community of inquiry, let's look at modes of communication. There are two basic modes of communication: synchronous, which occurs at the same time, and asynchronous, which occurs at different times. Interactions can be one-to-one or one-to-many, depending on the type of tool. Both synchronous and asynchronous communications allow learners to collaborate with each other to exchange opinions, experiences, and interpretations of course content. The challenge is to provide the appropriate types of communication modes to help learners achieve the intended outcomes of a learning activity.

Asynchronous communication allows learners and instructors to communicate anytime, anywhere, and thus offers flexibility to learners to engage in the course materials at a time that fits with their lifestyle and commitments. The benefits of asynchronous communication include opportunities to think about course content and to address a diverse set of topics in more depth than can be done in a synchronous environment (Weasenforth, Biesenbach-Lucas, & Meloni, 2002). This allows learners the opportunity to conceptualize a topic from multiple viewpoints and contribute to each other's understanding.

Jonathan Finkelstein (2006) describes five functions that real-time synchronous communication serves, including instruction, collaboration, support, socialization and information exchanges, and extended outreach. Synchronous communication allows for more dynamic communication due to the immediacy of the interaction. According to Finkelstein (2006), "the active construction of knowledge by learners through a process of real-time give-and-take is well-served in a live online setting" (p. 3). Synchronous communication provides a venue for instruction through real-time presentations and demonstrations. It allows learners to ask questions with an immediate response and follow-up questions to clarify understanding. Collaboration in the online environment through real-time synchronous communication gives immediacy of exchange and supports group work. Being able to provide just-in-time support through live interaction when learners have issues is critical to helping them persist, which is an important advantage of synchronous communication. Opportunities for learners to socialize and develop interpersonal relationships can also increase motivation and help learners develop a network of peers to support one another. Finally, opportunities to extend outreach beyond the classroom can increase motivation by providing learners with an opportunity to build a community.

There are some general characteristics of online interaction that need to be considered when choosing appropriate modes of communication. Interaction in an online environment is in some respects anonymous because it protects the learner's identity. Many learners are attracted to the online environment because it puts them on the same level as other learners because their physical presence is unknown. Other learners are attracted to the online learning environment because they can accommodate learning in their busy schedule by being able to participate anytime and anywhere. Synchronous communication modes may not meet the needs of learners who want to be anonymous or want to participate on their own schedule. In both synchronous and asynchronous communications, a learner's lack of good writing skills can also hinder his or her ability to communicate equally. In addition, if a learner is not a good typist, the text communications in some synchronous environments may move too quickly for him or her to be able to keep up. As you begin to consider the types of interactions to support the learning outcomes of the course, it is important to understand that learners' ability to interact equally may be affected by their personal needs, time restrictions, and writing skills. Being able to offer learners a number of different types of communication modes can support the diversity of individual learning styles and help meet the needs of all learners.

COMMUNICATION TOOLS AND APPLICATIONS

There is a wide variety of communication tools for both synchronous and asynchronous communication. Exhibit 14.1 describes the tools and their applications.

Exhibit 14.1   Communication Tools and Applications.

Mode of Communication	Tool Type	Applications	Examples (Manning and Johnson, 2011)
Synchronous	Chats or Instant Messengers	Virtual office hours, learner-to-learner social networking, group projects	Google Chat at http://www.google.com/talk/ Yahoo! Messenger at http://webmessenger.yahoo.com/ AOL Instant Messenger at http://www.aim.com
Synchronous	VoIP	Virtual office hours, learner-to-learner social networking, group projects	Skype at http://www.skype.com Google Talk. For talk alone go to http://www.google.com/talk/ To add video to your talk, visit http://www.google.com/chat/video TinyChat at http://www.tinychat.com
Synchronous	Web conferencing	Group projects, document sharing and editing, presentations, demonstrations, lectures, virtual office hours, desktop sharing	Elluminate at http://elluminate.com/ Adobe Connect at http://www.adobe.com/products/acrobatconnectpro/ DimDim at http://www.adobe.com/products/acrobatconnectpro/ Vyew at http://www.adobe.com/products/acrobatconnectpro/
Synchronous	Virtual worlds	Group projects, real-world applications, knowledge construction	Quest Atlantis at http://atlantis.crlt.indiana.edu/ Fantage at http://www.fantage.com/ Reaction Grid at http://www.reactiongrid.com/ Second Life at http://secondlife.com
Asynchronous	E-mail	Group projects, instructor-learner communications, learner-to-learner social networking	Pegasus Mail at http://www.pmail.com/ Eudora at http://www.eudora.com/email/features/windows/
Asynchronous	Discussion forums	Group projects, collaboration, self-reflection, community building, learner-to-learner social networking	Ning discussions at http://www.ning.com/ Yahoo groups at http://groups.yahoo.com/ Voicethread audio discussion at http://voicethread.com/ Wimba voice audio discussion at http://www.wimba.com/products/wimba_voice/

(continued)

Exhibit 14.1 *(continued)*

Mode of Communication	Tool Type	Applications	Examples (Manning and Johnson, 2011)
Asynchronous	Blogs	Self-reflection	Wordpress at http://wordpress.com Blogger at https://www.blogger.com/start Edublogs at http://edublogs.org/ Posterous at http://posterous.com/
Asynchronous	Wikis	Group projects, collaboration, document sharing, organization	Wikispaces at http://www.wikispaces.com/ PBWorks at http://pbworks.com/ Google Docs at http://docs.google.com/
Asynchronous	Social networking and microblogs	Learner-to-learner social networking	Facebook at http://www.facebook.com/ LinkedIn at http://www.linkedin.com/ Ning at http://www.ning.com/ Microblog: Twitter at http://www.twitter.com Tumblr at http://ww.tumblr.com Edmodo at http://www.edmodo.com

Chat or Instant Messaging

Chat or instant messaging is an excellent tool for generating communications on the fly. It requires a chat platform such as Google Chat, Yahoo! Messenger, and AOL Instant Messenger and allows for one-to-one and one-to-many communication (Manning & Johnson, 2011). Most course management systems have chat messenger technologies available. This form of communication is synchronous and, therefore, place and time dependent. It provides a spontaneous environment for learners to develop an involvement mode of presence through interactions with peers and you. It can be used in an online environment for virtual office hours and other personalized support for learners. In addition, it can be used as a tool for collaborating between learners and building community within a course. Some issues with chat relate to the speed at which messages appear and disappear, so it requires learners to have good typing skills as well as be able to think quickly to continue engaging in the discussion. Learners who want more social presence in the course can use chat to talk informally to other learners when they are online at the same time. Thus it provides a social component of the learner-to-learner relationship, which can improve persistence by helping them feel affiliation with their peers.

VoIP

VoIP stands for Voice over Internet Protocol whereby voice communications are delivered over an IP network such as the Internet. This technology allows for synchronous one-to-one or one-to-many communications. Skype, Google Talk, and TinyChat are a few examples of the VoIP tools available (Manning & Johnson, 2011). This, too, offers learners an opportunity to develop an involvement mode of presence through interactions with peers and you. The technology has the capability of both voice and audio, so it can help develop greater presence with learners because they are able to see you during a conversation. It also has the capability of conferencing with a number of individuals in a single session for group interactions on projects and virtual office hours. VoIP is free, so learners can interact with peers and you without incurring costs. Currently, most computers come with built-in audio and video; however, if learners are using an older computer they may have to purchase a webcam and speakers to use VoIP. One of the issues with VoIP can be the quality of the connection. Sometimes you may feel as though you are talking to someone in the next room; other times voices may fade in and out, thus diminishing communication and causing frustration.

Web Conferencing

Web conferencing is a synchronous one-to-one or one-to-many communication tool that allows a group to interact, share documents, make presentations, present demonstrations, and edit documents, to name a few of its applications. In addition, conferencing systems offer audio and video components to establish presence. Elluminate, Adobe Connect, DimDim, and Vyew are a few of the web conferencing tools available (Manning & Johnson, 2011).

The value of a conferencing system is that it is live and provides opportunities for involvement and interaction by replicating the capabilities of the traditional face-to-face classroom. This is an excellent tool for you to use to deliver lectures with the opportunity for learners to interact during the presentation. It can also be used by instructors to demonstrate concepts that are more suitable for visual representation. Learners can also actively participate by asking questions or making demonstrations of their own through a feature that allows anyone in the conference to share their desktop or upload documents. Web conferencing can be an excellent tool to use one-on-one with learners who are having issues because it allows you to show the course environment and demonstrate to learners how to navigate the course. It can be used to help troubleshoot issues learners have with saving templates and files. It can also be used to show learners how to flesh out the ideas and reasoning of an author by displaying a research article and going through it paragraph by paragraph with learners to help them understand the author's reasoning.

It can support group work by allowing teams to meet synchronously to go over a group project and discuss individual tasks and deliverables. It also supports construction of documents by allowing a team to show a document and have someone be the scribe while others edit, as the group builds out specific deliverables for the project. One of the obvious drawbacks is that it is time dependent, so everyone needs to be available to meet at the same time. This requirement can be challenging if learners are in different time zones and especially difficult if they are widely distributed throughout the world. In addition, there is a cost for web conferencing as well as long-distance fees for the telephone conference if your institution cannot provide a toll-free number. There are also limits to the number of learners who can actively interact in a live conference. If you use the built-in audio feature, everyone must have special equipment, such as a microphone. The video is great for establishing presence, but again, it requires everyone to have a camera for his or her computer.

Virtual Worlds

Virtual worlds are simulated real-world environments that allow learners to interact with other learners in a real-world context. Virtual worlds are shared spaces that depict a space visually, usually in 2D or 3D, and interactions occur in real time. They allow users to build objects and add functionality to an object. Learners inhabit the virtual world via avatars, which is a learner's representation of himself or an alter ego, and interact in the environment by performing roles and activities related to that environment. This tool allows presence to be developed through immersion. It can also be used to develop the suspension of disbelief mode of presence, depending on the application. Quest Atlantis, Fantage, Reaction Grid, and Second Life are examples of virtual worlds (Manning

& Johnson, 2011). The benefit of using virtual worlds is that it allows learners to apply the knowledge and skill they gain from the learning content within a real-world environment. It also allows learners an opportunity to understand the complexity of the real world, as well as how individual differences affect outcomes. The interactive nature of virtual worlds makes this type of tool exceptional for being able to construct meaning and new knowledge through the shared ideas of learners.

E-mail

E-mail is an electronic mail tool that allows one-to-one or one-to-many communication. It is asynchronous, therefore not time and location dependent. There are free e-mail clients available including Pegasus and Eudora. E-mail can be used for learner-to-learner presence and faculty presence. You can provide personalized and continuous feedback to learners with e-mail or a course mail feature. This allows learners to understand whether they are meeting the course expectations and provides an opportunity for interaction to help improve learners' performance. In addition, e-mail can be used among learners to involve them in collaborative projects to exchange ideas, share documents, and build relationships. Some e-mail clients, such as Microsoft Outlook, include tools that allow you to create distribution lists and template e-mail messages, so you can send communications to a number of individuals by using basic message templates, customized as needed. This can be a timesaver and assures consistency in messaging.

Discussion Forums

Discussion forums are the most common communication tool used in online learning. They provide a way for learners to interact asynchronously one-to-one or one-to-many to discuss topics and freely exchange thoughts and ideas. Discussion forums use threaded discussions to organize discourse so that replies to learners' posts fall under the main post and are indented to show to whom the post is replying. There are many discussion forums available, including Ning, Yahoo groups, Voicethread audio discussions, and Wimba voice audio discussions (Manning & Johnson, 2011). In addition, most course platforms include discussion forums with simple interfaces that allow you to organize the discussion forum into categories and topics within categories. Discussion forums give learners an opportunity to develop presence through involvement. You can include an informal space where learners can discuss topics unrelated to the learning activities or create a space where learners can ask questions about a topic of interest. You can create a discussion thread where you can post guides and additional resources for learners, or hold discussions where learners can post questions they have. You can also include private forums for groups to interact with one another to complete group projects or private spaces for you to interact with individual learners. The main disadvantage of forums is that threads can get long, and if you are interacting with a group on a project, it can be difficult to construct team deliverables in a threaded discussion.

Blogs

Blogs are individual collections of writings from an individual with the capability of allowing others to comment on the writings and ideas of the author of the blog, thus establishing a sense of involvement. Wordpress, Blogger, Edublogs, and Posterous are a few examples of the available blogs (Manning & Johnson, 2011). In addition to these blogs, individual blogs can be set up by using some management systems.

Blogs can be used in your course to disseminate information that may not be specific to an individual course. They can also be used to establish involvement with learners outside of the course to further their interest in the field of study by sharing current topics. Blogs can also be used as a medium for learners to publish their writings (Manning & Johnson, 2011) and allow others to comment on them.

Blogs are an excellent reflective tool for learners to communicate about their learning experiences in the form of an online journal. Individual blogs can be set up for your course to allow learners to post thoughts about the course and reflect on how well they are achieving the course goals, knowledge gained and its relevance, areas that need improvement, how they have improved or changed because of course activities, and future goals.

Wikis

A wiki is a collaborative workspace that has the capability of being organized as a collection of linked pages. Wikispaces, PBWorks, and Google Docs are examples of wiki environments (Manning & Johnson, 2011). They provide learners opportunities for involvement with one another to increase presence. I have tried to have groups work in threaded discussions and found that keeping a number of different threads organized can be difficult. Collaborating to create and edit documents can be difficult as well. Each time a change is made to a document, a new version has to be uploaded to the discussion, which can create confusion regarding which version of the document is the most recent. Wikis provide more structure and can help learners organize information better with linked pages and navigation menus. Pages can be created for individual tasks and deliverables and can be linked together. In addition, most wikis have navigation bars to access pages on the wiki. Wikis provide a place to post comments, so there is a collaborative feature to each page that allows learners to comment on the information being presented, make recommendations, and share ideas. Learners can also edit documents, so all learners have the opportunity to contribute to the deliverables of the project. Because of the asynchronous nature of wikis, learners can engage in the activities according to their own schedule. An additional benefit is that learners can control the space, which can enhance their sense of responsibility.

Wiki Matrix (wikimatrix.org) is an excellent site to look at the variety of wikis available and compare wikis based on the features that interest you. It compares general features, hosting features, system requirements, data storage capabilities, security and anti-spam features, development and support, common features, special features, and media and files, to name a few. James West and Margaret West (2009) have written a book dedicated to the use of wikis for online projects, titled *Using Wikis for Online Collaboration,* which can give you a more detailed description of how to design projects using wikis.

Social Networks and Microblogs

One of the most popular modes of asynchronous communication used by people around the world is social networking applications. These include Facebook, LinkedIn, and Ning, as well as microblogs such as Twitter, Tumblr, and Edmodo (Manning & Johnson, 2011). Social networking has transformed the interactions that people have with family, friends, and colleagues, and has made it possible for people to connect who may not have been in touch for years. Social networking also provides an environment to share information, develop professional contacts, and collaborate with peers on course projects and research. Microblogs, the newer type of social networking tool, allow individuals to post short messages to capture someone's attention or communicate just-in-time information.

Social networking tools can be used to organize information for a project and allow interactions among group members. They can also be used in individual courses to extend the dialogue on topics of interest to learners by allowing them to continue a discussion once a unit has ended. Social networking tools can build a community within a discipline outside of an individual course. They can provide learners a space where they can engage with peers, faculty, and experts in the field to ask questions, discuss courses they have taken, talk about what's in the news, discuss career goals, network to create job opportunities, and share resources, to name just a few of the opportunities a social networking site can offer.

Microblogs can be used to communicate with learners just in time. For instance, I have used Twitter to tweet messages about due dates, upcoming assignments, and new resources for learners to check out, conferences I am attending, presentations I am making, and other short messages that help develop presence and build relationships with learners. Learners can use microblogs to call out specific tasks or updates if they are working in a group, post questions, send short messages to other learners to describe their state of mind as they engage in learning activities, or even to begin developing personal relationships with one another.

EMERGING TECHNOLOGIES

The Horizon Report (Johnson, Levine, Smith, & Stone, 2010), a collaboration between the New Media Consortium and the Educause Learning Initiative, identifies and describes emerging technologies that are likely to have an impact on teaching and learning within the next five years. The 2010 report describes mobile computing as the technology that will grow the fastest, because most learners already carry some form of mobile device and more are able to connect to a cellular network through these devices, which will allow for more just-in-time communications with faculty and peers. The smart phone, which has advanced computing ability and connectivity, can be thought of as a computer that you can hold in your hand. Smart phones have a large collection of applications that allow someone to learn just in time. These applications include basic tools for e-mail, communication, and managing a calendar, as well as applications for collaborating, sharing documents, accessing social networks, and downloading content from a course management system. "The portability of mobile devices and their ability to connect to the Internet almost anywhere makes them ideal as a store of reference materials and learning experiences, as well as general-use tools for fieldwork, where they can be used to record observations via voice, text, or multimedia, and access reference sources in real time" (Johnson, Levine, Smith, & Stone, 2010, p. 10). For more information on emerging tools, please read the most recent *Horizon Report*, available at the New Media Consortium website (www.nmc.org).

COMMUNICATION TOOLS PLAN

Before you begin teaching your online course, consider the different technologies discussed in this chapter and how they can be used in your course to develop presence, build community, improve collaboration, and help learners construct knowledge in the subject domain. Bates and Poole (2003) recommend asking the following questions when selecting communication technologies for interaction and interactivity:

1. What kind of activities by the student would most facilitate learning of this subject?
2. What media or technology would best facilitate this interaction?
3. How can technology enable scarce teaching resources to be used and supported by less scarce resources, with respect to increasing the amount and quality of learner interaction? (p. 102)

Using the communication plan in Exhibit 14.2, consider the course activities and determine what types of communication tools would be appropriate to accomplish each of the activities. Take into consideration the needs of learners for flexibility as you look at both synchronous and asynchronous tools to facilitate interaction. Also consider how you can increase the amount and quality of learner interactions using a variety of tools. Think about activities within the course, as well as activities outside of the course, that can help develop a community of inquiry.

Exhibit 14.2 Communication Plan.

Course Activities	Interaction Tools That Can Best Facilitate Activities	Goal of Interaction: Knowledge Construction, Develop Presence, Feedback, Community Building	Choice of Tool
E.g., Course introduction	Discussion forum, e-mail, instant chat, web conferencing	Develop presence, community building	
E.g., Team activity	Discussion forum, e-mail, instant chat, web conferencing, wiki	Knowledge construction, develop presence, community building	
E.g., Learner feedback	E-mail, blog (private journal)	Feedback	
E.g., Extended discussions	Social networking tool, blog	Knowledge construction, community building	
E.g., Critical thinking activity	Discussion forum, virtual world	Knowledge construction	
Activity			
Activity			
Activity			
Activity			

In this chapter we explored the types of communication tools available to increase presence, build community, and support knowledge construction. We discussed the importance of understanding the needs of individual learners, including personal needs and time restrictions. We also addressed the need for good writing and typing skills for some synchronous and asynchronous modes of communication, because poor skills can inhibit some learners from communicating equally with other learners. As you begin to develop communication strategies for your online course, carefully consider the types of interactions that you will use to build community, promote learning, and provide a variety of tools to meet the needs of all learners. The more deliberate you are in planning the interaction for your online course, the greater opportunity you will have to build a learning community that will assist learners in staying motivated, persisting, and ultimately achieving the learning outcomes of the course.

Part 4 looked at how you can develop cognitive, social, and teaching presence in your online course through the development of a community of inquiry that engages learners in active learning, critical thinking, and reflection. Chapter 11 presented strategies for developing cognitive presence with active learning strategies to support critical thinking and knowledge construction. Chapter 12 described learner-to-learner interaction strategies to help develop social presence to establish learners as individuals and, in turn, to help build interpersonal relationships to build a community of inquiry where learners engage in critical thinking and knowledge construction as a collaborative activity. Chapter 13 described strategies to help you develop teaching presence to support learners and facilitate learning. Finally, Chapter 14 described communication tools that can be used to establish cognitive, social, and instructor presence. The strategies from these chapters can provide you with a solid foundation to engage learners in a community of inquiry that supports critical thinking and knowledge construction.

PART 5

Strategies for Managing Your Online Course

We have looked at the profile of the online learner and developed an understanding of the foundations of cognition and learning that influence the instructional strategies you choose. We also looked at specific instructional strategies, including cognitive scaffolding tools to support learning and active learning strategies to develop presence through learner interactions with the content, instructor, and peers. This book would not be complete if we did not discuss strategies to help you manage your online course, which include specific strategies to manage your teaching activities, behavior issues you may encounter, and ethical issues as they arise.

Chapter 15 describes specific strategies to help you organize and manage the online course environment. It examines how you set expectations for your online course and an array of strategies to help you develop a routine and streamline teaching activities. Behavioral issues may manifest themselves differently in the online learning environment, so Chapter 16 describes behavioral problems that arise in the online environment and offers ideas on how to deal with them effectively. Chapter 17 discusses ethical issues that you will need to manage in your online course, presents strategies for overcoming plagiarism in your course, and offers important information on copyright. Chapter 18 concludes the book and ends with a reflection on your online teaching philosophy. This philosophy can serve as your guide as you engage with learners online to help them successfully reach their educational goals.

15

Strategies for Managing Your Online Teaching Activities

The online learning environment is different from the traditional learning environment in many ways. One important difference is that in a traditional classroom, the time commitment is finite in that most interaction occurs during the class and office hours. In an online environment, the course is available 24/7. The continuous accessibility of the online classroom demands that you develop new time management strategies. How you manage your online course not only affects your workload, it also has an impact on persistence. Learners need to understand the expectations of your course to be successful and avoid frustration from not understanding your requirements. Learners also need opportunities to ask questions to help them understand specific activities. This can take a lot of time, so finding ways to communicate with learners as a group can improve the efficiency and effectiveness of your communication and help learners persist. We also understand that learners are managing many different responsibilities in their life, which can cause them to have low interaction, so being able to track and monitor learners' progress is important to help them stay engaged. In this chapter, we look at strategies to help you develop a routine for streamlining your teaching activities, develop effective ways to track learner progress, and manage the increased amount of interaction that you will have with learners.

SETTING EXPECTATIONS FOR THE COURSE

At the beginning of the course, you will need to spend time interacting with individual learners, answering their questions, and helping them understand what will be expected of them in the course. In an online learning environment, it is critical to set expectations for the course, so learners have a complete understanding of the format and structure of the course, as well as the expectations for engaging in the course (Palloff & Pratt, 2007; Boettcher & Conrad, 2010). Chapter 7 described expectation and orientation scaffolds to help learners understand procedures for the course. These are important tools to help learners understand the layout of the course, how to navigate the course environment, and the expectations for engaging in the course. An expectation scaffold is also an important tool to help you proactively manage expectations of learners and keep them from making inaccurate assumptions about the course. This can reduce the time you have to spend helping learners meet expectations or change their own expectations because of misunderstanding. It can also be used as a tool to remind learners, if issues arise, that you clearly set out expectations at the beginning of the course. It is important that you post your faculty expectations in the discussion and have each learner post a reply to your expectation indicating that he or she understands your expectations and does not have any questions about them.

DEVELOPING A ROUTINE TO STREAMLINE TEACHING ACTIVITIES

Developing a routine for all of the teaching activities during the course can help you manage your time and effort. By developing a routine, you can control the workload, which can keep you from feeling overwhelmed. Exhibit 15.1 is a time management worksheet that you can use to organize your teaching activities each week and manage your available time.

To begin, consider all of the activities that are involved in teaching your course. Using the template in Exhibit 15.1, keep the listed activities that are relevant to your course, delete the ones that are not, or add additional activities based on the design of your course. Next establish how much time you will need to allocate to accomplish each of the activities. If you are new to teaching, take a best guess. Generally speaking, with an average of 20 learners, an online course can take anywhere from 10 to 15 hours per week; however, that figure varies greatly

Exhibit 15.1 Time Management Worksheet.

Example of Course with Units That Begin on Monday and End on Sunday Each Week	Day/Times [Mon.]	Day/Times [Tues.]	Day/Times [Wed.]	Day/Times [Thurs.]	Day/Times [Fri.]	Day/Times [Sat.]	Day/Times [Sun.]
Unit activity setup Unit overviews, due dates, supplemental materials etc. [30 minutes weekly]					8:30 AM–9:00 AM		
Posting weekly discussion summaries [15 minutes]	10:30 AM–10:45 AM						
Managing discussions E.g., participating in discussions, tracking discussions [2–3 hours weekly]		9:00 AM–10:00 AM		7:00 PM–8:00 PM		11:00 AM–12:00 AM	
Grading discussions/assignments [10 minutes per learner discussion/15 minutes per learner assignment]	8:30 AM–10:30 AM	7:00 PM–9:00 PM					
Managing learner questions/issues E.g., e-mail/course mail, question and answer discussion, technical issues discussion [15 minutes daily]	8:00–8:15 AM 4:00–4:15 PM	8:00–8:15 AM 4:00–4:15 PM	8:00–8:15 AM 4:00–4:15 PM	8:00–8:15 AM 4:00–4:15 PM	8:00–8:15 AM 4:00–4:15 PM	8:00–8:15 AM 4:00–4:15 PM	8:00–8:15 AM 4:00–4:15 PM
Sending proactive communications [15 minutes per learner]	8:15 AM–8:30 AM	8:15 AM–8:30 AM			8:15 AM–8:30 AM		

depending on the structure of the course. It is important to track the time it takes for you to complete each of the activities, but remember that over time, you will build efficiencies that will reduce the time you spend on each activity. Continue to update your time allocations as you teach the course from one quarter or semester to the next, and adjust your schedule accordingly.

Next allocate your time throughout the week for the different activities, including setting up the units, managing discussions, managing learner questions and issues, grading discussions and assignments, proactively communicating with learners at risk, posting weekly summaries, and so on. In the template, mark the specific day you will complete the activity. You may also want to include a specific time to better organize your schedule.

Unit Setup Activities

If your course requires weekly setup, I recommend that you try to set up your course on the Thursday or Friday prior to the start of a new unit of study. This allows learners who are caught up with work to have an extra weekend to work ahead. It also will keep you from having to rush in on the first day of the unit and post information about the activities. You will also need to determine whether you will introduce and close a unit of study. A good strategy is to introduce a unit of study by presenting an overview of the unit. Discuss any issues that you have found that learners have in the studies, and point out ways to overcome them. Once the unit has closed, posting a summary of the unit activities can signal that the unit has officially ended and can provide an opportunity to summarize activities and discussions and post your reflections. If you do not participate in discussions, this is an opportunity to demonstrate to learners your awareness of what took place in the discussion activities. The unit overview can be posted as part of your setup on Thursday or Friday, but I recommend that you post summary discussions following the close of a unit of study.

Managing Discussion

Discussions can take a lot of time to manage. Creating specific strategies for participating in weekly discussions can help reduce the time you spend responding to individual discussion posts. Consider strategies for how you participate in discussions, how you will monitor instructor-to-learner and learner-to-learner interactions, and other discussion strategies to reduce the time that you have to spend managing discussions.

There are several strategies you can use to participate in discussions. One strategy is to choose specific discussions to participate in and communicate with learners where you will be interacting. Another is to respond to key discussion posts from learners and weave themes or point out areas where learners are not on target. You can also interact with different learners in different discussions, and make sure that you interact with every learner at least once.

You may also want to consider a strategy of learners' taking on the role of moderator in the discussion, which alleviates the need for you to engage in discussions. Your role can move to monitoring the discussions to make sure they are on target and provide feedback to the moderator to keep the discussion focused and engaged. As discussed earlier, if you choose not to participate in discussions, a discussion summary can help demonstrate your awareness of what took place during the discussions, give learners your personal perspective, and point out any misunderstandings of the topic. The important thing is to communicate to learners the strategies you will be using. Once you have an understanding of how you will engage in the discussion, you can determine how much time to allocate to participate in them.

You may want to develop a system for tracking learners' responses to discussions, as well as interactions you have had with individual learners in the discussion and other important information to help you manage the discussions and reduce the time needed each week to grade discussions. Exhibit 15.2 is a sample of a spreadsheet you can use to track discussions. For each discussion, post a score for the quality of a learner's discussion post based on the discussion-grading rubric you are using. Include comments regarding the quality of the response and make notes if you ask the learner to elaborate on something. Include comments if you have received communications from learners indicating they are sick, out of town, or have other reasons that they cannot participate in the discussion. Also include communications from learners indicating problems they are having with understanding the materials or activities for the unit. This will help you develop a clear understanding of how the learner is doing and where to focus your feedback to learners when you grade discussions at the end of a unit. It also will remind you of communications from learners regarding not being able to participate, so

Exhibit 15.2 Course Roster and Tracking Spreadsheet.

Learner Name	Learner E-mail	Unit 1 Discussion 1	Comments	Unit 1 Discussion 2	Comments
E.g., Tom Jones		3 points	Excellent response	3 points	Excellent response
E.g., John Smith			Father died—out of class this week		
E.g., Jane Johnson		1 point	Short response; no arguments; no evidence; sent e-mail that she does not understand the discussion question. Posted to discussion and asked her to elaborate on arguments, evidence. Gave her concrete examples of how to do this.		
Learner					
Learner					
Learner					
Learner					
Learner					
Learner					

you do not end up sending communications at the end of a unit asking why they did not participate in the discussion.

Grading Discussions and Assignments

By being organized and using tools to help you manage discussions, you will be able to allocate less time to grading discussions. At the beginning of a course, learners do not have a sense of your grading style and may be unsure whether they are meeting your expectations in discussions. Providing feedback frequently during the first few weeks of the course can help learners understand the extent to which they are meeting the discussion requirements. Once learners have an understanding of your grading, you can post grades for discussions to a grade book (if available) and reduce the number of times you send out individual written feedback. Encourage learners to become more independent and use the grading rubrics and scoring guides, as well as the feedback they have received from you on past discussions, to evaluate their own performance. For assignments, I recommend that you give detailed feedback along with a grade each time, and try to return feedback within 48 to 72 hours. Feedback templates can help reduce the amount of time you spend grading discussions and assignments, discussed in detail in an upcoming section of the chapter.

Managing Learner Questions and Issues

Much of your time can be taken up communicating to individual learners about questions they have regarding course activities. There are several communication strategies that can help you organize and reduce the number of such individual communications, including question-and-answer threads, technical question discussions, and frequently asked question posts.

Although learners often have the same questions, they e-mail you separately about them. Posting a question-and-answer discussion thread such as "Ask Your Instructor" is an effective strategy to encourage learners to ask questions. By posting them to a public discussion thread, all learners are able to read each question and your reply, which will reduce the number of individual replies you need to make. When you receive individual questions that are not specific to an individual learner, copy and paste the question or issue and your response into your "Ask Your Instructor" discussion. This can help prevent this same question being asked again by another learner. Encourage learners to review posts to the

"Ask Your Instructor" discussion before asking questions to see whether it was already answered, as well as to review other questions and answers that may be helpful to them.

Many learners have technical issues throughout the course, so providing a space for asking questions related to technical issues can help communicate answers to common technical issues in the course. A separate thread can also allow you to bring in a technical support person to monitor and answer questions that you may not have the expertise to answer. You may also provide a link to your technical support site in the discussion, so learners can quickly get answers to questions that you are unable to answer.

Frequently asked question (FAQ) documents are another excellent way to answer questions proactively. As you teach a course several times, you will begin to get an understanding of the kinds of questions and specific issues that occur during learning activities. Developing a FAQ document that answers some of the most frequently asked questions can be helpful. Documenting all questions asked throughout the course can help you regularly update your FAQ document. It can also be used to reflect on the course activities and help you determine important edits that need to be made to resolve issues that frequently occur in the course. You may want to post the FAQ document to the "Ask Your Instructor" thread, so it is handy for learners to review prior to asking a question.

Most course management systems have a built-in mail feature. In order to manage the number of communications from learners in a course, use this feature in your course and communicate with learners that this will be the main tool for communicating privately with them throughout the course. Many of the available course mail tools allow you to forward any mail that comes into the inbox of the course mail to your regular mail, which will allow you to see immediately when you have mail in the course. They do not allow you to reply to the mail from your regular e-mail account, so you will need to log into the course to reply. The benefit of using this tool is to track all learner correspondences. If your course management system does not have a course mail system or you prefer your regular e-mail, you may want to consider creating a rule that automatically moves incoming e-mail from a distribution group to a specific folder. In the tools menu you can create rules and add all of your learners to a distribution group, so they are automatically organized into a single folder. This will allow you to manage learner e-mails more efficiently and allow you to track individual learner communications. This can be especially important if a learner challenges a grade at the end of the course or files a complaint, because it will help you organize learner communications that you may need to demonstrate you clearly communicated the learner's standing in the course.

Another option is to use private discussion threads for learner communications. Most course management systems allow you to designate a discussion as private or public. At the beginning of the course, you can set up private discussions for each learner and post all of your communications to their private discussion thread. The advantage of this type of communication strategy is that you can organize your communications with unique threads for different types of communications. For instance, you can have a private question thread, a thread for feedback on discussions and assignments, and a thread for announcements, to name a few. Compiling all of the communications to and from an individual learner can also help you if you are trying to determine how to manage a particular learner issue. It allows you to review what you have discussed with the learner and make recommendations to help him overcome issues.

Managing Proactive Communications

You will need to manage proactive communications that you send out each week. It is important to send proactive communications weekly to all learners who do not participate in discussions or turn in assignments. Prior to grading discussions and assignments, determine which learners did not interact in discussions or did not turn in assignments. You can review your tracking spreadsheet for any communications from inactive learners, indicating a reason for their absence. For learners who have not communicated with you, send out a communication (Exhibit 15.3) to each learner that indicates the activities they did not participate in and the time line for completing them and submitting them for a grade. It is very important to be specific about the time line and what will happen if learners are not able to turn in late work within the agreed-upon time line.

You will also need to consider sending proactive communications to at-risk learners. Exhibit 15.4 describes the components for proactive communicating with at-risk learners. For learners who are not participating, I recommend that you send them the weekly communications that we discussed and if they do not respond to your communications after a week, send them a more formal communication. Be specific about the issue and their current standing in the

Exhibit 15.3 Late Work Communication Example

Hi John,

We have finished the activities for Unit 3 and it appears that you were not able to participate in the activities for this unit. There were two graded activities, the Unit 3 Discussion on the use of deception in research and the Unit 3 Assignment, which is a draft of issue paper.

I will accept your initial post to the discussion question and the draft of your paper through midnight, Wednesday, September 15, 2010. If you do not turn them in by that date and you do not communicate with me regarding your ability to make that deadline, your grade for these activities will become 0 and you will not have another opportunity to make up the grades.

Please let me know how you are doing and if there are any issues or concerns that you are having that are keeping you from actively engaging in the course. I am here to support you☺

Dr. Smith

---

course. There are additional issues that you may want to formally communicate with learners about. These include writing issues, failing grades, or technology issues that are putting the learner at risk of not passing the course. This template should be used to communicate with learners after you have reached out to them informally to help them with the issue they are having. An "at risk" communication is a stronger message to learners. It should include a description

Exhibit 15.4 At-Risk Proactive Communication Template.

Type of issue	Include a heading that indicates the type of issue you are communicating about: Nonparticipation Failing grades Writing issues Technology issues
Details of issue and previous solutions recommended	Describe the issue in detail, including any solution strategies that you have previously recommended.
Actions needed	Describe what actions need to be taken by the learner to overcome issue.
Time line	Include a specific time line for resolving issue.
Results	Describe what will happen if appropriate actions are taken. Describe what will happen if appropriate actions are not taken.
Name and e-mail address	Include your name and e-mail address.

of the issue and details about the issue, including any recommendations you have previously made to help the learner resolve the issue. Also describe specifically what actions need to be taken, the time line in which they must be taken, and the results of what will happen if they are taken or not taken. By proactively communicating with learners you can provide them with specific information about the issue and how to resolve it and make it clear what the results will be if they do not take action. This will protect you at the end of the course if learners come back and state they had no idea there was a problem or that they were never told they were failing the course.

TEMPLATES FOR MANAGING INSTRUCTOR INTERACTIONS AND COMMUNICATIONS

The first time you teach a course online is the most time consuming. If you set up your interactions using basic templates, you will be able to communicate more effectively and efficiently with all learners in a reasonable amount of time. As you teach the course over several quarters or semesters, you can reuse the templates and continue to enhance them. In addition, you can personalize communications by weaving specific information from the current course into an existing template.

Part 3 of the book describes the use of learning scaffolds to support learners as they engage in learning activities. Worksheets, templates, and worked examples can support learners as they engage in activities. They can also help reduce the time you will spend answering individual questions regarding specific learning activities. In addition to the worksheets, templates, and worked examples, consider additional strategies for managing learning activities such as unit overviews, grading rubrics, and feedback templates.

Unit Overviews

Unit overviews can easily be reused each time you teach the course and are an excellent way for you to support learners as they begin a unit of study (Exhibit 15.5). Begin your overview by stating something positive about the behaviors you have seen with learners in general. For instance, you may want to say, "I really enjoyed the discussion last week and appreciate that you are getting into the discussions early and extending the dialogue with your peers. There were multiple perspectives shared and I appreciated how everyone used their critical thinking skills as you engaged in the discussion." If you post a summary of the discussion each week, then you do not need to go any further into the previous week. If not, then you may want to provide a little more detail about the multiple perspectives that were shared and any issues that learners had in general, along with your perspective on the issue. Next connect the previous unit with the upcoming unit. If you are introducing a new topic or project, offer a general overview of the topic or project and provide a high-level review of the upcoming units involved. You can then describe each of the individual activities for the unit, pointing out important resources, due dates, and time estimates if you have them. If you have taught the course before, point out any issues learners had in the past and recommend ways to keep learners from having the same issues. Close by encouraging learners to contact you if they have any questions or issues. Once a unit of study has ended, I recommend that you go back to your unit overview and add any information in your details of the unit activities based on the issues learners had. The next time you teach the course, you will have

Exhibit 15.5 Components of Unit Overview.

Introduction	Begin by encouraging learners about the behaviors they have been demonstrating.
	E.g., "I really enjoyed the discussion last week and appreciate that you are getting into the discussions early and extending the dialogue with your peers." "There were multiple perspectives shared and I appreciated how everyone used their critical thinking skills as you engaged in the discussion."
Summary of Previous Unit	If you do not post an individual summary at the end of each unit, include a summary of the previous unit.
Connect Previous Unit to Current Unit	Connect what learners did in the previous unit to the current unit and show how they fit together.
Make Transition to New Topic or Project	If the unit is a transition to a new topic, discuss the transition to the new topic.
	If the unit is a transition to a new project, describe the project, along with an overview of the units the project will cover.
Unit Activity Description	Describe each learning activity.
	Describe resources learners will use to complete activities.
	Discuss the due date for each activity.
	If you have time estimates for activities, describe a time line for completing each of the activities.
	If you have taught the course in the past, point out anything about the topic or activity that previous learners have had issues with and suggest ways to prevent learners from having the same issue.
Closing	Encourage learners to contact you if they have questions or issues.

your unit overview complete and you can simply change the information in the introduction to personalize it.

Grading Feedback Templates

Grading rubrics can help you provide timely feedback to learners. Rubrics are a quick way to give learners specific feedback and allow you to develop consistent grading practices from one learner to the next. A grading rubric feedback template can help you develop individual feedback and manage the actual time it takes to provide individual feedback to every learner. Exhibit 15.6 is an example of a grading rubric feedback template.

Along with feedback on the criteria in the grading rubric, additional personal feedback can provide more information regarding the specific issues with the learner's work.

Detailed feedback should include

- Specifics of where the learner excelled
- Specifics of where the learner needs improvement
- Actionable ways to improve performance
- Final positive statement on learner's behavior

Begin with specific details regarding where the learner excelled. Next, discuss areas where the learner can improve and include specific, actionable ways to improve performance. End with a final positive statement regarding the learner's behavior to encourage and motivate them. Follow up with a positive statement about their behavior to leave them feeling good about themselves and with specific actionable ways they can continue to improve their performance. If you develop templates with specific types of responses, you can easily copy and paste specific comments into your grading rubric template, which can save time developing individual feedback for learners' assignments.

Microsoft Word Forms

You can also create feedback templates with Microsoft Office 2007 Word forms. A form allows you to include general information that you will use in all

Exhibit 15.6 Grading Rubric Feedback Template.

Criteria	Performance	Comments	Comment Choices
Criteria 1 E.g., states a position with at least 3 arguments that are supported by evidence	Level of performance on grading rubric E.g., nonperformance, basic, proficient, distinguished	*Specific feedback on performance including:* Where learner excelled on criteria Where learner needs improvement Actionable ways to improve on criteria	*Where learner excelled:* You did a great job of analyzing the issue. You did a good job of stating your position on the issue. You did a great job of weaving the multiple perspectives on this issue into your line of reasoning. *Where the learner needs improvement:* Please try to incorporate more arguments to support your position along with evidence. You can do this by analyzing specific arguments made in the readings and the evidence used to support the arguments. As you continue to build your critical thinking skills, consider using a number of different pieces of evidence from a variety of sources to support your arguments. You can do this by finding additional resources on the issue in peer-reviewed journals and looking at the evidence experts use to support their arguments. Also consider data and real-world examples to support your arguments. As you continue to build your understanding of the issue, look at underlying assumptions, as well as the implications for following your line of reasoning. To do this, ask yourself what things have to be true for this argument. Ask yourself if someone follows my line of reasoning, what impact it will have immediately and in the future. Also, ask yourself how and where the impact will be felt (persons, places, things).
Criteria 2			
Criteria 3, etc.			
Overall Comments: Address learners by name and give an overall comment on their performance. Sign your comment with your name and make sure that your last comment motivates the learner to want to improve his or her performance.			E.g., Jim, I really appreciate the effort you have put into this assignment. Please be sure to review my individual comments above for how you can continue to improve on the grading criteria. I look forward to your continued growth! Dr. Jones

communications and specific information based on criteria that you use to grade discussions or assignments. For instance, when grading discussions, you may grade learners based on the quality of their response to the discussion, the number of learners they interact with, spelling and grammar errors, number of days in the course, and so forth. For each of these variables, you can create

Exhibit 15.7   Microsoft Word Form for Discussion Feedback

Hi [insert learner name],

   This week's discussion asked you to consider the issue of the use of deception in research and describe your position on this issue, using arguments and evidence to support your position.

Choose an item (drop-down menu).
Choose an item (drop-down menu).
Choose an item (drop-down menu).
Choose an item (drop-down menu).
Choose an item (drop-down menu).
Choose an item (drop-down menu).

   Please let me know if you have any questions. I appreciate your efforts☺ [insert instructor name]

---

drop-down menus that allow you to choose the appropriate feedback to learners. Exhibit 15.7 shows an example of a discussion feedback form.

You will see in the template that there are six "Choose an item" elements, which are drop-down menus from which you can choose the response that fits the learner's performance in the discussion.

The choices include

- The quality of the learner's initial post to the discussion question.

- The quality of the learner's interactions with other learners.

- The number of points he or she received for the discussion.

- The next three include choices for point deductions.

The first one describes the quality of the initial post to the discussion. There are several choices, as shown in Figure 15.1.

Once you select all of the drop-down menu choices, your form is complete. Exhibit 15.8 demonstrates the completed feedback form.

It takes time to create the forms, but once you have developed them, you can use them repeatedly each time you teach the course. It is very easy to add choices to the list, so you can easily accommodate additional response types as you grade and find that the current choices do not fit. One caveat is that if you paste

Figure 15.1 Microsoft Form—"Choose an Item".

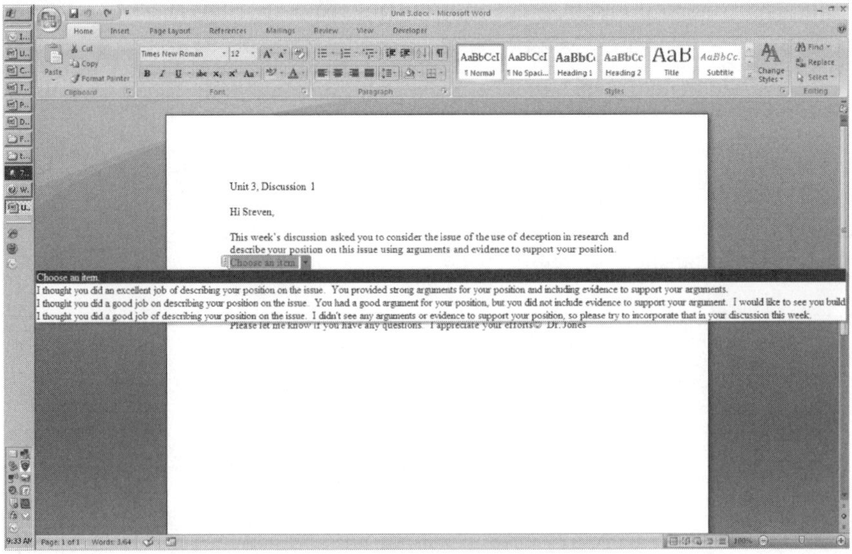

Exhibit 15.8   Microsoft Form—Completed

Hi Cheryl,

This week's discussion asked you to consider the issue of the use of deception in research and describe your position on this issue, using arguments and evidence to support your position. I thought you did an excellent job of describing your position on the issue. You provided strong arguments for your position and included evidence to support your arguments.

I appreciate the interactions you had with other learners and thought you did a great job of using your critical thinking skills.

You received 9/9 points for this discussion and I have recorded it in the grade book.

Please let me know if you have any questions. I appreciate your efforts☺ Dr. Jones

---

your form into a Word document, the drop-down menu choices will appear. You should complete the form and paste it into an e-mail, so the drop-down menus are not visible or clickable. To access information on how to create a form in Microsoft Office 2007, click on the question mark in the upper right-hand corner of a new Word document and use the search string "Create forms," and you will find a link to how to "Create a form that users complete in Word." Follow the directions for inserting a "drop-down list" to create the different choices of wording in your feedback template. Once you have completed your form, you can use it as a template to create forms for all of the feedback you will give on specific activities. You can simply delete fields that are not applicable and add new ones that reflect the type of feedback you want to give.

COURSE PLATFORM CAPABILITIES

Course platforms have a number of capabilities that will help you gain efficiency in managing your online course. Two features that I find the most valuable are the grading features and tracking reports.

Grading Features

Three grading tools that can save you time are the discussion grading tool, assignment submission and grading tool, and the grade book. Many course management platforms have a discussion grading tool that allows you to pull up all of the responses from an individual learner in a discussion and evaluate the quality of responses and interactions with other learners. You can enter a grade for a discussion that is automatically populated in the grade book. You can also send course mail with feedback from the discussion grading tool. An assignment box tool allows learners to submit assignments in one location, and you can grade assignments and send feedback to learners within the tool. The assignment grade automatically populates in the grade book. The grade book feature allows you to track enrollment of learners, enter grades, and automatically calculate midterm and final grades for individual learners. Many also have statistical features that allow you to look at the distribution of grades to determine the overall performance of learners. The release feature allows you to release the grade as soon as you have entered it or you can release it once you have finished grading all of the learners' assignments.

Tracking Data

Many platforms have built-in tracking reports that can help you determine how active learners are in your course. Reports often include information such as overall course activity, tool usage, course items that are being used, course entry and exit pages, frequency of use of specific files, as well as detailed activity of individual learners. When learners enter the course environment, you can track which content areas they access, how much time they spend in each area, what documents they have viewed and compiled, and if they have read e-mails or accessed their grades. I use tracking data to determine the last time a learner has been in the course. If learners have not accessed the course for a period of time, it would not make sense to try to communicate via the course mail feature. A better choice would be to send communications via their personal e-mail. I also use tracking data when learners communicate with me that they are confused and do not understand what to do. One of the first things I look at is where the learners have been in the course and the amount of time they have spent in different content areas. Often I find that confused learners spend the majority of their time in the discussions. They spend a lot of time compiling all of the discussion posts but very limited time in the learning unit where the content is found. This may indicate a learner who is trying to figure out what to post by looking at other learners' posts instead of spending the needed time going through the content in the learning unit. By reviewing learners' interactions in the course, I can make recommendations to view specific resources they have not viewed and spend more time in the learning unit prior to trying to respond to discussions and assignments.

It also allows me to track the amount of time the learner is spending in the course and the number of times per week he or she is logging into the course. Throughout the years of teaching online, I have found a direct correlation between the number of days and hours a learner spends in the course and his or her final grade. Learners who spend the most time in the course generally get higher grades than learners who engage in the course less frequently.

Prior to teaching online, review all of the capabilities of your course platform and consider the features that fit your course structure. If these features are not available to you in your course management system, you will want to develop strategies to track and communicate learner progress in the course.

Before you begin to teach online, you may want to consider creating a course management plan that takes into consideration some of the strategies that have been discussed in this chapter. The more time you can take before the course begins developing specific strategies and routines for managing your online course, the more efficient and effective you can be in facilitating it. In addition, how you manage your online course can have a direct impact on persistence because it will allow you to streamline activities in order to demonstrate presence in the course, help learners overcome issues, and provide them with quality feedback to help them continue to improve their performance.

16

Strategies for Managing Behavioral Issues

Managing learner issues can be more difficult in the online learning environment than in a traditional learning environment. For some learners, the fact that they do not have to look a person in the eye makes it easier to act differently and exhibit inappropriate behaviors. In addition, the online environment can be a place for some individuals to "hide out" because they do not have to reveal themselves personally. The anonymity can give them braveness to say whatever they want. Behavioral issues can destroy a course environment if not managed. If offending behavior is left unchecked, it can cause a deterioration of discussions and team projects and lead learners to drop out. In addition, behavioral issues that are a result of learning problems must be recognized and managed to help learners overcome issues and persist. In this chapter, we look at specific learner personalities and types of behavioral issues and discuss strategies for dealing with learners when issues arise.

LEARNER PERSONALITIES

First, I would like to introduce you to some learners whom I have had in my online courses throughout the years. I think it will help you understand in a more concrete way the types of personalities you may find in your online course. For each personality, I describe solutions for managing this personality to help you deal with issues that may arise.

Co-Instructor

There always seems to be at least one learner who feels he or she has some excellent strategies to help you teach the course. Generally, he will send you an e-mail indicating the issues he has found in the course and let you know that he has some strategies that can help you. He also may volunteer to work with individual learners who are having problems.

Solution: The best way to deal with a learner who would like to take on the role of co-instructor is let him know how much you appreciate his ideas and leave it at that. Do not indicate that you will or will not use the advice, so the learner does not become offended by being turned down by the offer to help. Regarding the comments about wanting to help other learners, I recommend that you state your appreciation for volunteering to help a learner with problems, but indicate that you are working with the learner one-on-one. Let the learner know that you appreciate a supportive learning environment and the best way he can support other learners is to engage with them in the discussions in a respectful manner that does not point out problems or errors because it can cause embarrassment. Indicate that you monitor discussions and will work individually with any learner who needs additional support.

Know-It-All

This learner is the one in the course who always has the right answer and spends a great deal of time letting everyone else know they are wrong and she is right.

Solution: A good time to discuss this issue with the learner is in your regular feedback to her on her performance. Indicate in your feedback the value of multiple perspectives and let the learner know that in order to build community, it is important to respect diverging opinions and ideas. If your class has activities where learners take on different perspectives on a topic or issue, I recommend that you post "rules of engagement" to make sure that learners argue issues, not one another, and support ideas with evidence rather than opinions.

Bully

The bully is the person who tries to intimidate or offend another learner or sometimes even the instructor. The bully's language tends to appear to be a "rant" rather than a discussion, and he sometimes uses offensive language to communicate his ideas.

Solution: Communicate with the learner that this behavior is not tolerated and remove any posts in which this occurs. Let him know that the post has been removed and the reason for removing it. In addition, cite the learner code of conduct to support your decision. When communicating with the bully, keep your statements neutral (without personal comments), short, and to the point.

Helpless

Many learners come into the course and let everyone else know that he or she has no idea what to do. The learner tries to get sympathy from other learners and will ask other learners for help. Rarely do such learners reach out to the instructor, but instead feed on the attention they get from other learners who are willing to help them.

Solution: The best way to deal with this learner is to post directly to the learner's post and let her know that you are there to support her. Also send a personal communication to the learner and in the discussion, respond to the learner and ask her to review your personal correspondence in the course mail area or e-mail (if your course does not have a built-in mail feature). This way you can demonstrate to other learners that you are working with the learner and you can work one-on-one through private correspondences with the learner to deal with the issues.

Chatty Kathy

These learners post too much personal or off-topic information to the discussion that is irrelevant to the discussion topic. Their focus is on building personal relationships with other learners rather than learning.

Solution: All personal discussions should be moved to a café or lounge discussion area. Copy and paste the posts to your café or lounge discussion and communicate to the learners via course mail or e-mail what you have done. I also recommend that you post to the discussion a general comment to all learners reminding them to focus on the discussion and use the café or lounge discussion for interactions not related to the discussion.

The Offender

Once in awhile you will have a learner who posts offensive words to communicate their ideas. They may be right on target with the focus of their response to the discussion, but the offensive language distracts from their ability to communicate.

Solution: I recommend that you post a general statement to the discussion board regarding professionalism in discussions and remind learners that posting offensive language is against the student code of conduct. Then contact the learner individually and politely ask him to edit his post and remove the offensive language.

Sarcastic/Humorous

This learner uses sarcasm or humor in her posts. Generally, it is not meant to be malicious but many learners misunderstand the sarcasm or humor and are offended because there are no visual cues.

Solution: If learners show concern about the "sarcastic" learner's posts, then you should let them know that you will deal with it immediately. The best way to deal with the learner with the issue is to let her know that her post has offended another learner and to try to keep her statements neutral. Since the act was not meant to be malicious, there is no need to review the learner code of conduct. Simply ask her to review her responses prior to posting them and consider her tone.

Challenger

This learner challenges the learning activities as well as the solutions offered by the instructor. Generally, the challenger will receive feedback about an activity and instead of accepting the comments and making appropriate changes to improve his performance, he will challenge the instructor asking why he needs to do this and states his disagreement.

Solution: It takes a lot of patience to work with a challenger but the best response is to discuss specifically why the activity is important and how it relates to the overall goals and objectives of the course. Although the challenger may want to continue the debate about the relevance of the activities, it is best not to continue a dialogue.

Complainer

This learner complains about the course in public forums and tries to encourage others to feel the same. She openly describes activities as worthless and a waste of time. She may state that this is basic information that everyone should know or information that she learned when she was in high school.

Solution: Communicate with the complainer privately and give her an opportunity to be heard. Show empathy for how she feels and work through a resolution that makes the learner feel she has been heard. However, make it clear that a public forum is not the appropriate place to complain.

These are just a few of the many personalities that you may find as you teach your online course. As a summary to the solutions, consider the following as you manage behavioral issues:

- Keep your tone neutral. Do not use language that demonstrates a personal feeling about the issue, such as I am sad or disappointed, but stick to the facts.

- If appropriate, site your organization's code of conduct policy to ensure learners understand what behavior is not appropriate.

- If the behavior occurs in a public forum, intervene quickly, so other learners are able to see that you recognize the problem and are in control of the situation.

- Do not argue with the learner. Stick to the policies within your institution and the expectations that you have set for your course.

- Contact the learner exhibiting the behavioral problem privately and give the learner an opportunity to discuss the issue that is causing the behavior.

- Remove offending posts immediately. If other learners have responded to the post you removed, their post will also be removed. Contact all learners whose posts will be removed and state the policy to justify the removal of the offending post along with the responses.

- Do not discuss the behavioral issue with other learners in the course but focus on the expectations for creating a professional course environment.

- Set up a time to discuss the issue via telephone. Being able to have a synchronous conversation can alleviate a problem faster, especially if you let the offending learner talk and you show concern for the learner.

FLAMING

Many of the behaviors described above fall under the category "flaming". In the online environment, where learners do not have to look someone in the eye to communicate, there can be a rise in the number of offensive statements made between learners and between the learner and the instructor. *Flaming* is a term used when discussing inappropriate posts in an online environment. It generally refers to someone posting remarks that include personal attacks in the form of insults, swearing, or other intense language, which many times is signified by the use of ALL CAPS. David Plotnikoff (1994) describes five types of flaming that occur in bulletin boards, which also occur in online learning environments. The types of flames include the ad-hominem attack, the spelling-grammar flame, the "you have no business being here" flame, the sneak flame, and the surgical-strike flame.

The *ad-hominem attack* refers to attacks on persons who are unsure of themselves in the online environment. Generally such flames are thrown when learners post questions in the discussions that, to the flamer, appear to be ridiculous. For instance, a learner who has not learned the different areas of the course may be asking where the information is that relates to the discussion question. A flamer may sarcastically make a comment about how ridiculous it is that the learner does not know where the course content is.

The *spelling-grammar flame* is common in the online environment because there is a wide range of writing skills among learners. Some learners may become agitated about the poor writing skills, especially if they feel they are being allowed to post compositions that contain spelling and grammar errors. If learners do not see the instructor pointing out the errors, they can become aggressive in the discussions and point them out to the learner in a way that is critical and embarrassing. It can be a double-edged sword. If too much focus is placed on spelling and grammar, learners can start to flame that anyone can correct spelling and grammar errors and question your expertise for teaching the course if your main contributions are corrections to spelling and grammar.

The *"you have no business being here" flame* is generally posted when learners are perceived as not having the prerequisite academic skills to engage in the course. You may find learners posting responses to discussion questions that indicate they are confused by the discussion questions because their response does not relate to what is being asked. Learners can become sarcastic and flame that the learner needs to pay attention and answer the question rather than wandering off in another direction.

The *sneak flame* appears to be friendly and helpful, by pointing out an error in the learner's discussion post but ends with something sarcastic such as "I hope this doesn't happen again" or "You better put your thinking cap on next time." It is important to note that I have also seen this in discussion posts from instructors, so it is very important that you are aware of how these types of comments can be flames.

Finally, the *surgical-strike flame* is made by a learner to refute statements made by another learner regarding an issue being discussed. It is generally considered a flame when the flamer continues to pick on a learner refuting every single statement the learner makes and becomes more taunting in nature. Generally, it moves from arguing a point to arguing an opinion and then arguing a person.

Many flames result from situations in which learners feel that another learner is not working as hard or is not at the same level as they are, and they feel that the situations need to be called out because they do not see the instructor taking action. Therefore, regardless of the type of participation that you have with learners in the learning activities, it is critical that you monitor discussions to ensure that issues are being addressed and learners are being respectful to one another. If you address issues with grammar and spelling, off-topic posts, and other issues relating to the quality of individual learner posts, you will find fewer occurrences of flaming. You also need to monitor all of the interactions that go on between learners to ensure that flaming is not occurring and to catch it as soon as possible in order to deescalate the situation.

Most institutions have a written "learner code of conduct" policy, so make sure that you are familiar with the policy. It is critical not only for you to understand it, but also learners. Be sure to include information regarding the learner code of conduct at the beginning of the course, as well as consequences for any violations. Code of conduct violations generally relate to learners whose interactions with the instructor or other learners contain verbal abuse, threats, intimidation, harassment, coercion, and other conduct that makes other learners uncomfortable and feel unsafe. I recommend that as soon as you find language from a learner that is unacceptable, immediately remove the post and send a communication to the learner. Include the copied language along with the specific language from your institution's learner code of conduct that the learner has violated. Ask the learner to review the code of conduct in its entirety to make sure he or she understands why the language posted is in violation of the policy. As stated earlier, you can resolve an issue faster by setting up a time to talk with the learner via telephone to better understand the learner's situation and answer any questions he or she may have. In addition, try to focus on solutions and give learners ways to manage situations that arise, so they do not post messages in the heat of the moment.

If the interaction that you remove contains other responses from learners, it will be important that you send the learners involved in the interaction a communication letting them know that their responses have been removed due to a violation of the learner code of conduct policy. If they are not involved in any misconduct, simply assure them that you are working through the issue with the learner but do not share any additional details about the issue or situation.

Often a learner will challenge your authority, so it is important to remain in control and assertive instead of defensive or argumentative. Address such learners in a respectful way and allow them to express their feelings and views. By acknowledging their views and feelings, you can deflate the situation and work toward a resolution. Allow learners to help solve the issue in order to help them feel not only a part of the problem, but also a part of the solution.

NETIQUETTE

There are proactive strategies you can use to prevent inappropriate behavior in learner-to-learner interactions and create an environment where learners feel safe to express their feelings and ideas. According to Brookfield and Preskill (2005), "rules of conduct and codes of behavior are crucial in determining whether or not students take discussion seriously" (p. 52). Developing ground rules for discussions can set expectations for how learners will conduct themselves in course interactions. In the online environment, *netiquette* refers to a set of rules for how to behave in an online learning environment (Shea, 1994). Virginia Shea has developed a set of core rules of netiquette that should be followed when interacting with people in cyberspace. These rules can be adapted to the online learning environment to provide an environment where learners feel safe to express themselves without fear of criticism. The core rules are

1. Remember the human
2. Adhere to the same standards online that you follow in real life
3. Know where you are in cyberspace
4. Respect other people's time and bandwidth
5. Make yourself look good online
6. Share expert knowledge
7. Help keep flame wars under control
8. Respect other people's privacy
9. Don't abuse your power
10. Be forgiving of other people's mistakes (p. 32)

These rules should be followed by you and learners as you interact in the online learning environment. Remember that there is a person behind the written posts who has feelings and can be hurt by what and how you interact. It is easier to say something online when you do not have to look the person in the eye. Shea recommends that you never post anything that you would not say to the person face-to-face. In addition, you should adhere to the same standards of behavior online that you follow in real life, which includes acting ethically and following rules and regulations. If you would not steal in real life, you should not steal online by taking other people's ideas and using them as your own. Knowing where you are in cyberspace is important because depending on the environment, there may be different rules of netiquette. Respecting other people's time and bandwidth relates to taking the time to understand the requirements of discussion and do the preparatory work prior to responding to discussion questions. It also includes not wasting people's time by asking questions that are not relevant to the discussion or questions whose answers can readily be found with a little effort. It also encourages staying away from disagreements that lead to personal attacks. "Make yourself look good

Exhibit 16.1 Expectations and Guidelines for Interacting in the Online Environment

The following guidelines should be followed each time you interact in the course to ensure your interactions are respectful and professional:

1. In all of your interactions, remember that there is a person behind the written post, who has feelings and can be hurt by what and how you interact with him or her.
2. It is easier to say something online when you do not have to look the person in the eye, so never post anything that you would not say to the person face-to-face.
3. Adhere to the same standards of behavior online that you follow in real life, which includes acting ethically and following rules and regulations. If you would not steal in real life, then you should not steal online by taking other people's ideas and using them as your own.
4. Respect other people's time and bandwidth:
   a. Take time to understand the requirements of a discussion.
   b. Do not waste people's time by asking questions that are not relevant to the discussion or questions whose answers can readily be found in the course with a little effort.
   c. Refrain from disagreements that lead to personal attacks.
5. Make yourself look good online:
   a. Take time to check your spelling and grammar.
   b. Prepare for discussions prior to engaging in them.
   c. Refrain from inappropriate language and remarks.
6. Share your knowledge by offering help to learners who have questions.
7. Help keep flame wars under control by not posting flames and not responding to flames—keep discussions professional.
8. Forgive other learners' mistakes and be patient and compassionate of all learners in the course.

Source: Adapted from Shea, 1994.

online" relates to taking time to check your spelling and grammar, preparing for discussions prior to engaging in them, and not flaming. By sharing expert knowledge you offer help to learners who have questions. Helping keep flame wars under control means you do not post flames and do not respond to flames; you keep discussions professional. When you respect other people's privacy you do not read other people's private e-mail, which is generally not an issue in the online learning environment. Finally, be forgiving of other people's mistakes—be patient with and have compassion for all learners in the course. These are excellent rules for engaging in the online environment.

Exhibit 16.1 is an adaptation of Shea's netiquette guidelines to the online learning environment. Palloff and Pratt (2005) recommend that you review netiquette guidelines and have learners discuss and agree to these rules at the beginning of a course to ensure that learners understand the expectations and guidelines and agree to them. The following discussion can give learners an opportunity to discuss and agree to the rules:

> *Discussion Question:* Review "Expectations and Guidelines for Interacting in the Online Environment" (Exhibit 16.1). Once you have reviewed the guidelines, post a message to this discussion indicating your understanding of what is expected of you as you interact with others in the course. Indicate your agreement to follow these guidelines throughout the course to ensure a respectful and professional course experience.

PLAGIARIZING OTHER LEARNERS´ IDEAS

Another issue that arises in the online environment is a learner's taking ideas from another learner and using it as his or her own. I discuss the issue of plagiarism in more detail in Chapter 17; however, in this section, I would like to discuss how to manage the behavior side of the issue.

The most common issue of plagiarism occurs in learners' assignments, so you can manage the issue one-on-one. Plagiarism also occurs in discussions. The most common plagiarism is when learners post a response that is copied from another source. Another type of plagiarism that I have seen is learners copying discussion posts from other learners in the course. They may take another learner's post to the discussion question, change a couple of words, and post it as their own. Learners can be very clever at how they plagiarize other learners' ideas. They will take several ideas from a number of different learners in the course to compose their response to the discussion so it will not be recognized as plagiarism.

Most of the time, the learner whose ideas have been taken will report the misconduct to the instructor, but there may be times the learner whose ideas have been taken is not aware of the situation. Closely monitor discussions and observe any similarities in learners' posts to ensure learners are not copying from one another. Also look for language that is more sophisticated than the learner to uncover plagiarism of other sources. You may also want to compile all discussions each week and run the compiled discussion through a plagiarism detection tool to check for posts that have been plagiarized.

It is critical that you act swiftly when learners take other learners' ideas as their own without credit. When the situation arises, immediately notify the offending learner and let him or her know that it is a violation of the academic honesty code. If the offending learner has taken another learner's ideas, also cite the code of conduct. I recommend that you remove all plagiarized posts and notify the learner that it has been removed. In your communication with the learner inform him or her that you have removed the post and discuss whether you will give the learner an opportunity to repost. If other learners have posted to the learner's discussion post, you will have to notify the individual learners that their response to the learner has been removed. If you grade interactions between learners, I recommend that you give the nonoffending learners credit for their interactions.

TONE OF FACULTY WHEN MANAGING LEARNER ISSUES

It is important that regardless of the issue, you consider the tone and language you use when dealing with learner issues. I have seen posts from instructors such as "I will not tolerate this in my course" or "I can't believe you said that," which can be inflammatory and escalate the situation. Please be sure to follow the "Expectations and Guidelines for Interacting in the Online Environment" (Exhibit 16.1) in your own interactions with learners. One of the most important things to remember when communicating with learners is to try to keep your communications neutral and not include personal thoughts or reactions to the learner.

Consider the following components when composing messages to learners regarding issues:

1. State the specific issue that has occurred and the action that has been taken. Include a specific example by copying the comment made by the learner or describing the issue in detail.

2. If the issue violates a specific policy in the course or institution, copy the specific language from the policy (i.e., learner code of conduct, academic honesty).

3. Allow the learner an opportunity to provide his or her understanding of the issue and reasoning for what happened. This can include an offer to talk with the learner via telephone to clarify the issue.

4. Allow the learner an opportunity to solve the issue by making him or her part of the solution (not just a part of the problem).

This structure can help you keep your communications regarding learner behavior neutral by focusing on the problem and action you have taken, making learners aware of the policies that have been violated, allowing learners to express their own feelings about the situation and why it occurred, and allowing them to be a part of the solution.

MANAGING LEARNER MOTIVATION ISSUES

Learners also display personal behavioral issues that may impact their motivation to persist. Sharon Bender and Eileen Dittmar (2006) describe ten learner types including arrogant, careless, delinquent, disjointed, irresponsible, overachiever, stubborn, surprised, unmotivated, and unskilled. These learner behaviors may be expressed as a result of motivation issues. Some learners may lose motivation because their expectations are not being met by the course, while others may lose motivation because they are not able to meet the expectations of the course.

Arrogant Learner

The arrogant learner *lacks appreciation* (Bender & Dittmar, 2006). These learners barely meet assignment requirements, turn in assignments late, do not integrate instructor feedback, and feel their educational experience is a waste of time.

Solution: The best recommendation I can give for managing arrogant learners is to call them on the phone and give them an opportunity to share their thoughts. Ask them how you can help make their time in the course satisfying. Be very specific about their need to meet the expectations and requirements for the course but be willing to negotiate areas that will not have an impact on the course outcomes or be unfair to other learners.

Careless Learner

The careless learner *lacks attention* (Bender & Dittmar, 2006). These learners do not follow directions and details for completing assignments and skip reading required resources. Their assignments are weak and they fail to correct grammar and spelling errors in their papers.

Solution: Many times careless learners who *lack attention to details* indicate a learner with poor academic skills. Part 3 describes scaffolding strategies to support learners who have poor thinking skills. Learners who have strong thinking skills but are careless in their work for other reasons can be managed by providing feedback on the needs for a standard of work. Grading rubrics can be used to communicate the standards to learners, and reduced scores can motivate them to pay more attention to details to improve their grade. You may also want to contact learners prior to assignment deadlines to review the grading rubrics to ensure their work meets the requirements of the assignment.

Delinquent Learner

The delinquent learner *lacks devotion* (Bender & Dittmar, 2006). These learners post to discussions and assignments at the 11th hour, and the result is a rushed product.

Solution: Managing delinquent learners is critical because it can cause you to have to spend additional time grading work submitted by learners after the due date. It is important to set guidelines for late submissions at the beginning of the course and follow through on point deductions in order to help delinquent learners overcome the behavior. In addition, a delinquent learner may have motivation issues, so take the time to determine the issue and provide encouragement to support the learner and help him or her engage in activities in a timely manner.

Disjointed Learner

The disjointed learner *lacks direction* (Bender & Dittmar, 2006). These learners do not know where to begin and may be considered field dependent in that they are not sure how to break down the big picture into manageable chunks of work. These learners suffer from a lack of direction, resulting in poor time management and poorly completed work that is submitted late or not at all.

Solution: Throughout the book, we have discussed several strategies for working with disjointed learners who lack direction. Course road maps, unit overviews, unit checklists, and graphic organizers are a few of the scaffolding tools you can use to support disjointed learners. Having these supports available in the course can help them avoid difficulties and can be used to work with learners one-on-one to overcome problems with course activities.

Irresponsible Learner

The irresponsible learner *lacks accountability* (Bender & Dittmar, 2006). They are unable to meet responsibilities and resort to complaining. They show an external locus of control by blaming everything and everyone else for their inabilities.

Solution: The irresponsible learner who lacks accountability may actually be covering up learning problems, which are characteristic of the disjointed learner. Try using the strategies described for disjointed learners. Also consider strategies that we have discussed in the book about working with learners who have an external locus of control by helping them understand they can control their learning by the effort they put into the activities.

Overachiever Learner

The overachiever learner *lacks patience* (Bender & Dittmar, 2006). These learners perform well but their field independent cognitive style makes them want to take control of their learning to the point of not following processes and procedures for the course.

Solution: The overachiever is the advanced learner who is self-directed. When overachievers become dissatisfied with the course, they can become impatient and exhibit a behavioral issue. When interacting with such learners, recognize their achievements and ask them what they need to have a satisfying learning experience. It is important to make sure they understand that all learners have to demonstrate the outcomes of the course, so there are not opportunities to skip activities they find boring or mundane. In addition, it is important that the alternatives for overachievers are fair and help them find ways to engage in activities at a higher level. For instance, you may want to suggest additional reading at a more advanced level, allow them to dig deeper into a particular perspective or theory to develop expertise, or apply coursework in a more real-world application.

Stubborn Learner

The stubborn learner *lacks flexibility* (Bender & Dittmar, 2006). When you provide feedback to stubborn learners, they refuse to consider your feedback. They will not make necessary changes to meet the requirements of an assignment or course activity.

Solution: Stubborn learners may exhibit some of the same behaviors as the previous behaviors described; however, no matter what you do, they remain uncooperative. The best way to manage stubborn learners is to listen to them, ask them for ways to resolve the issue, evaluate their solution, and make a final decision on the resolution. The key to managing a stubborn learner is once the resolution has been determined, if the learner is not happy with it, you need to be firm and exhibit your authority to ensure the learner understands your expectations.

Surprised Learner

The surprised learner *lacks self-confidence* (Bender & Dittmar, 2006). These learners are not prepared for online learning and are dependent on the instructor to lead them through the course activities. You may recognize this learner by communications that state, "I don't know what to do." These learners also tend not to take advantage of additional resources you provide them to support building their skills.

Solution: In Chapter 6, we discussed motivation theory and how to raise learner' self-confidence. Successes raise efficacy, whereas failures lower them. Early in the course, develop activities that provide opportunities for learners to be successful. For a learner who is unfamiliar with the content area, the amount of content can be overwhelming and create anxiety, so consider techniques to support learners and maximize success to increase self-confidence. This can be done using templates, examples, and clear instructions to increase the likelihood of the learner succeeding in completing the course activities. Verbal persuasion by the instructor and peers can also have a positive influence on self-confidence.

Unmotivated Learner

The unmotivated learner *lacks enthusiasm* (Bender & Dittmar, 2006). These learners turn in work on time and meet expectations; however, they are not involved in the course outside of meeting the requirements.

Solution: All of the learner types described can result in learners' becoming unmotivated; however, this is a specific type of motivation issue because the lack of enthusiasm doesn't impact their grades, but ultimately may lead to learners' becoming bored with the course and eventually dropping out. The key to motivating learners is to help them understand how the course activities will help them build their thinking skills and discuss the importance of creating knowledge as part of a community of inquiry. They may have an external locus of control and only care about the grade, so helping them see how building skills and knowledge through interaction with peers in the course activities can affect them personally is critical.

Unskilled Learner

The unskilled learner *lacks prerequisites* (Bender & Dittmar, 2006). These learners do not possess the necessary academic skills to be successful in any learning environment, but they especially have difficulties in the online learning environment, where learners need good reading and writing skills.

Solution: It is very important to manage unskilled learners because their behavior can affect other learners and you in the course. Throughout the book, we have discussed strategies for managing learners who may not have strong academic skills. Scaffolds that have already been described for other behaviors can support them. In addition, you will need to continuously monitor unskilled learners and provide just-in-time feedback to help them overcome difficulties as they engage in learning activities. It is also important to consider your grading and be honest with unskilled learners about their performance. It may be difficult to fail learners who are making an effort; however, it does not do them any good to be passed from one course to the next. This could lead to them graduating without the necessary skills and knowledge to perform in a professional environment.

Behavioral problems that are a result of unmet expectations can lead to low motivation and may result in the learner dropping out of the course. Being able to identify the root cause of the issue can help you work with learners to overcome motivation issues to help them successfully complete your course. In this chapter, we looked at specific learner personalities and types of behavioral issues and discussed strategies for dealing with offending learners. Each of the behaviors described in this chapter are real and have been reported in the online environment. Behavioral issues can take up the majority of your time. Managing these behaviors effectively is essential to allow you also to engage with learners who are not exhibiting behavioral problems. How you manage behavioral issues has a direct impact on the satisfaction of the learning experience for all learners and can lead to higher persistence. In addition, behavioral issues resulting from learning problems must be recognized and managed to help learners overcome issues and persist. By considering the strategies in this chapter, you can proactively plan for the different behavioral issues you may confront in your online course and can manage them more effectively and consistently without reacting in the moment. You will save time and ensure that all learners feel comfortable engaging in your online course. You can also help learners overcome issues quickly, which can have an impact on their ability to persist and successfully complete your course.

17

Strategies for Managing Ethical and Legal Issues

The online environment is ripe with ethical and legal issues that need to be considered. One key ethical issue of growing concern is plagiarism because of the rise in reported cases across the country. Copyright is a critical legal issue in the online environment that must be carefully considered when using resources in an online course. In this chapter we look at the issue of plagiarism and discuss strategies for detecting and preventing plagiarism in your online course. We also consider the legal issue of copyright and develop an understanding of when fair use is and is not applicable in the online learning environment.

Throughout the book, we have focused on strategies to help learners persist. Plagiarism can be a strong indicator of a learner at risk, and it has a direct impact on the learner's ability to persist. Here we examine plagiarism to uncover reasons learners plagiarize and look at strategies to help learners overcome the issue. Understanding the legal issue of copyright can also affect the resources we use, so we discuss the copyright law specific to online learning environments.

PLAGIARISM

Plagiarism has always been an issue; however, with the rapid growth of the Internet, learners now have available to them an endless source of materials with the capability to copy and paste work directly into their assignments. To prevent

Exhibit 17.1 Levels of Plagiarism.

Levels of Plagiarism	Description
Level 1: Minimum plagiarism	Result of misunderstanding how to cite sources correctly
Level 2: Partial plagiarism	Mix of the use or replication of the words and ideas of another author along with some original writing from the learner
Level 3: Complete plagiarism	Complete work copied from another source without giving credit to the original author

plagiarism, you need to be able to recognize potential cases and be armed with an array of tools and strategies to manage plagiarism issues.

Plagiarism Defined

Plagiarism occurs when the author of a paper uses someone else's words and ideas in his or her writing without giving credit to the original author of the ideas. By not giving credit to the original author, the reader of the paper assumes that these ideas can be attributed to the writer of the paper, which is why it is considered an act of stealing. This is a serious act of fraud and needs to be addressed immediately if a learner is found to have committed this act.

Types of Plagiarism

The use of another author's thoughts, ideas, and words can take on many different forms. In my experience I have found plagiarism on three levels, described in Exhibit 17.1, ranging from minimal acts of plagiarism to complete plagiarism.

Level 1: Minimum Plagiarism   Most of these types of plagiarism are a result of misunderstanding how to cite sources correctly. In this type of plagiarism, learners

1. Use an author's ideas word-for-word and include a citation, but forget to use quotations around the words.

2. Include a citation in the paper but forget to cite the source throughout the paper, so there is no differentiation between the author's ideas and their own.

3. Neglect to include citations due to poor note taking and inadvertently use the author's words without a proper citation.

Level 2: Partial Plagiarism   In this type of plagiarism, there is a mix of the use or replication of the words and ideas of another author along with some original writing from the learner. Learners

1. Take large paragraphs from several sources and piece them together into a paper with minimal original thoughts.
2. Use large portions of another author's work and substitute words with synonyms. May change language by altering key words and phrases to keep plagiarism tools from finding it.
3. Take the entire format of an author's paper and construct a similar paper.
4. Cite some resources but then use the arguments made about the cited sources from another source that has not been included in the reference list and properly cited in the paper.

Level 3: Complete Plagiarism   Here, the complete work is copied from another source without giving credit to the original author. Learners

1. Take a complete post or paper from the Internet or library verbatim.
2. Take a post or paper from another learner.
3. Work with another learner (from the same course or from a learner who was previously in the course) and use the same post or paper.
4. Use discussion post or paper from a previous course.

I am sure you have seen many of these types of plagiarism issues with learners; however, understanding that plagiarism occurs is not enough to be able to tackle the issue head-on. It is also important to understand *why* learners plagiarize in order to begin to develop strategies to decrease the number of occurrences of plagiarism in your courses.

Why Learners Plagiarize

Not all learners know they are actually plagiarizing in their writing because they are not familiar with the proper way to give credit to authors, which is reflected in level 1 plagiarism. Many learners also lack the understanding of how to use specific styles such as MLA and APA, which compounds the issue of properly citing sources they use in their paper. In addition, different resources may use different style guides, which further confuse learners, so they are not sure what examples to follow.

Another major issue is that learners may not understand the difference between paraphrasing and plagiarizing. They may feel that as long as they do not copy the ideas exactly, they are not plagiarizing. According to McCabe, Treviño, and Butterfield (2001), "although most students understand that quoting someone's work word for word demands a citation, they seem to be less clear on the need to cite the presentation of someone else's ideas when the students present them in their own words" (p. 221).

There also may be confusion with the use of a bibliography versus a reference list. A bibliography contains all resources consulted but not necessarily cited in the paper. A reference list contains all of the resources cited in the body of the paper. Because learners may not have used reference lists in the past, they may not be aware that each source listed in the reference list needs to be cited in the body of the paper and every source cited in the body of the paper should have a corresponding reference.

Learners can also inadvertently commit plagiarism because of the way they compile notes as they review resources. Instead of summarizing information in their own words, they may simply copy the information with the intention of going back and summarizing the information as they begin to develop their draft. Once they begin drafting their paper from the notes they have collected, there may be confusion between what they have copied and what they have written. Copied text ends up inadvertently being incorporated into their draft without proper citations. They also may not have noted where the information came from, and instead of eliminating the information, make the decision to include it without a proper citation.

Another reason learners end up plagiarizing when they write is a lack of good writing skills. McCabe and Treviño (1997) found that students with lower GPAs report more cheating than students with higher GPAs (as cited in McCabe, Treviño, & Butterfield, 2001).

If learners have been told that their writing is poor, they may feel pressure to use another author's ideas as their own in order to avoid criticism for poor writing skills. If they have not performed well on previous assignments, they may also fear they will fail the assignment.

Another factor may be poor time management. In the online environment, many learners have to balance coursework with many other responsibilities. The amount of time they have to dedicate to coursework is limited. This may cause them to panic near the deadline and put together a paper without considering the ramifications of taking someone else's ideas and attributing them as their own.

Finally, there are learners who plagiarize intentionally. There are sites on the Internet that sell papers, which can be very tempting to learners who are poor writers or who have run out of time to develop their own paper. Learners also work together, taking the same courses and sharing assignments, to reduce the amount of individual work. I have also witnessed a rise in the number of learners copying the responses of other learners as their own from the same class. I have seen a variety of ways that learners do this. Some learners copy and paste the entire response of another learner, while others are more clever and copy and paste one or two sentences from a number of learners and cobble them together to develop a response to the discussion question.

How to Identify Issues of Plagiarism

Depending on the level of skill for covering up acts of plagiarism, either it can be readily detected or you can have a strong suspicion but not be able to prove that plagiarism has occurred without spending a lot of time going through each of the sources provided by the learner in his or her reference list. If the learner used sources he or she did not report and cleverly changed the wording, it will be nearly impossible to catch. There are several clues, however, you can look for to identify issues of plagiarism:

1. Sophistication of writing
   a. Voice
   b. Terminology
2. Copy and paste anomalies

a. Different writing style in the body of paper

b. Different fonts

c. Different spacing

d. Embedded hyperlinks

e. Different citation styles

3. Lack of flow from one topic to another

a. Unorganized topics

b. No transitions between paragraphs

One indication of plagiarism can be the sophistication of the writing. Most learners do not write like a scholar, so when you notice more sophisticated language and terminology being used in a paper, you should investigate further. This is especially true if the learner has demonstrated poor writing skills elsewhere in the course.

There are many clues that indicate that learners have copied and pasted information into their paper. Clues include different writing styles within the body of the paper, or different fonts and spacing. You may also find hyperlinks and other anomalies left in the paper from a copy and paste or different citation styles throughout the paper. If a learner has taken time to change the words, it may be more difficult to discover. You may have to investigate the case more closely by searching the actual text of the documents they have cited in their paper.

Another critical clue is if the paper does not flow from one topic to another. You may find similar topics being discussed in different sections of the paper. Additionally, there may not be clear transitions that link the information together in a coherent way. This is evidence of a learner taking information from a number of sources without a clear understanding of how to organize the information cohesively.

Strategies to Deter Plagiarism

It is very important that learners understand the implications of plagiarism. If they feel they can get away with careless or illicit acts of plagiarism, it will set the stage for additional violations throughout the course and possibly their entire

Exhibit 17.2   Example of Discussion on Academic Honesty

After reviewing the Academic Honesty Policy in the syllabus, please acknowledge that you understand the policies and procedures by stating: "I acknowledge that I have read and understand the academic honesty policy. I understand that plagiarism is a violation of the academic honesty policy and understand the policies and procedures, should the instructor find that I have committed plagiarism in my work." If you have questions regarding the policy and procedures, use this thread to dialogue with the instructor; otherwise, indicate that you have no questions about the policy.

---

program of study. Consider specific strategies both proactive and reactive as you begin teaching to try to deter learners from plagiarizing.

To begin with, as a part of your proactive strategies, it is important that your syllabus include an academic honesty statement that discusses plagiarism and the procedures for handling infractions. It is a good practice to have learners acknowledge they have read your academic honesty policy and understand it. An online discussion works well for this and provides learners an opportunity to dialogue about the policy and ask questions. Exhibit 17.2 is an example of a discussion you can post to discuss academic honesty.

Having this acknowledgment from learners at the beginning of the course can help ensure that all learners have read and understood the policy and set the expectation that plagiarism will not be tolerated.

You will also need to consider the policies and procedures that you have put in place when plagiarism is found. This will include a decision on whether you will allow a learner an opportunity to submit another paper once you have found the original submission has been plagiarized. Consider a process for managing and communicating issues with plagiarism. Exhibit 17.3 is a template for communicating plagiarism to learners when they occur in your course. The strategies include a variety of recommendations that can be considered; however, please be sure to review the policies and procedures in your institution's academic honesty procedure, and adjust your communication plan to fit your institution.

My personal opinion is that it is important that all learners understand the repercussions of committing acts of plagiarism. According to McCabe and Trevino (1997, as cited in McCabe, Treviño, & Butterfield, 2001), a significant

Exhibit 17.3   Plagiarism Communication Template

1. Submit paper to a plagiarism detection tool to determine percentage of match text.
2. Communicate to learner:

   Assignment in which plagiarism was found

   Discuss the percentage match from plagiarism detection tool and include report if available or detail what the report found and how to include proper citations and references

   Include a copy of the academic honesty policy and the potential actions that can be taken if plagiarism is found in the future

3. Indicate action you will take:

First occurrence	Second occurrence	Third occurrence
Actions can include:	*Actions can include:*	*Actions can include:*
Opportunity to resubmit assignment	0 grade for assignment	0 grade for assignment
Reduction in grade on assignment	Report incident to school	F grade for the course
0 grade for assignment	Indicate to learner actions that will be taken if another incident is reported, including the potential of earning a 0 for the course or being brought before a board to hear the case with the possibility of being dismissed from the institution (if appropriate)	Report incident to school for further action
Ask learner to submit all future assignments to plagiarism detection tool and not accept papers that fall above a specific percentage that you determine is agreeable		Other
Indicate to learner what will happen if a second occurrence of plagiarism is found		
Other	Other	

factor that is a deterrent to cheating is the "perceived severity of penalties for cheating" (p. 222). If learners receive a zero on their papers, it will send a clear message to learners that plagiarism is not tolerated. If learners are given an opportunity to redo an assignment, the repercussion will not affect their grade, so they may be more likely to plagiarize their work in the future. Of course, there has to be consideration for the type of plagiarism and for learners who are at risk and may drop the course due to low confidence. You will have to determine why a learner is plagiarizing and find ways to support learners to overcome issues involving poor academic skills while setting high expectations and standards for properly citing all sources.

Another proactive strategy is to address the issue of plagiarism in course activities. You may want to consider including in your course an activity that describes the types of plagiarism that can occur as well as strategies to help them prevent plagiarism in their writing. In addition, helping learners check their own work for missing or improper citations and references can help them be proactive in evaluating their own work. Also consider a topic on paraphrasing to help learners understand how to properly paraphrase what they read. Consider having learners submit their paper drafts to a plagiarism detection tool and report their percentage match. Although it takes time for you to review all submissions, it is an important learning tool to help learners evaluate their own writing and build their understanding of the use of citations and references.

Some learners clearly plagiarize because of not understanding how to use research to analyze issues. Instead, they use research to describe issues and lack analysis and synthesis in their writing. The research analysis worksheet described in Chapter 11 can help learners analyze the ideas of an author to help them develop a clearer understanding of the issue from that person's perspective. This helps learners understand how to analyze academic papers and provides a structure that allows them to draw comparisons between different authors' perspectives on an issue. For learners who plagiarize because they do not understand how to use research to support their writing, the worksheet can help support their research and provide a more complete understanding of how it can be used to support their ideas.

Another strategy is to structure the course materials so learners first research a topic or issue, then discuss the topic or issue, and finally write about it. Having learners participate in discussion on the topic or issue prior to beginning their writing will keep them from rushing through the analysis of research. Then, when they begin the writing portion of the activity, they have a solid understanding of the issue, as well as the arguments made to support multiple perspectives on the issue. This greater level of preparedness prior to the beginning of a writing assignment may keep learners from committing plagiarism because of a lack of understanding of the issue. With a strong foundation for how to analyze and synthesize research and form opinions, you can help learners move away from simply constructing papers that cobble together the ideas and thoughts of authors to a more thoughtful analysis of an issue.

During the writing activity, another strategy to consider is building out individual deliverables such as a problem statement, outline, introduction, first draft, and final draft. This will keep learners on a time line and help them avoid the rush of pulling together a writing assignment in the 11th hour, a rush that can lead to purposeful or inadvertent plagiarism.

Plagiarism Detection Tools

Plagiarism detection tools can be used to identify plagiarism in learners' assignments. There are a wide variety of services and tools available, which can make it difficult to determine which tool is appropriate for your purpose. The University System of Georgia has developed a comparison of major plagiarism detection tools, including Turnitin, MyDropBox, PAIRwise, EVE2, WCopyFind, CopyCatch, and GLATT. The categories of comparison include type (web-based, download, CD), price, company, licensing structure, databases, papermills, Internet searches, number of previously submitted papers, turnaround time for reporting, reporting features, training, support, and integration with course management systems. With this comparison chart you can review a number of plagiarism detection tools to determine which is most appropriate for your environment. The comparison chart is available at http://net.educause.edu/ir/library/pdf/SER07017B.pdf. Also, consult your institution to determine what tools are available for instructors to use to help detect plagiarism.

There is some controversy over the use of plagiarism detection tools regarding potential infringement on learner copyright and privacy. When learners submit their assignments to a plagiarism detection service, a copy of their submission can be stored in a database, which could possibly infringe on learners' copyright. In addition, if the copying is done without the permission or knowledge of the learners or without consent, this may be an issue of invasion of learners' privacy. Most services have circumvented this problem by asking for permission from the person submitting the paper to include his or her submission in a database, but it is important to make sure that this is the case for any tool you decide to use.

Search engines such as Google can also be used as a plagiarism detection tool. If you suspect a phrase, sentence, or paragraph has been plagiarized word for word, then put quotations around the suspected section and Google will return selections that exactly match the order of the words. An alternative is to use the advanced search option, and choose the specific phrases that you believe have been plagiarized and select the "with the exact phrase" option to find a match for the plagiarized phrase.

Plagiarism is a serious issue that needs to be addressed in the online learning environment. After considering the information presented in this section of the chapter, you may want to develop a process guide for plagiarism to help you determine the appropriate strategies for alleviating the issue with learners. As you begin developing your plagiarism process guide, consider developing a set of strategies for hindering plagiarism, which can include an academic policy statement and other resources to inform learners of the issue, as well as the procedures if plagiarism is found.

In addition, having learners acknowledge their understanding of the academic honesty policy can assure you that all learners understand the policies and procedures for plagiarism. In addition, specific learning activities can help learners evaluate their work and use research and writing strategies to alleviate unintentional plagiarism, which can be a proactive way to prevent plagiarism from occurring. There are some excellent resources available online to help learners understand plagiarism, as well as resources to help you consider policies and procedures for managing plagiarism. A review of the following resources may be a good place to start:

Purdue Online Writing Lab—Avoiding plagiarism

http://owl.english.purdue.edu/owl/resource/589/01/

University of Maryland University College—Plagiarism resources. Retrieved November 1, 2010

http://www.umuc.edu/distance/odell/cip/links_plagiarism.shtml

"What Is Plagiarism," available from Plagiarism dot org at

http://www.plagiarism.org/

Center for Academic Integrity—a consortium of more than 200 colleges and universities involved in an effort to initiate and maintain a dialogue among students, faculty, and administrators on the issue of academic integrity. Retrieved November 1, 2010

http://www.academicintegrity.org/

COPYRIGHT AND INTELLECTUAL PROPERTY

Copyright is an important subject to understand for anyone who is teaching in an online environment. I do not consider myself an expert in copyright law, but I do want to touch on some important considerations when using resources for your online course.

Definitions of Copyright

According to the U.S. Copyright Office (2006), "Copyright is a form of protection grounded in the U.S. Constitution and granted by law for original works of authorship fixed in a tangible medium of expression. Copyright covers both published and unpublished works" (Para. 1). As you can see from the definition, it protects the creative works of an individual from being used without permission. It keeps individuals from being able to copy or reproduce the work, develop derivatives of the work, distribute the work, and display or perform the work in public. To use works of another author requires you to receive permission from the author or the publisher in some cases. In the educational environment, there are several exemptions to having to receive copyright clearance.

Exemptions to Copyright

The Copyright Act of 1976 offers several exemptions from having to receive copyright clearance in sections 107 and 110. These exemptions include fair use, face-to-face classroom teaching, and distance education.

Fair Use   Fair use is covered in Section 107 of the Copyright Act of 1976, which allows instructors in nonprofit institutions to use works without obtaining copyright clearance. In determining whether fair use is appropriate, the following factors should be considered:

1. The purpose of the use and whether it is for nonprofit educational purposes—if the purpose is not educational in nature or is being considered in a for-profit educational institution, you will not be able to use fair use as a defense for not receiving copyright clearance.

2. The nature of the work copyrighted—generally, if the work is fiction or unpublished, or if the work is intended for the educational environment, for example, in the form of a case study or workbook, it will be difficult to use fair use as a defense.

3. The portion of the work used—if you are considering a large portion of the original work or a portion of the work that is central to the work, then fair use is not an acceptable defense unless it is being used for a critical analysis.

4. The effect the use has on the market or value of the work—if you make the information available to the public, keep it available for a long time, or are planning to make many copies, all of which could replace sales or diminish the market of the copyrighted work, fair use is not an acceptable defense. In addition, if getting copyright clearance is not very costly or timely, you have less of a defense for fair use.

Face-to-Face Classroom Teaching   In Section 110(1) of the Copyright Act of 1976, there is an exemption for nonprofit institutions from copyright infringement when works are used by teachers in the face-to-face classroom. This allows teachers to display or perform works but does not take into consideration making copies of works. In addition, there was no affordance for educators teaching in an online environment to use works for educational purposes. It also does not allow posting works electronically on a server, which would be the means of displaying or performing works in an online environment.

TEACH Act   In November 2002, the Technology, Education, and Copyright Harmonization Act (TEACH Act) was passed to allow online instructors some of the same opportunities as face-to-face instructors. This is included in Section 110(2) of the Copyright Act. There are limitations to the amount of materials within specific types of works that can be used, so you will want to consult this section of the Copyright Act when determining limitations for the specific works you are interested in using. In addition, there are requirements to assure protections, so only learners in the course have access to the materials and cannot retain copies of the materials or disseminate copies to others. In addition, institutions must have copyright policies in place and display them in the course regarding copyrighted materials.

If you are teaching for a nonprofit institution, these three exemptions should be considered as you determine the use of resources in your online course. Consult your institution's copyright policies in detail to get a clear understanding of how your own institution has interpreted these exemptions to make sure that you are in accordance to their policies and procedures.

Exhibit 17.4 is a summary of the sections of the Copyright Law that are important to the online environment. You should become familiar with how copyright, depending on the type of educational institution you work for, affects the resources you use in your online course.

Exhibit 17.4 Summary of Copyright Law for the Online Environment.

Nonprofit Educational Institutions	For-Profit Educational Institutions
Section 107 of the Copyright Act of 1976 — Fair Use	
Allows instructors in nonprofit institutions to use works without requiring copyright clearance. In determining whether fair use is appropriate, the following factors should be considered:	
1. The purpose of the use and whether it is *for nonprofit educational purposes* — if the purpose is not educational in nature or is being considered in a for-profit educational institution, you will not be able to use fair use as a defense for not receiving copyright clearance.	If you are teaching an online course at a for-profit institution, it is important to understand that fair use does not cover "for-profits" because the language is specific to nonprofit institutions.
2. The nature of the work copyrighted — generally, if the work is fiction or unpublished, or if the work is intended for the educational environment, for example, in the form of a case study or workbook, it will be difficult to use fair use as a defense.	
3. The portion of the work used — if you are considering a large portion of the original work or a portion of the work that is central to the work, then fair use is not an acceptable defense unless it is being used for a critical analysis.	
4. The effect the use has on the market or value of the work — if you make the information available to the public, keep it available for a long time, or are planning to make many copies, all of which could replace sales or diminish the market of the copyrighted work, fair use is not an acceptable defense. In addition, if getting copyright clearance is not very costly or timely, you have less of a defense for fair use.	
Section 110(1) of the Copyright Act of 1976	
Exemption for nonprofit institutions from copyright infringement when works are used by teachers in the face-to-face classroom.	
Face-to-Face: This allows teachers to display or perform works, but does not take into consideration making copies of works.	Does not apply to for-profits.
Online: It does not allow posting works electronically on a server, which would be the means of displaying or performing works in an online environment, so there was no affordance for educators teaching in an online environment to use works for educational purposes.	
Section 110(2) of the Copyright Act of 1976 — TEACH Act	
The TEACH Act allows online instructors some of the same opportunities as face-to-face instructors. If you are teaching for a *nonprofit institution*, these three exemptions should be considered as you determine the use of resources in your online course:	
There are limitations to the amount of materials within specific types of works that can be used.	If you are teaching an online course at a for-profit institution, it is important to understand that the TEACH Act does not cover "for-profits" because the language is specific to nonprofit institutions.
In addition, there are requirements to assure protections, so only learners in the course have access to the materials and cannot retain copies of the materials or disseminate copies to others.	
In addition, institutions must have copyright policies in place and display them in the course regarding copyrighted materials.	

Teaching for a For-Profit Institution   If you are teaching an online course at a for-profit institution, it is important to understand that fair use and the TEACH Act do not cover your usage because the language is specific to nonprofit institutions. If you work in a for-profit institution, you should be very careful in using any works without proper copyright clearance. In many for-profit institutions, faculty are not allowed to post supplemental resources or include URLs to resources on the Internet, so I recommend that you work with your institution to understand the limitations of posting resources without copyright clearance to assure compliance.

Posting Example Assignments from Learners   Often learners ask instructors for examples of assignments because they have difficulty understanding the requirements of the assignment. It is very common for an instructor to provide examples; however, learners' works are also copyrighted and you need permission to use their assignments as examples. You should have learners sign a release form that gives permission for you to use their assignment submissions as examples in your course. Exhibit 17.5 is a sample of a permission letter template that can be used to request permission to use learners' works. The permission letter should state specifically what you are interested in using. Provide a copy of the assignment if possible and describe specifically how the work will be used. Include a statement that they are not obligated to agree to the use of the works, and indicate that the acceptance or denial of permission will have no impact on their current standing in the course (if they are still currently in the course) or later standing (if they are not currently in the course). The permission letter should also include a statement about the amount of time the assignment will be used or state that the release will allow unlimited use of the work. Finally, the consent form should include sections for the learner to sign and date.

Use of Your Own Works

You do not need to get permission to use your own works. Be very careful, however, that anything you create does not include resources, images, or tables from other sources. Historically, if you use your own works in a course you are teaching, they are considered to be owned by you as a part of academic freedom. Legally, any materials prepared by employees in the course of their employment are owned by the company by whom they are employed. I bring this up because

Exhibit 17.5   Permission to Use Student Work Template

Date:
  Name of institution:
  Name of course:
  Name of instructor:
  Name of student:
  Title of work:
  I hereby grant my instructor permission to use my work listed above for the purpose of [insert purpose]. I grant permission for [choose one of two statements: unlimited use or limited use for the time] of the work listed above.
  Initial one of the following:

_____ I would like my name removed from the work before being used.
_____ I would like to include my name and be credited with the creation of the work in
        all cases of use.
_____ I would rather not have my instructor use my work for any purpose.

  I understand that I am not obligated to agree to the use of the works and understand that the acceptance or denial of permission will have no impact on my current standing or future standing in the course.

Student signature   Date

_____   _____

Instructor signature   Date

_____   _____

---

of the dynamic nature of distance learning. Policies are continuing to evolve and what you may have considered a part of academic freedom in a land-based institution may not be the same for the online institution. It is important to understand your institution's position on this before posting your own works to a course you are teaching.

As I stated at the beginning of this section, I do not consider myself an expert in copyright law, but I wanted to touch on some important considerations when using resources for your online course. There are excellent resources available if you would like to learn more about the copyright law.

1. The University of Minnesota libraries have created a Fair Use Analysis Tool to help you determine whether the use of a work falls under fair use. In addition they have a resource that discusses fair use in the online environment.

   a. Fair Use Analysis Tool:
   http://www.lib.umn.edu/copyright/checklist.phtml.

   b. Fair Use and Teaching Online:
   http://www.lib.umn.edu/copyright/teachon.phtml

2. Georgia Harper from the University of Texas System's Office of General Counsel is an expert in copyright law and a member of the Copyright Advisory Board of the Association of American Universities. She developed the following sites to explain copyright law:

   a. Copyright Crash Course:
   http://www.utsystem.edu/ogc/intellectualproperty/cprtindx.htm

   b. Copyright Law in Cyberspace:
   http://www.utsystem.edu/ogc/intellectualproperty/distance.htm

3. Janis Bruwelheide has authored a number of excellent resources on copyright specific to the online learning environment. She authored the following titles:

   a. Bruwelheide, J. H. (1994). Copyright concerns for distance educators. In B. Willis (Ed.), *Distance Education: Strategies and Tools*. Englewood Cliffs, NJ: Educational Technology Publications.

   b. Bruwelheide, J. H. (1997). Copyright: Opportunities and restrictions for the teleinstructor. In T. Cyrs (Ed.), *New Directions for Teaching and Learning: Distance Education*, No. 71. San Francisco: Jossey-Bass.

   c. Bruwelheide, J. H. (1997). Myths and misperceptions. In L. Gasway (Ed.), *Copyright Growing Pains: Adopting Copyright for Libraries, Education, and Society*. Littleton, CO: Fred B. Rothman, pp. 287–314.

   d. Bruwelheide, J. H. (1995, reprinted with 1997 update). *The Copyright Primer,* (2nd ed.) Chicago, IL: ALA Editions, American Library Association. http://www.ala.org

In this chapter, we discussed the ethical issue of plagiarism and looked at reasons why learners plagiarize, as well as strategies for preventing plagiarism in your online course. We also examined copyright issues and the application of fair use when using resources in your online course. As you consider these issues, review the policies available at your own institutions to make sure that you understand them before implementing specific strategies to combat plagiarism and ensure that the resources you are using are protected under the United States Copyright Act.

18

Developing an Online Teaching Philosophy

After reading this book, I hope that you have developed a body of knowledge about teaching online to help you develop effective instructional strategies for your online course(s). We looked at the profile of online learners, including their diversity, how they want to learn, and the challenges they face learning online. We also discussed learning and cognition and how the online environment affects learning. We have considered a number of strategies to support learners' thinking in the online environment and considered ways to develop cognitive, social, and instructor presence online to build a community of inquiry that is grounded in active learning, critical thinking, and reflection. We have also looked at the issues associated with managing the online environment, including managing teaching activities, the behaviors of learners, as well as the ethical issues of plagiarism and copyright that have an impact on the learning environment. All of the strategies in the book have been learner focused to help learners overcome the challenges of learning in a computer-mediated environment in order to persist and achieve their educational goals.

It has been recognized that the process of identifying a personal philosophy of teaching and continuously examining this philosophy can lead to a change of teaching behaviors and to professional and personal growth (Developing a Teaching Portfolio, n.d.). The final activity in the book is intended to foster reflection on your views of teaching and how teaching online is different from

Exhibit 18.1   Online Teaching Philosophy Worksheet

Component	Statement
Conceptualization of Learning Online	
How do primary and secondary diversity characteristics affect learning?	
How do learning styles affect learning?	
What impact does the environment have on learning?	
What impact does motivation have on learning?	
What impact does self-directedness have on learning?	
Conceptualization of Teaching Online	
What is your role in teaching with respect to diversity characteristics of online learners?	
What is your role in teaching with respect to learning styles?	
What is your role in teaching with respect to support learners to develop cognitive thinking skills?	
What is your role in teaching with respect to motivating online learners?	
What is your role in teaching with respect to developing cognitive presence in the online environment?	
What is your role in teaching with respect to developing social presence in the online environment?	
What is your role in teaching with respect to developing teaching presence in the online environment?	
Goals for Online Learners	
What are the roles and responsibilities of learners?	
What skills should learners obtain as a result of learning?	
How do learners obtain these skills?	
What ways do you facilitate learners' obtaining these skills?	
Implementation of Your Online Teaching Philosophy	
How do you operationalize your philosophy of teaching in the online classroom?	
What personal characteristics in yourself or your learners influence the way in which you approach teaching online?	
Professional Growth Plan for Online Teaching	
What goals have you set for yourself as an online instructor?	
How will you continue to develop your skills as an online instructor to reach your goals?	

Adapted from "Developing a Teaching Portfolio" at http://ucat.osu.edu/portfolio/philosophy/ Phil_guidance.html teaching in a traditional face-to-face learning environment. Using the Teaching Philosophy Worksheet in Exhibit 18.1, consider each of the components of the worksheet as you reflect on your online teaching philosophy and compose statements for each of the components of your philosophy, including your

- Conceptualization of learning
- Conceptualization of teaching
- Goals for learners
- Philosophy implementation
- A professional growth plan

This philosophy can serve as your guide as you engage with learners online to help them successfully reach their educational goals.

References

Aldrich, C. (2009). *Learning online with games, simulations, and virtual worlds strategies for online instruction.* San Francisco: Jossey-Bass.

Allen, I. E., & Seaman, J. (2009). *Learning on demand: Online education in the United States.* Needham, MA: Sloan Consortium.

Anderson, T., Rourke, L., Garrison, D. R., & Archer, W. (2001). Assessing teaching presence in a computer conferencing context. *Journal of Asynchronous Learning Networks, 5*(2).

Ausubel, D. P. (1960). The use of advance organizers in the learning and retention of meaningful verbal material. *Journal of Educational Psychology, 51,* 267–272.

Ausubel, D. P. (1963). *The psychology of meaningful verbal learning.* New York: Grune & Stratton.

Ausubel, D. P. (1968). *Educational psychology: A cognitive view.* New York: Holt, Rinehart and Winston.

Bandura, A. (1986). *Social foundations of thought and action: A social cognitive theory.* Englewood Cliffs, NJ: Prentice Hall.

Bandura, A. (1997). *Self-efficacy: The exercise of control.* New York: Worth.

Barrows, H. S., & Kelson A. M. (1993). *Problem-based learning: A total approach to education* [Monograph]. Springfield, IL: Southern Illinois University School of Medicine, 1993.

Bates, T. (2001). International distance education: Cultural and ethical issues. *Distance Education, 22*(1), 122–136.

Bates, A. W., & Poole, G. (2003). *Effective teaching with technology in higher education. Foundations for success.* San Francisco: Jossey-Bass.

Bean J. R., & Metzner, B. (1985). A conceptual model of nontraditional undergraduate student attrition. *Review of Educational Research, 55,* 485–650.

Bender, S. L., & Dittmar, E. (2006, August). Dealing with difficult online learners. *International Journal of Instructional Technology and Distance Learning, 3*(7), 55–59.

Bloom, B., Englehart, M., Furst, E., Hill, W., & Krathwohl, D. (1956). *Taxonomy of educational objectives: The classification of educational goals. Handbook I: Cognitive domain.* New York, Toronto: Longmans, Green.

Boettcher, J. V., & Conrad, R. M. (2010). *The online teaching survival guide: Simple and practical pedagogical tips.* San Francisco: Jossey-Bass.

Bransford, J., Brown, A., & Cocking, R. (1999). *How people learn: Brain, mind, experience, and school* [Online]. Retrieved November 1, 2010. Available: at http://www.nap.edu/openbook.php?record_id6160

Brookfield, S. D. (1987). *Developing critical thinkers: Challenging adults to explore alternative ways of thinking and acting.* San Francisco: Jossey-Bass.

Brookfield, S. D., & Preskill, S. N. (2005). *Discussion as a way of teaching, tools and techniques for democratic classrooms.* San Francisco: Jossey-Bass.

Bruwelheide, J. H. (1994). Copyright concerns for distance educators. In B. Willis (Ed.), *Distance education: Strategies and tools.* Englewood Cliffs, NJ: Educational Technology Publications.

Bruwelheide, J. H. (1995, reprinted with 1997 update). *The copyright primer* (2nd ed.) Chicago, IL: ALA Editions, American Library Association. http://www.ala.org.

Bruwelheide, J. H. (1997a). Copyright: Opportunities and restrictions for the teleinstructor. In T. Cyrs (Ed.), *Teaching and learning at a distance.* New Directions for Teaching and Learning, No. 71. San Francisco: Jossey-Bass.

Bruwelheide, J. H. (1997b). Myths and misperceptions. In L. Gasaway (Ed.), *Growing pains: Adopting copyright for libraries, education, and society* (pp. 287–314). Littleton, CO: Fred B. Rothman.

Chang, S. L., & Ley, K. (2006). A learning strategy to compensate for cognitive overload in online learning: Learner use of printed materials. *Journal of Interaction Online Learning, 5*(1), Spring.

Conrad, R. M., & Donaldson, J. A. (2004). *Engaging the online learner: Activities and resources for creative instruction.* San Francisco: Jossey-Bass.

Craik, F., & Tulving, E. (1975). Depth of processing and the retention of words in episodic memory. *Journal of Experimental Psychology: General, 104,* 268–294.

Dabbagh, N. (2007). The online learner: Characteristics and pedagogical implications. *Contemporary issues in technology and teacher education* [Online serial], *7*(3). Retrieved November 1, 2010, from http://www.citejournal.org/vol7/iss3/general/article1.cfm

Developing a teaching portfolio (n.d.) Retrieved November 1, 2010, from http://ucat.osu.edu/portfolio/philosophy/Phil_guidance.html

Dille, B., & Mezack, M. (1991). Identifying predictors of high risk among community college telecourse students. *American Journal of Distance Education, 5*(1), 24–35.

Elder, L., & Paul, R. (2010). *The thinker's guide to analytic thinking.* Dillon Beach, CA: Foundation for Critical Thinking Press.

Finkelstein, J. (2006). *Learning in real time: Synchronous teaching and learning online.* San Francisco: Jossey-Bass.

Gagne, R. (1985). *The conditions of learning* (4th ed.). New York: Holt, Rinehart & Winston.

Garrison, D. R., Anderson, T., & Archer, W. (2001). Critical thinking, cognitive presence, and computer conferencing in distance education. *American Journal of Distance Education, 15*(1).

Grasha, A. F. (1996). *Teaching with style.* Pittsburgh: Alliance Publishers.

Grow, G. O. (1996). Teaching learners to be self-directed. *Adult Education Quarterly, 41*(3), 125–149. Expanded version available online at http://www.longleaf.net/ggrow

Hannifin, M., Land, S., & Oliver, K. (1999). Open learning environments: Foundations, methods and models. In C. M. Reigeluth (Ed.), *Instructional-design theories and models: A new paradigm of instructional theory, 2,* pp. 115–140. Mahwah, NJ: Erlbaum.

Hofstede, G. (May 8, 2008). *Cultural differences in teaching and learning.* FUHU conference on Education and Training in the Multicultural Classroom, Copenhagen.

Hofstede, G., & Bond, M. H. (1984). Hofstede's culture dimensions: An independent validation using Rokeach's value survey. *Journal of Cross-Cultural Psychology, 15,* 417.

Ijsselsteijn, W. A., de Ridder, H., Freeman, J., & Avons, S. E. (2000). Presence: Concept, determinants, and measurement. In Human Vision and Electronic Imaging Conference, proceedings of the International Society for Optical Engineering, 3959, 520–529.

Johnson, L., Levine, A., Smith, R., & Stone, S. (2010). *The 2010 Horizon Report.* Austin, TX: The New Media Consortium.

Kehrwald, B. (2008). Understanding social presence in text-based online learning environments. *Distance Education, 29*(1), 89–106.

Knowles, M. (1992). Applying principles of adult learning in conference presentations. *Adult Learning, 4*(1), 11–14.

Knowles, M. S., Holton, E. F., & Swanson, R. A. (1998). *The adult learner.* Houston: Gulf Publishing.

Kolb, D. A. (1976). *The learning style inventory: Technical manual.* Boston: McBer.

Kolb, D. A. (1999). *Learning style inventory, version 3.* Boston: Hay Group. haytrg@haygroup.com

Krathwohl, D. R. (2002). A revision of Bloom's taxonomy: An overview. *Theory into Practice, 41*(4), 212–218.

Lehman, R. M., & Conceição, S.C.O. (2010). *Creating a sense of presence in online teaching: How to "be there" for distance learners.* San Francisco: Jossey-Bass.

Lenburg, C. (1999). The framework, concepts and methods of the Competency Outcomes and Performance Assessment (COPA) model. *Online Journal of Issues in Nursing, 4*(2), Manuscript 2. Retrieved November 1, 2010, from www.nursingworld.org/MainMenuCategories/ANAMarketplace/ANAPeriodicals/OJIN/TableofContents/Volume41999/No2Sep1999/COPAModel.aspx

Manning, S., & Johnson, K. (2011). *The technology toolbelt for teaching*. San Francisco. Jossey-Bass.

McCabe, D. L., Treviño, L. K., & Butterfield, K. D. (2001) Cheating in academic institutions: A decade of research. *Ethics & Behavior, 11*(3), 219–232.

Merriam, S. B. (2001). Andragogy and self-directed learning: Pillars of adult learning theory. In S. Merriam (Ed.), *The new update on adult learning theory*. New Directions for Adult and Continuing Education, No. 89 (pp. 2–13). San Francisco: Jossey-Bass.

Miller, G. A. (1956). The magical number seven, plus or minus two: Some limits on our capacity for processing information. *Psychological Review 63*(2), 81–97.

Moore, M. (1980). Independent study. In R. Boyd, J. W. Apps, & Associates (Eds.), *Redefining the discipline of adult education* (pp. 16–31). San Francisco: Jossey-Bass.

Moore, M. (1991). Editorial: Distance education theory. *The American Journal of Distance Education, 5*(3), 1–6.

Noel-Levitz, Inc. (2005). *The 2005 national online learners priorities report*. Iowa City, IA: Noel-Levitz, Inc. Retrieved November 1, 2010, from https://www.noellevitz.com/NR/rdonlyres/1CB71B9D5E9A-42CBA757AB6DFA69889F/0/NatSatisfactionReportOnlineLearners09.pdf

Noel-Levitz, Inc. (2009). *The 2009 national online learners priorities report*. Iowa City, IA: Noel-Levitz, Inc. Retrieved November 1, 2010 from https://www.noellevitz.com/NR/rdonlyres/36724DC0 CE12459D-9D70–3E0E76E47A70/0/2005OnlineLrnrPriorrpt.pdf

Palloff, R. M., & Pratt, K. (2001). *Lessons from the cyberspace classroom: The realities of online teaching*. San Francisco: Jossey-Bass.

Palloff, R. M., & Pratt, K. (2005). *Collaborating online: Learning together in community*. San Francisco: Jossey-Bass.

Palloff, R. M., & Pratt, K. (2007). *Building online learning communities: Effective strategies for the virtual classroom*. San Francisco: Jossey-Bass.

Pascarella, E. T. (1985). *College environmental influences on learning and development: A critical review and synthesis*. In J. C. Smart (Ed.), *Higher education*: Handbook of theory and research (Vol. 1.). New York: Agathon.

Pavlov, I. P. (1927). *Conditioned reflexes: An investigation of the physiological activity of the cerebral cortex* (G.V. Anrep, trans.). London: Oxford University Press.

Piaget, J. (1985). *The equilibration of cognitive structures*. Chicago: University of Chicago Press.

Plotnikoff, D. (1994). *Flaming in cyberspace. Neophytes beware: Online assaults can be devastating*. The Salt Lake Tribune [Online].

Rovai, A. P. (2003). In search of higher persistence rates in distance education online programs. *The Internet and Higher Education, 6*(1), 1.

Savery, J. R., & Duffy, T. M. (1995). Problem based learning: An instructional model and its constructivist framework. *Educational Technology, 35*, 31–38.

Shea, V. (1994). *Netiquette*. San Francisco: Albion Books.

Skinner, B. F. (1938). *The behavior of organisms*. New York: Appleton-Century-Crofts.

Smith, R. M. (2008). *Conquering the content. A step-by-step guide to online course design*. San Francisco: Jossey-Bass.

Snow, R. (1997). Individual differences. In R. D Tennyson, F. Schott, N. Seel, & S. Dijkstra, *Instructional design: International perspective*. Vol. 1, *Theory, research, and models*. Mahwah, NJ: Erlbaum.

Spady, W. (1970). Dropouts from higher education: An interdisciplinary review and synthesis. *Interchange 1*, 64–85.

Stavredes, T. (2011). *Study strategies handbook*. Hoboken, NJ: Wiley.

Sweller, J., & Chandler, P. (1994). Why some material is difficult to learn. *Cognition and Instruction, 12*, 185–233.

Tennant, M. (1997). *Psychology of adult learning*. London and New York. Routledge.

Tennyson, R. D., & Schott, F. (1997). Instructional design theory research and models. In R. D. Tennyson, F. Schott, N. Seel, & S. Dijkstra. *Instructional design: International perspective*. Vol. 1, *Theory, research, and models*. Mahwah, NJ: Erlbaum.

THE Journal. (2004). Faculty training for online teaching. *THE Journal*. Retrieved November 1, 2010, from http://thejournal.com/articles/2004/09/01/faculty-training-for-online-teaching.aspx

Tinto, V. (1975). Dropout from higher education: A theoretical synthesis of recent research. *Review of Educational Research, 45*, 89–125.

Tinto, V. (1993). *Leaving college: Rethinking the causes and cures of student attrition research* (2nd ed.). Chicago: University of Chicago.

University of Delaware Problem-Based Learning Clearinghouse: https//:primus.nss.udel.edu/Pbl

U.S. Copyright Office (2006). Retrieved November 1, 2010, from http://www.copyright.gov/help/faq/faq general.html

Vygotsky, L. S. (1978). *Mind in society*. Cambridge, MA: Harvard University Press.

Weasenforth, D., Biesenbach-Lucas, S., & Meloni, C. (2002). Realizing constructivist objectives through collaborative technologies: Threaded discussions. *Language Learning & Technology, 6*(3), 58–86. Retrieved November 1, 2010, from http://llt.msu.edu/vol6num3/pdf/vol6num3.pdf

West, J. A., & West, M. L. (2009). *Using wikis for online collaboration: The power of the read-write web*. San Francisco: Jossey-Bass.

Witkin, H. (1950). Perception of the upright when the direction of the force acting on the body is changed. *Journal of Experimental Psychology, 40*, 93–106.

Workman, J. J., & Stenard, R. A. (1996). *Student support services for distance learners*. DEOSNEWS 6(3). Retrieved November 1, 2010, from the Distance Education Online Symposium website: http://www.ed.psu.edu/acsde/deos/deosnews/deosnews6_3.asp

Index

C

Careless learners, 218
Center for Academic Integrity, 233
Challenger (learner personality), 208
Chandler, P., 51
Chang, S. L., 52, 53
Characteristics of online learners, 3–11
Chat or instant messaging, 171, 172–173
Chatty Kathy (learner personality), 207
Checklist, communication, 163–165
Checklist, unit, 89, 90, 103
Circular response, 138–139
Cocking, R., 59, 61, 65, 87
Code of conduct violations, 211–212
Cognitive constructivism, 38
Cognitive load, 51–53
Cognitive presence, defined, 107, 168
Cognitive styles: defined, 53; Field
    Dependence/Independence dimension of,
    53–55; Kolb Learning Style Inventory of,
    53, 55–58
Cognitivism, 35–37
Co-instructor, learner who behaves as, 206
Collaborative learners, 18, 19
Collaborative learning strategies: discussions,
    132–141; group projects, 141–145;
    importance of, 131–132; peer reviews,
    145–149
Collaborative strategies, and problem-based
    learning, 123–124
Collectivism, 7, 8, 9
Communication checklist, 163–165
Communication tools: blogs, 172, 176; chats or
    instant messaging, 171, 172–173; discussion
    forums, 171, 175–176; e-mail, 171, 175,
    192–193; social networks and microblogs,
    172, 177–178; virtual worlds, 171, 174–175;
    Voice over Internet Protocol (VoIP), 171,
    173; Web conferencing, 171, 173–174; wikis,
    172, 176–177
Communication tools plan, 179–181
Comparison charts, 99, 100
Competitive learners, 18, 19
Complainer (learner personality), 209–210
Complete plagiarism, 224, 225

Conceição, S.C.O., 132, 169
Concept maps, 99, 100
Conceptual scaffolding, 95–100, 103
Conflict management, and group projects,
    144–145, 146, 147
Conrad, R. M., 77, 84, 97, 186
Constructivism, 37–40
Convergers, 56, 57
Copyright Act of 1976, 234, 235, 236
Copyright and intellectual property, 223, 233–240
Course platform capabilities: grading features,
    201; tracking reports, 201–202
Craik, F., 47
Credibility criteria, for evaluating resources, 121,
    122
Critical thinking: activities, 112–113; description
    of, 107, 108–109; in discussions, 135,
    136–137, 139; four components to, 108;
    pedagogical approach to, 109–111
Cultural differences of learners: description of,
    5–7; impact of, 8–10
Cycle, as graphical organizer, 98, 100

D

Dabbagh, N., 21
de Ridder, H., 168
Debates: as active learning strategy, 125;
    instructor role in, 128–129; organizing,
    125–126; pre-debate activities, 126;
    preparation worksheets for, 126, 127–128;
    standards for posting, 128, 129, 130
Definitions, as advance organizers, 95, 97
Deliberation, and discussions, 137, 138
Delinquent learners, 218
Dependent learners, 18–19, 161
Dille, B., 64
Discussion forums, 171, 175–176
Discussion questions, types of, 133–134
Discussions: critical thinking in, 135, 136–137,
    139; dispositions of, 138; grading, 140–141,
    187, 191; how learners interact in, 134;
    importance of, 132–133; learner-to-learner
    interactions in, 135, 137–139; managing, 187,
    188–189, 191; protocol for, 79, 82
Disjointed learners, 218–219

O

Offender (learner personality), 208
Offensive language, handling, 207, 208
Oliver, K., 73, 90, 95, 102
Online learners: demographic characteristics of,
 3–11; learning attributes of, 13–19;
 personalities of, 205–210; ten types of, 217–222
Organization charts, 99, 100
Orientation scaffold, 75–77, 103, 186
Overachievers, 219–220

P

Palloff, R. M., 77, 131, 143, 144, 186, 215
Partial plagiarism, 224, 225
Participation: in discussions, 135, 138;
 interactions to encourage, 153, 164
Participative learners, 18, 19
Pascarella, E., 22, 24, 25
Pascarella's General Model for Assessing Change,
 23, 24
Paul, R., 109, 110, 124, 135, 139, 154
Paul-Elder Model of Critical Thinking, 109–111,
 135, 136–137
Pavlov, I., 34, 41
Peer reviews: benefits of, 146; instructor role in,
 149; process for, 146–148
Permission to use student work template, 237,
 238
Persistence: models, 22–29; retention versus,
 21–22
Personal discussions, 207
Personalities, learner: and behavioral issues,
 205–210; ten learner types, 217–222
Philosophy Worksheet, Teaching, 241–243
Piaget, J., 38, 41
Plagiarism: as behavioral issue, 215–216; defined,
 224; detection tools, 84, 103, 216, 232–233;
 identifying, 227–228; policy, 80, 83; reasons
 for, 226–227; strategies to deter, 228–231;
 types of, 224–225
Planning strategies, 87–90
Plotnikoff, D., 210
Poole, G., 8, 179
Power distance, 5–6, 8, 9, 145
Pratt, K., 77, 131, 143, 145, 186, 215

Presence, four modes of, 168–169
Preskill, S. N., 132, 133, 134, 135, 137, 138, 139,
 140, 212
Proactive communications, managing, 187,
 193–195
Probing questions, 102, 103
Problem analysis worksheet, 121
Problem-based learning: and collaborative
 strategies, 123–124; description of, 117–118;
 instructor role in, 124–125; pedagogical
 approach to, 118–119; process, 119, 121–123
Problem-Based Learning Clearinghouse, 119
Procedural memory, 44, 46, 47
Procedural scaffolding: defined, 73, 75, 103;
 expectations scaffold, 77–84, 103, 186;
 orientation scaffold, 75–77, 103; resource
 scaffolds, 84–85, 103
Progress, monitoring, 158–159, 164
Prompts, 154, 157
Purdue Online Writing Lab, 233

Q

Questions: discussion question format, 133–134;
 management of, 187, 191–193

R

Ranting or offensive language, 207, 208. *See also*
 Flaming
Realism, 168
Redundancy, 52
Reflection, 113–117
Reflective scaffolds, 93
Research Analysis Worksheet, 112, 113, 122
Resource scaffolds, 84–85, 103
Retention, persistence versus, 21–22
Riechmann, S., 17
Road map, course, 88–89, 103
Roster and tracking spreadsheet, 189, 190
Rourke, L., 153, 154
Rovai, A., 25, 27, 28, 151
Rovai Composite Persistence Model, 26, 27

S

Sarcastic students, 208
Savery, J. R., 117